The Protective Intelligence Advantage

The world reacted in horror to the graphic security camera footage of United Healthcare CEO Brian Thompson being gunned down on a Manhattan sidewalk as he was on his way to attend a scheduled investor conference. Contrary to many reports, his murder was not the first attack against a CEO on American soil, and it won't be the last.

Since this murder has already spawned copycat attacks, *The Protective Intelligence Advantage: Mitigating the Rising Threat to Prominent People* is especially needed at this moment in time. In it, the authors outline various case examples of other executives, VIPs, and high-profile figures who were victims of such attacks. The goal is to learn key elements from them, then outline exactly how individuals and security teams can utilize protective intelligence tools—and their own behaviors, mindfulness, and awareness to protect themselves and their families from threats and imminent harm. This book will detail the essential security and awareness tools that any executive can learn: what the authors dub protective intelligence-led security, a model they designed. Since 1998, the authors have trained billionaires and Fortune 100 protection teams on the concept.

After a lifetime of investigating attacks on high-profile persons, heads of state, and celebrities—and training others to prevent them—the authors will be the first to examine the murder of Brian Thompson in detail, and use the lessons learned from that attack (and others) to illustrate how protective intelligence can be used to identify threats and prevent attacks.

Fred Burton is one of the world's foremost experts on protective intelligence, global security, and terrorism. He is a former State Department counterterrorism deputy chief and DSS special agent, who investigated the kidnapping of the hostages held captive by Hezbollah and many other acts of terror. He is the author of *Ghost: Confessions of a Counterterrorism Agent* and *Chasing Shadows: A Special Agent's Lifelong Hunt to Bring a Cold War Assassin to Justice,* and coauthor with Samuel M. Katz of the *New York Times* bestseller *Under Fire: The Untold Story of the Attack in Benghazi.*

Scott Stewart is the Vice President of Protective Intelligence at TorchStone Global. He is a veteran protective intelligence practitioner with four decades of analytical, investigative, and security experience in the government, corporate, and NGO sectors. Prior to joining TorchStone, Scott led Stratfor's global analysis of terrorism and security topics from 2004 to 2020. He also served as the protective intelligence coordinator at Dell and spent ten years as a special agent with the U.S. State Department where he conducted hundreds of terrorism, criminal, and protective intelligence investigations.

The Protective
Intelligence Advantage
Mitigating the Rising Threat to
Prominent People

Fred Burton and Scott Stewart

CRC Press
Taylor & Francis Group
Boca Raton London New York

CRC Press is an imprint of the
Taylor & Francis Group, an **informa** business

Front cover image: Kyle Mazza/Anadolu via Getty Images

First edition published [2026]
by CRC Press
2385 NW Executive Center Drive, Suite 320, Boca Raton FL 33431

and by CRC Press
4 Park Square, Milton Park, Abingdon, Oxon, OX14 4RN

CRC Press is an imprint of Taylor & Francis Group, LLC

ISBN: 978-1-041-08960-5 (hbk)
ISBN: 978-1-041-08961-2 (pbk)
ISBN: 978-1-003-64774-4 (ebk)

DOI: 10.4324/9781003647744

Typeset in Sabon
by codeMantra

This book is dedicated to all the agents and analysts we have had the good fortune to learn from over the decades— and to those who will follow after us to further advance the art and science of protective intelligence.

Contents

Acknowledgments

Scott and Fred would like to thank Ben West, Kori Sidwell, and Scott's amazing wife Jackie for their input on early drafts of this book. Scott would also like to thank Frank Rodman and the TorchStone Global team for their support and encouragement. Finally, we would like to thank Mark Listewnik and the team at Taylor and Francis for all their advice and assistance in helping us craft this book.

Introduction

The world reacted in horror to the graphic security camera footage of United Healthcare Chief Executive Officer (CEO) Brian Thompson being gunned down on a Manhattan sidewalk as he was on his way to attend a scheduled investor conference. The camera dispassionately recorded the scene as Mr. Thompson approached the hotel door and a hooded lone gunman stepped from the shadows, raised his pistol, and fired at the CEO's back at close range. As a bystander watched, the shooter approached Mr. Thompson and fired two more rounds before walking away from the scene of the attack (Figure 0.1).

The murder of Mr. Thompson has sent shock waves through the C-Suites and board rooms of America that continues to reverberate today, fueled by the viral coverage of the assassination—and in many cases, the realization that the gunman could have targeted them, or another executive within their company, due to their negligent or non-existent executive protection programs. This awareness has led many companies to conduct reviews of their security and executive protection programs.

This is a good thing, because Mr. Thompson's murder provided an operational roadmap for those harboring grievances or extremist ideologies. The video of his assassination demonstrated to the world that with a little effort and determination, it is possible for an untrained individual to stalk and kill a prominent person armed with an easy-to-acquire 3D printed "ghost Glock." In addition to being a "proof of concept" operation, the public reaction to Mr. Thompson's murder has been quite disturbing. Amid the viral coverage of the murder in the mainstream press and social media, the murderer, Luigi Mangione, has been venerated and

FIGURE 0.1   X post encouraging people to kill CEOs and billionaires.

Source: X.com, accessed April 29, 2025, https://x.com/biology35376069/status/1888659359242113132.

DOI: 10.4324/9781003647744-1

held up as an example for others to follow.[1] In fact, as seen in the post from the X social media platform above, his name has become a verb used to describe the assassination of a prominent person.

These calls to imitate the killer come as we are witnessing a surge of anti-capitalist and anti-corporate sentiment and vitriol that shows no sign of ebbing. In the wake of Mr. Thompson's murder, anti-capitalist extremists pasted CEO "wanted posters" at various locations in Manhattan,[2] and a Socialist clothing company announced they were publishing a deck of "most wanted CEO" cards akin to those the U.S. military issued in Iraq for wanted terrorists.[3] The four suits of cards in the deck featured executives from different sectors. Clubs focused on chemicals, agriculture, and logistics; diamonds on finance, tech, and the media; hearts on healthcare, real estate, and retail; and finally, spades on weapons, energy, and pharmaceuticals. New York City Police Commissioner Jessica Tisch was the joker.

We regularly see social media posts denouncing prominent individuals and identifying them as targets worthy of being attacked. And this is not just an American phenomenon; social media posts and graffiti have appeared all over the globe calling for the murder of CEOs, as seen in the graffiti in the X post below that appeared in Athens, Greece. This threat will not subside anytime soon, and interest in Luigi Mangione will continue well through his upcoming state and federal trials (Figure 0.2).

But anti-corporate/anti-capitalist sentiment, anti-technology grievances, and climate extremism stemming from anarchists and other left-wing extremists are not the only factors driving the rising threat to prominent people, and CEOs are not the only ones facing the threat. Celebrities continue to be stalked by unstable admirers, denounced by detractors, and targeted by criminals. In countries around the globe, the political environment is contentious and highly polarized, leading to threats and attacks against politicians at all levels of government, judges, and even political donors. In many cases this political strife is being stoked by information operations conducted by hostile intelligence services and dramatically amplified by social media.[4]

Even as this book was in production in June of 2025, a lone gunman conducted a string of attacks targeting Democratic politicians in Minnesota at their residences, killing one lawmaker and her husband and seriously wounding another politician and his wife. According to the federal indictment, the killer had also attempted to attack another politician who was not home at the time, and was spotted outside the home of yet another presumed target.[5]

Right-wing extremists such as the Proud Boys, Oath Keepers, and Three Percenters have been emboldened by the election of President Donald Trump, and the pardons he issued for the extremists who had been convicted for their involvement in the January 6, 2021, storming

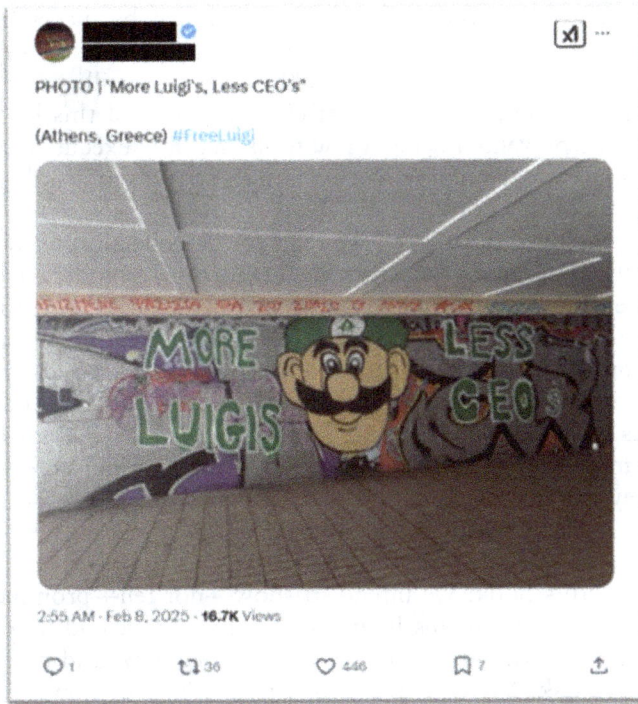

FIGURE 0.2 X post of graffiti in Greece illustrating the spread of the Luigi phenomenon.

Source: X.com, accessed April 29, 2025, https://x.com/ultras_antifaa/status/1888134536078217290.

and ransacking of the U.S. Capital Building. Likewise, anti-abortion extremists, Q Anon adherents, white supremacists, and sovereign citizens all pose threats to government officials and others they identify as enemies.

Anti-establishment grievances are being propagated by both extremes of the political spectrum, and they are focused not just on the government, but on the entire democratic and free market system in the West. Extremists seek to destroy the entire current world order, and one way to do that is to target the prominent people who are the figureheads of this system.

In this book we will share protective intelligence lessons we have learned over our combined eight decades of executive protection and protective intelligence experience. Using these lessons as a lens, we will examine the attacks against Brian Thompson and other prominent individuals to illustrate the need for protective intelligence tools. One of the things we have learned over the years is that once the shooter or group deploys for an attack, they will, in all probability, be successful unless the target is very lucky or the attacker extremely inept; it is very difficult to stop a bullet once it has been fired. However, as we illustrate through the case studies outlined in the first eight chapters of this book, these attacks can be prevented using a few tools that any executive can learn and any company can employ. We explain these tools in detail in the last eight chapters of this book.

When employed in concert, we refer to the collection of those tools as *protective intelligence-led executive protection*, a model we designed in the government and brought to the private security world in 1998. In the ensuing years, we have trained many prominent people and their executive protection teams on this model.

Another important lesson we learned by investigating and analyzing attacks is that *the how is more important than the why or the who*. It doesn't matter what motivates a hostile actor planning to conduct an attack, they can be detected, and their efforts thwarted by focusing on how attacks are conducted and by exploiting vulnerabilities in those processes.

Through this book, we intend to show—not tell—prominent people and their security teams how threat actors work and how to look for danger, assess threats, enhance personal security, and determine if THEY are at risk. Most people don't know where or how to look for danger or how to escape the notice of a threat actor, but this book will give them the tools they need to recognize and avoid threats to keep themselves and their families safe.

NOTES

1 https://www.threads.com/@spaceboy_eurotrash/post/DHuLqHG tKHA/luigi-is-the-best-example-for-all-of-us-to-follow.
2 https://abcnews.go.com/US/executive-hit-lists-wanted-posters-nypd-warns-threats/story?id=116662519.
3 https://www.newsweek.com/ceo-card-game-brian-thompson-luigi-mangione-2001973.
4 https://www.rusi.org/explore-our-research/publications/commentary/russia-winning-global-information-war.
5 https://www.torchstoneglobal.com/minnesota-zattacks-protective-intelligence-lessons/

CHAPTER **1**

Denial in New York

Brian Thompson didn't bother to put on a coat before he left the lobby of the luxurious Conrad Midtown Hotel. As he stepped out onto the sidewalk he didn't give much thought to the pre-dawn chill. He only had to cross the street and walk down the block to arrive at the New York Hilton that morning, so with such a short walk it really wasn't worth the time and effort to wear a coat he'd just have to check. Besides, as an Iowa boy who had lived in Minnetonka, Minnesota for many years, 33 degrees didn't feel all that cold.[1]

As Thompson walked down the street, he quickly checked his phone and then began to think about the busy day ahead at his company's annual investor conference. Thompson was the Chief Executive Officer (CEO) of United Healthcare, the insurance division of the United Health Group, and one of the largest health insurers in the United States. He assumed the helm of United Healthcare in 2021, and as a veteran executive, was familiar with these conferences, so there was little to be anxious about. Besides, his company had logged record profits since he took charge—$16 billion on $281 billion in revenues in 2023[2]—and the forecast for 2025 was also looking very positive. It was always easy to give analysts and institutional investors good news.

Thompson was also very familiar with Midtown Manhattan, having stayed there countless times over the past couple of decades, and especially now as a senior executive, he frequently visited Manhattan for business. With the Hilton only half a block down 54th Street from his hotel, he didn't need a car and driver to get him from his hotel to the meeting.

Still thinking about his schedule and remarks, Thompson used the crosswalk to get to the south side of 54th Street, the side of the street the Hilton was on. Although he was in a part of Manhattan that is normally very busy, 6:45 AM was still early enough that traffic was light, and he had little problem making his way across the street.

With the streets nearly deserted, Thompson also knew from experience that he was unlikely to encounter any of the aggressive panhandlers who would haunt Manhattan's streets later in the day. Most of them

DOI: 10.4324/9781003647744-2

were still crashed, sleeping off the booze or drugs they purchased with yesterday's proceeds. Besides, he was a strong guy, a wrestler who frequently challenged people to arm wrestle[3]—he did not need close protection to simply cross the street and walk down the block from one hotel to another. He could take care of himself. Unconcerned, he kept his focus on the sidewalk—and his mind on the day ahead.

Because of this, as Thompson approached the 54th Street entrance of the Hilton, he didn't notice the hooded figure who was standing in the shadows across the street from the hotel's entrance. He also failed to detect when the shadowy form began to move toward him and hurried across the street. Still focused ahead, Thompson was oblivious to the fact that as the man in the hood cut between two parked cars, he drew a gun and fired a shot at his back (Figure 1.1).

Although the hooded gunman was only 20 feet behind Thompson, it appears the excitement of the moment caused him to jerk the trigger—driving the first shot down and to the right—striking Thompson's right calf. Although the pistol had a suppressor that muffled the sound of the shot, Thompson still heard the pistol's report. The surprise and shock of the shot, and the bullet's immediate impact on the back of his leg, caused him to stumble to his right and fall down next to the building. The gunman's pistol malfunctioned as a result of the suppressor not allowing the pistol to cycle fully and keep firing, but he kept walking toward the wounded Thompson. While struggling to clear the malfunctions of his

FIGURE 1.1   A still frame from the CCTV footage of Brian Thompson being shot. United States of America v. Luigi Nicholas Mangione, sealed complaint, accessed April 24, 2025, https://www.justice.gov/d9/2024-12/signed_complaint_mangione.pdf.

pistol caused by the suppressor, he ejected three live rounds, but he was nevertheless able to fire two more shots at his prone victim, one of which fatally struck him in the chest. The hooded and masked shooter then crossed back across 54th Street and disappeared down an alley.

The shooter did not attempt to stop and rob Thompson, nor did he attempt to take his watch or wallet after he had been incapacitated.[4] This shooting was clearly a murder, an assassination, not a robbery attempt gone wrong, and the killer had escaped from the scene.

Murders in New York City are not unusual, and high-profile shootings outside Manhattan hotels are not entirely unheard of. In March of 2022, a wealthy French Cryptocurrency investor was shot five times outside The Fifty Hotel and Suites in Midtown, only a little over a half mile from the Hilton.[5] But that was a case of robbery with the thieves targeting the victim's $450,000 Richard Mille watch. He was only shot after he refused to relinquish his expensive timepiece and struggled as the criminals unsuccessfully attempted to wrestle it from his wrist.

The cold-blooded assassination of a health insurance CEO outside a Midtown hotel by an unknown killer, however, was unusual—and chilling. The killing was also captured on the Hilton's security camera system and the grainy video of Thompson being brazenly gunned down quickly went viral on social media.[6] Unfortunately for investigators, the video did not provide much help in identifying the murderer. He had been hooded and masked, which concealed much of his face. The dramatic, true-life crime mystery portrayed in the video also rapidly came to dominate national and international media.[7] The resulting hype only increased as police launched a nationwide manhunt for the escaped killer.

Police retrieved a few items discarded by the shooter, including the spent cartridge casings, three unfired bullets ejected as he attempted to clear the malfunctioning pistol, a water bottle, a cell phone, and a snack bar wrapper. These items were documented and then rushed to forensic labs for examination.[8]

Word soon leaked to the press that the three shell casings had words inscribed on them: "Deny," "Defend," and "Depose."[9] These words were quickly linked to a 2010 book by Jay Feinman, *Delay, Deny, Defend*, that criticized how insurance companies handle claims, providing a potential motive for the murder.[10]

The items bearing forensic evidence retrieved from the murder scene were not the only leads NYPD was working on. Manhattan is one of the most heavily saturated cities in the world in terms of surveillance cameras,[11] with the camera networks of the New York Police Department (NYPD) and the Metropolitan Transit Authority augmented by thousands of cameras owned by other entities, businesses, and private citizens. While this proliferation of cameras in New York has caused privacy advocates to protest,[12] they are a powerful investigative tool, and NYPD detectives were able to conduct a painstaking canvas of video footage to trace the killer's steps before the murder[13] as well as document his escape.[14]

By the next day, NYPD investigators were able to trace the gunman back to the Manhattan hostel where he had paid cash to stay. Identifying the hostel also provided a significant lead when detectives were able to obtain photos of the shooter's face as he flirted with the receptionist at the hostel front desk.[15] Two days later, on December 6, NYPD announced that their review of video feeds led them to conclude the killer had left New York.[16]

After an extensive search of Central Park, NYPD also found a distinctive backpack the suspect wore at the time of the shooting. It had been abandoned with a pile of Monopoly money inside it.[17] The fake money again hinted at a motive, but NYPD failed to identify the suspect as the national manhunt for the unknown killer continued.

The mysterious shooter was finally apprehended on December 9, after a customer at a McDonald's Restaurant in Altoona, Pennsylvania, saw him remove his mask as he ate, and recognized him from the hostel photos NYPD had provided to the media.[18] The customer alerted a restaurant employee, who called the Altoona Police Department. After a quick field interrogation, the responding officers quickly determined that they had detained the mysterious suspect wanted in connection with the Thompson murder. They even found him in possession of a weapon and suppressor matching those seen in the video, and the fake New Jersey ID he had used to check into the hostel. They were also able to finally identify the mysterious suspect as 26-year-old Luigi Mangione (Figure 1.2).[19]

Mangione was the scion of a wealthy Maryland family. He had been the valedictorian at the Gilman School, an elite private high school in Baltimore, who had gone on to earn bachelor's and master's degrees in computer science from the prestigious University of Pennsylvania. The fact that the suspect was an Ivy League tech grad further fueled the media frenzy surrounding the case.[20]

Raised to a life of privilege, Mangione traveled widely and lived for a period in a trendy co-living space called "Surfbreak" just off Hawaii's Waikiki Beach.[21] During this time Mangione reportedly suffered a serious back injury during a surfing accident. In 2023, he had surgery to fix his back, and it is speculated this may have some nexus to his grievance against the health insurance industry,[22] even though he was not a patient of United Healthcare.[23] At any rate, the surgery does not appear to have had an adverse financial impact on Mangione or his family. He spent several months backpacking alone through Asia after recovering from the surgery.[24]

In retrospect, the solo backpacking excursion appears to have been a sign of Mangione beginning to withdraw from his friends and family.

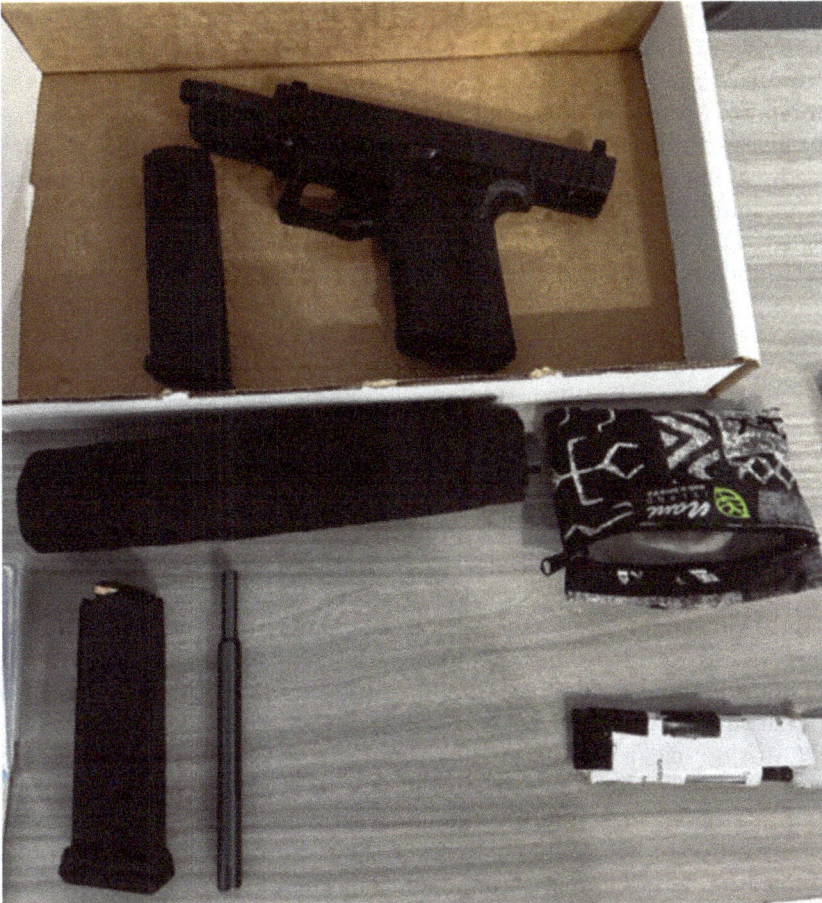

FIGURE 1.2 Ghost Glock and suppressor found in Mangione's back-pack when he was arrested.

After his surgery he appears to have become progressively reclusive, and he began to focus on materials that were critical of society. In January Mangione posted a review on his Goodreads account of the Unabomber's manifesto, giving a four-star rating.[25]

Over 2024, he progressively detached from his friends and family, with friends desperately reaching out to him on social media.[26] By November, he had completely dropped off the radar. On November 18, just 16 days before the murder of Brian Thompson, Mangione's mother filed a missing person's report for him with the San Francisco Police Department.[27]

At the time of Mangione's arrest, Altoona police found a notebook in his backpack in which he had outlined his grievances against society and the outline of his plans for murdering Brian Thompson. These writings vividly illustrated how Mangione's journey followed what we in the protective intelligence community call "the pathway to violence."[28] In the notebook Mangione described going to a "bean-counter" conference—an investor's meeting—to kill a health care executive. Another passage read: "What do you do? You wack (sic) the CEO at the annual parasitic bean-counter convention. It's targeted, precise, and doesn't risk innocents." He also ranted in the manifesto that the "parasites" in the health care industry "had it coming."[29]

PROTECTIVE INTELLIGENCE LESSONS

While Thompson's wife told NBC News that he had been receiving threats, ostensibly related to health care coverage,[30] a review of the video shows the CEO was not practicing good situational awareness on the morning of his murder and never saw his attacker coming. The exact nature of the threats leveled against Thompson is unknown to the authors. We also do not know if Thompson was offered protection due to the threats, or attendance at the conference, and declined coverage. However, from his actions we can conclude with certainty that Thompson did not think he would be targeted for an attack at that time and at that location.

It is not clear if Mangione had considered other targets during the target identification and selection phases of his attack cycle,[31] or if he had attempted to conduct surveillance of Thompson at his residence or his office in Minnesota. However, since both are known locations associated with Thompson, it would not surprise us to learn he had. It is important to recognize that some threat actors travel to stalk their prey, gathering locational information via social media or event announcements.

We have been working to piece together Mangione's attack cycle from press reporting, but we will likely not have enough detail to definitively outline his attack cycle until more information is released as evidence during his trial—assuming his case does proceed to trial. However, we have been able to uncover some information that sheds some light on how he planned his attack. According to the U.S. Department of Justice (DOJ),[32] Mangione began pre-operational surveillance of Thompson several months prior to the attack. This is not a surprise. Surveillance is a necessary component of the attack cycle, and an attacker will surveil the target and the attack site multiple times as he proceeds through the cycle, right up to the point of the attack.

The DOJ provided this glimpse into what the investigation had uncovered about Mangione's attack cycle.[33]

Mangione meticulously planned the execution of Brian Thompson in an effort to initiate a public discussion about the healthcare industry. Mangione targeted the victim, tracked his whereabouts, and traveled from out of state to New York City, where the victim was scheduled to attend the company's investor conference. After arriving in the city on Nov. 24, more than one week before the murder, Mangione performed reconnaissance in the area around the victim's hotel and the conference venue where the victim was scheduled to speak. Using a false identification, Mangione checked into an Upper West Side hostel.[34]

Threat actors often consider multiple targets during the target identification and selection phase of the attack cycle, and surveillance is used to help determine which potential target is the most vulnerable or accessible.[35] At this point it is not known if Mangione chose Thompson because he considered him a vulnerable target, or simply because of his profile and position.

But once Mangione selected Thompson as a target, it is not surprising that he also traveled to the investor conference in New York. He wrote in a notebook that the conference was a "windfall," indicating that he considered it an ideal opportunity to find and target Mr. Thompson.

Threat actors can be mobile, something that we've witnessed many times over the years. For example, while we were serving in the Protective Intelligence Division of the Diplomatic Security Service, we investigated a threat case involving a suspect who was focused on Secretary of State James Baker and who stalked him in several countries in Europe and the Middle East. We finally caught up with the suspect in Israel and were able to coordinate with the Shin Bet, Israel's domestic security service, to get him arrested. That case was a good illustration that some threat actors are mobile, and once a target is selected, it is not difficult for a fixated person to find their target at a publicized event or a known location if they have the means to travel. Steps can be taken to reduce this vulnerability, and we will discuss those later in this book.

REACTION TO THE MURDER

Shortly after the attack on Mr. Thompson, supporters of the unknown killer began to surface, claiming that Thompson deserved to die because of his role in leading a health insurance company.[36] This vile reaction first emerged on social media, but later spread to the physical world with graffiti, "wanted" posters, and signs all calling for additional executives to be murdered.[37]

Once Mangione was identified, the support for him only increased with some people on social media expressing their affection for him due to his looks, others praising him for doing a "noble" act for the people, hosting demonstrations outside the courthouse demanding that the government "Free Luigi,"[38] and even holding a Mangione look-alike contest.[39] The McDonald's where he was arrested received threats, and the Altoona Police Department website was hacked and their officers threatened (Figure 1.3).[40]

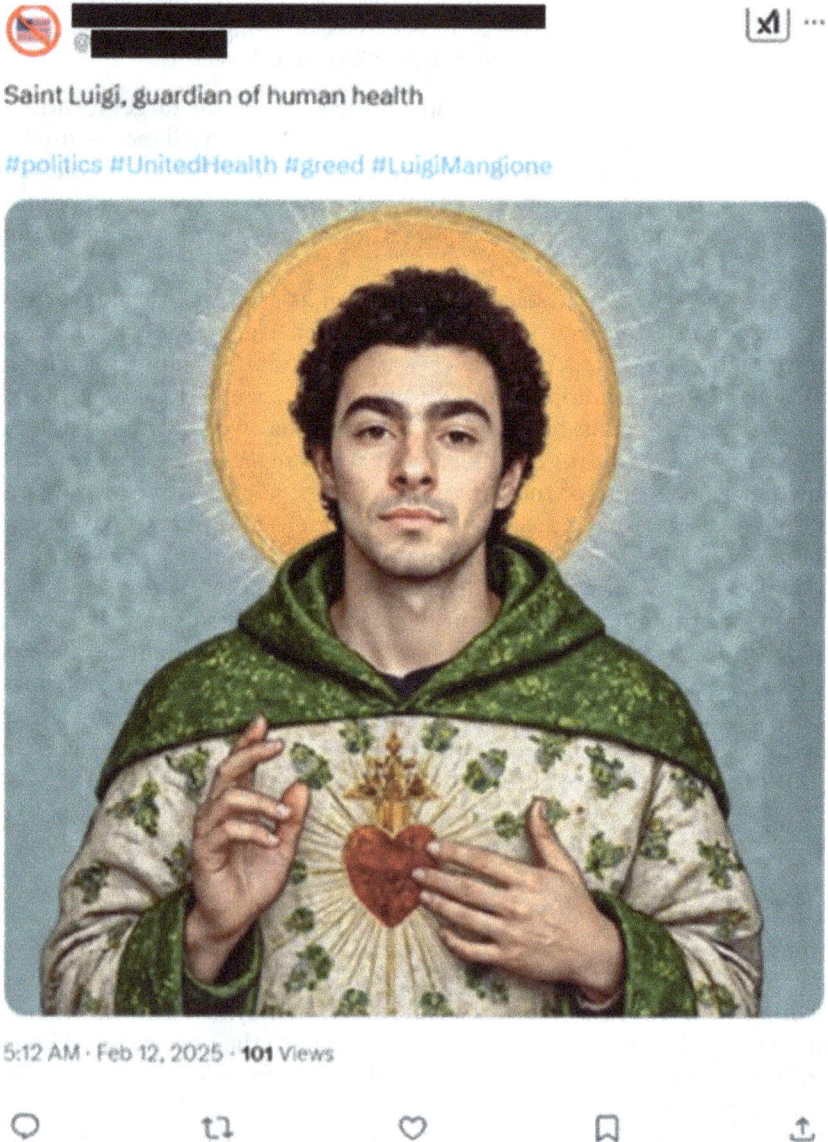

FIGURE 1.3 Post from X venerating Mangione as a "saint." @Grrl Scientist, Twitter (deleted), February 12, 2025, 5:12 AM.

The lionization of Mangione is a highly troubling development for those of us engaged as protectors in the protective intelligence and threat assessment industry. High-profile events, like this one, can inspire other copycat attacks and assassins—even more so when the murderer becomes a celebrity and the center of attention. We have seen copycats after past attacks when school shooters and other killers become celebrities and are deluged with fan mail.[41]

Hindsight is always 20-20, but we can learn important lessons from attacks that can help us prevent the next one. Our intent is to learn from the tragic murder of Brian Thompson. We are in no way attempting to point fingers or criticize him or the men and women of the United Healthcare security team. We will leave that up to their internal corporate after-action review.

That said, we firmly believe that the outcome of Mangione's plotting would have had a far different outcome if Thompson had been covered by close protection or a surveillance detection team. Firstly, Mangione may have reconsidered the attack, if he felt the presence of a close protection team made it too dangerous, or if he got cold feet because he believed the protection agents spotted him before he could cross the street for the attack. It is not unusual for attackers to get cold feet or to divert from a target they consider hard and choose one they believe is easier to attack.

Secondly, Mangione was not subtle as he deployed across the street from the hotel prior to the attack. A covert surveillance detection team or even a security advance agent at the hotel would likely have had very little problem spotting him due to his dress and demeanor.

An alert close protection agent walking with Thompson at the time of the attack would also have seen Mangione in time to prevent the attack. Even if the agent didn't spot Mangione until he began to approach Thompson, he would still likely have been in a position to react. A reaction such as lunging for Mangione's gun, returning fire after the first shot—as Mangione fumbled with his pistol before firing the fatal shot—or even screaming for Thompson to run for safety into the hotel while the agent covered him could have saved his life. At the very least, a trained protection agent with the proper equipment could have immediately begun to administer first aid minutes before the first responders arrived to do so.

In retrospect, the threats Thompson reportedly received before the attack also show the value of threat assessment teams, technology solutions to capture and triage threats, and the need for continuous monitoring of the threat landscape for any executive.

One of the elephants in the room is this: Did Thompson decline protection or call his agents off for this simple morning walking move? We don't know. However, the incident has been a watershed moment in corporate security and caused most, if not all, corporations to reevaluate protection protocols for their executives and board members.

Historically, tragedy has been the driver to force changes in our industry and caused the creation of new job categories, such as international security manager, protective intelligence analyst, executive protection teams, campus police, and others.[42]

We believe that the tragic killing of Thompson will create a new push for discreet, covert protection teams that can focus on surveillance detection and countersurveillance. These "shadow" teams are something we first used in the government to support low-profile protective details. Later we were the first to transfer this model into the private sector in the late 1990s. The model allows the person being protected to know that someone is always discreetly watching their backs, while also watching ahead for potential problems at their destinations.

KEY TAKEAWAYS

- Denial is deadly: "Not me, not here, not now" can cause people to neglect security.
- Threat actors can travel, and attack cycles can be completed across different geographies.
- Scheduled conferences and events require enhanced security that can include discreet countersurveillance.

NOTES

1 Reed Abelson, "Who Was Brian Thompson, the CEO of United Healthcare?" *The New York Times*, December 4, 2024, https://www.nytimes.com/2024/12/04/health/brian-thompson-unitedhealthcare.html/.

2 United Health Group, "UnitedHealth Group Reports 2023 Results," accessed April 17, 2025, https://www.unitedhealthgroup.com/content/dam/UHG/PDF/investors/2023/UNH-Q4–2023-Release.pdf.

3 Reed Abelson, "Who Was Brian Thompson, the CEO of United Healthcare?" *The New York Times*, December 4, 2024, https://www.nytimes.com/2024/12/04/health/brian-thompson-unitedhealthcare.html/.

4 Emily Mae Czachor, "After Fatal Shooting of UnitedHealthcare CEO Brian Thompson, Here's What We Know," *Cbsnews.com*, December 4, 2024, https://www.cbsnews.com/news/united-healthcare-ceo-shot-what-we-know/.

5 Jenny Stanton, "Crypto Expert, 33, Shot by Robber Targeting His $450k Watch Speaks Out," *Daily Mail*, March 29, 2022, https://www.dailymail.co.uk/news/article-10663677/Crypto-expert-33-shot-robber-targeting-450k-watch-speaks-out.html.

6 Shimon Prokupecz, "CNN Obtains Video of Fatal Shooting of UnitedHealthcare CEO," *CNN*, December 4, 2024, https://www.cnn.com/2024/12/04/us/video/surveillance-video-moment-of-shooting-unitedhealthcare-ceo-digvid/.

7 Christopher Maag, Ed Shanahan, and Andy Newman, "United Healthcare CEO Shooting: What We Know about Brian Thompson's Killing," *The New York Times*, December 4, 2024, https://www.nytimes.com/2024/12/06/nyregion/unitedhealthcare-brian-thompson-shooting.html.

8 Juliann Ventura, "Police Test DNA, Fingerprints on Bottle in Search for UnitedHealthcare CEO's Killer," *The Hill*, December 6, 2024, https://thehill.com/policy/healthcare/5025916-police-dna-testing-unitedhealthcare-ceo-shooting/.

9 Aaron Katersky and Meredith Deliso, "'Deny,' 'Defend' and 'Depose': Police Investigating Words Found on Shell Casings in CEO Shooting, Sources Say," *ABC News*, December 6, 2024, https://abcnews.go.com/US/deny-defend-depose-ceo-shooting-shell-casings/story?id=116530063.

10 Tom Murphy, "Words on Ammo in CEO Shooting Echo Common Phrase on Insurer Tactics," *AP News*, December 5, 2024, https://apnews.com/article/unitedhealthcare-ceo-shooting-delay-deny-defend-depose-ee73ceb19f361835c654f04a3b88c50c.

11 Paul Bischoff, "Surveillance Camera Statistics: Which City Has the Most CCTV Cameras?" *Comparitech*, May 23, 2021, https://www.comparitech.com/vpn-privacy/the-worlds-most-surveilled-cities/.

12 "Inside the NYPD's Surveillance Machine," Amnesty International, accessed April 17, 2025, https://banthescan.amnesty.org/decode/index.html.

13 Aaron Katersky, Emily Shapiro, Miles Cohen, and David Brennan, "New Photos of Suspect's Face Released as Police Race to Find Gunman Who Killed UnitedHealthcare CEO," *ABC11 Raleigh-Durham*, December 5, 2024, https://abc11.com/post/police-piece-together-shooting-suspects-escape-route-after-unitedhealth-care-ceo-brian-thompson-killed-outside-new-york-hilton/15623558/.

14 Anna Kutz, "New Video Shows CEO Shooting Suspect Enter Central Park," *NewsNation*, December 7, 2024, https://www.newsnationnow.com/us-news/northeast/exclusive-new-video-shows-ceo-shooting-suspect-enter-central-park/.

15 Michael Stallone and Alex Meier, "New Photos Show Alleged CEO Killer's Smile; NYPD Search NYC Hostels: Sources," *FOX 5 New York*, December 5, 2024, https://www.fox5ny.com/news/nyc-united-healthcare-ceo-brian-thompson-murder-midtown-shooting-hotel.

16 Aaron Katersky, Emily Shapiro, and Jon Haworth, "UnitedHealthcare CEO Shooting Latest: Manhunt for Killer Enters 3rd Day," *ABC News*, December 6, 2024, https://abcnews.go.com/

US/hearts-broken-unitedhealth-group-speaks-after-ceo-brian/ story?id=116515711.

17 Karina Tsui, Mark Morales, Brynn Gingras, John Miller, Shimon Prokupecz, Elise Hammond, Tori B. Powell and Ashley R. Williams, "Backpack Found in Central Park Believed to Belong to Suspect in Killing of UnitedHealthcare CEO, Source Says," *CNN*, December 6, 2024, https://www.cnn.com/2024/12/06/us/ brian-thompson-unitedhealthcare-gunman-search-hnk/index. html.

18 Jonathan Dienst, Tom Winter, Marc Santia and Jennifer Millman, "Manhunt in CEO Killing Leads to McDonald's Arrest: What We Know about Person of Interest," *NBC New York*, December 9, 2024, https:// www.nbcnewyork.com/news/local/ceo-killing-man-questioned- pennsylvania-suspect-gun-unitedhealthcare-brian-thompson- updates/6053340/.

19 Olivia Bosar, Bill Shannon, and Rebecca Parsons, "NEW DETAILS: Suspect in Deadly CEO Shooting Arrested in Altoona, Found with 3D-Printed Gun," *WTAJ*, December 9, 2024, https://www.wtaj.com/ news/local-news/murder-of-unitedhealthcare-ceo-leads-to-person- of-interest-in-altoona-pa/.

20 Corey Kilgannon, Mike Baker, Luke Broadwater and Shawn Hubler, "Luigi Mangione, Suspect in CEO Killing, Withdrew from a Life of Privilege and Promise," *The New York Times*, December 10, 2024, https://www.nytimes.com/2024/12/09/nyregion/united-healthcare- ceo-shooting-luigi-mangione.html.

21 Associated Press and Sean Murphy, "From Wealth and Success to Murder Suspect, the Life of Luigi Mangione Took a Hard Turn," *WHYY*, December 11, 2024, https://whyy.org/articles/luigi-mangione-united healthcare-ceo-brian-thompson-shooting/.

22 Daniel Gilbert, "Severe Pain Shaped UnitedHealth CEO Murder Suspect's View of Health System," *Washington Post*, December 11, 2024, https://www.washingtonpost.com/business/2024/12/11/luigi- mangione-back-pain-healthcare-shooting/.

23 Jonathan Dienst, Tom Winter, Marc Santia and Jennifer Millman, "Manhunt in CEO Killing Leads to McDonald's Arrest: What We Know about Person of Interest," *NBC New York*, December 9, 2024, https:// www.nbcnewyork.com/news/local/ceo-killing-man-questioned- pennsylvania-suspect-gun-unitedhealthcare-brian-thomp- son-updates/6053340/.

24 Dinah Voyles Pulver and N'dea Yancey-Bragg, "'Nothing More, Nothing Less': Writings Show Wandering Path across the Globe for Luigi Mangione," *USA Today*, December 14, 2024, https://www. usatoday.com/story/news/nation/2024/12/14/luigi-mangione- path-murder-asia-mystery/76980670007/.

25 Jason Ma and Amanda Gerut, "The Man Held in Connection with the UnitedHealthcare CEO's Killing Gave the Unabomber's Manifesto a 4-Star Review," *Fortune*, December 9, 2024, https://fortune.com/2024/12/09/luigi-mangione-unabomber-manifesto-reviewted-kaczynski-unitedhealthcare-ceo-brian-thompson/.

26 Jack Newsham and Katherine Long, "Luigi Mangione's Deleted Social-Media Posts Give Clues to His Politics," *Business Insider*, December 10, 2024, https://www.businessinsider.com/luigi-mangiones-deleted-social-media-posts-clues-politics-2024-12.

27 Aaron Katersky, Sasha Pezenik, Josh Margolin, Jon Haworth, Nadine El-Bawab, and David Brennan, "UnitedHealthcare CEO Killing Latest: Mangione's Mother Filed November Missing Report," *ABC News*, December 15, 2024, https://abcnews.go.com/US/unitedhealthcare-ceo-killing-latest-mangiones-mother-filed-november/story?id=116801461.

28 We discuss the pathway to violence in detail in Chapter 10.

29 Ashley Southall and Maria Cramer, "Police Have Luigi Mangione's Notebook Describing Rationale for UHC CEO Killing," *The New York Times*, December 11, 2024, https://www.nytimes.com/2024/12/11/nyregion/luigi-mangione-assassination-plan-notebook.html.

30 NBC New York Staff, "Brian Thompson's Wife Said Threats Had Been Made against UnitedHealthcare CEO before Shooting," *NBC New York*, December 4, 2024, https://www.nbcnewyork.com/manhattan/brian-thompson-united-healthcare-ceo-threats/6039242/.

31 We provide a detailed description of the Attack Cycle in Chapter 10.

32 Office of Public Affairs, "Luigi Mangione Charged with the Stalking and Murder of UnitedHealthcare CEO Brian Thompson and Use of a Silencer in a Crime of Violence," *Press Release*, December 19, 2024, https://www.justice.gov/opa/pr/luigi-mangione-charged-stalking-and-murder-unitedhealthcare-ceo-brian-thompson-and-use.

33 Office of Public Affairs, "Luigi Mangione Charged with the Stalking and Murder of UnitedHealthcare CEO Brian Thompson and Use of a Silencer in a Crime of Violence," *Press Release*, December 19, 2024, https://www.justice.gov/opa/pr/luigi-mangione-charged-stalking-and-murder-unitedhealthcare-ceo-brian-thompson-and-use.

34 Office of Public Affairs, "Luigi Mangione Charged with the Stalking and Murder of UnitedHealthcare CEO Brian Thompson and Use of a Silencer in a Crime of Violence," *Press Release*, December 19, 2024, https://www.justice.gov/opa/pr/luigi-mangione-charged-stalking-and-murder-unitedhealthcare-ceo-brian-thompson-and-use.

35 We have seen this in the study of past attackers, to include Sirhan Sirhan (RFK), Mark David Chapman (John Lennon), Arthur Bremer (Governor George Wallace).

36 Joe Joseph, "How an Insurance CEO's Killer Became a Symbol of American Anger," *The Hill*, December 6, 2024, https://thehill.com/opinion/5026570-unitedhealthcare-ceo-killed-criticism/.

37 Aaron Katersky, Peter Charalambous, and Josh Margolin, "Executive 'Hit Lists' and Wanted Posters: NYPD Warns about Threats to Executives," *ABC News*, December 11, 2024, https://abcnews.go.com/US/executive-hit-lists-wanted-posters-nypd-warns-threats/story?id=116662519.

38 Peter Charalambous, "'Catalyst': Luigi Mangione's Supporters Brave 11-Degree Arctic Blast to Air Healthcare Grievances," *ABC News*, December 24, 2024, https://abcnews.go.com/US/catalyst-luigi-mangiones-supporters-brave-11-degree-arctic/story?id=117064146.

39 New York Post, "New York Post Presents: Luigi Mangione Monster or Martyr? | Trailer (2025)," *YouTube*, January 2, 2025, https://www.youtube.com/watch?v=SuJm9i7ujwE.

40 Brian Niemietz, "Altoona Police Report Threats after Luigi Mangione Arrest," *New York Daily News*, December 11, 2024, https://www.nydailynews.com/2024/12/11/altoona-police-mcdonalds-threats-luigi-mangione-arrest/.

41 Brian Niemietz, "Altoona Police Report Threats after Luigi Mangione Arrest," *New York Daily News*, December 11, 2024, https://www.nydailynews.com/2024/12/11/altoona-police-mcdonalds-threats-luigi-mangione-arrest/.

42 The killing of JFK and Warren Commission, caused the U.S. Secret Service to dedicate protective intelligence advance agents, and the murders of the U.S. diplomats in Khartoum, Sudan, and Beirut, Lebanon, created the State Department Office of Security 24x7 command center and threat analysis group.

CHAPTER 2

Revenge Served Cold in DC

On the afternoon of May 14, 2015, the Washington, DC, Fire Department was called to respond to a fire that was engulfing a stately brick home in the city's upscale Woodley Park neighborhood. As firefighters battled the flames, they discovered the bodies of three adults and a child inside the home. As firefighters pulled the bodies out of the smoldering remains of the home, they made a horrific discovery—the victims had not been killed by the fire—the three adults had been secured to chairs, bludgeoned, strangled, and stabbed before the home was set alight. The child had been left tied to a bed in the room where the fire was initiated by pouring gasoline over his body and the mattress and then lighting it. There were puddles and spatters of blood all over the bedrooms. The firefighters quickly determined the fire had been started by someone attempting to destroy evidence of a grisly crime and cordoned off the home for police (Figure 2.1).

As the residence was transformed from a fire scene into a crime scene, investigators learned the home belonged to Savvas Savopoulos, the CEO of American Iron Works, a construction company specializing in building large commercial and government buildings. They were also able to identify the victims as the 46-year-old Savvas, his wife Amy, 47, their 10-year-old son Philip, and the family's housekeeper, Vera Figueroa, 57.[1]

Police reported that all four of the victims appeared to have been tortured prior to their deaths and had been beaten with a baseball bat, stabbed with a Samurai sword, and asphyxiated with a plastic bag. The three adults were all held captive in one of the upstairs bedrooms while the child was held in another. Investigators suspected the child may have been tortured to force his father to comply with the criminal's demand for money, but the torture inflicted on the victims appeared to have been far more severe than what would be required for this purpose—it was gratuitous.

The adult victims suffered significant head trauma, multiple stab wounds, and fire damage. In fact, the damage to the bodies was so severe that the medical examiner struggled to determine the exact cause of death for the adults, as the head trauma and stab wounds could have

DOI: 10.4324/9781003647744-3

FIGURE 2.1   Crime scene photo of the Savopoulos residence (Courtesy of U.S. Attorney's Office for DC).

both been responsible. The medical examiner was also unable to establish how many times young Philip had been stabbed, or if he had still been alive when he was set alight (Figure 2.2).

Ultimately, whatever amount of compulsion the captor used appears to have been sufficient because police learned that Mr. Savopoulos' personal assistant delivered $40,000 in cash to the residence shortly before it was set alight. Mrs. Savopoulos' Porsche 911 was found burning in a church parking lot in New Carrollton, MD, later that afternoon.

The brutal murder of a family and their housekeeper in an affluent area of the nation's capital garnered a great deal of media attention, and the case soon became known in the media as "the D.C. mansion murders."[2]

As the investigation into the murders continued, it was determined that the Savopoulos family was taken captive on the evening of May 13 and held overnight until Mr. Savopoulos could arrange for the cash to be delivered to the home.

One piece of evidence supporting the theory that the family had been held overnight was the fact that two pizzas were delivered to the home on the evening of May 13, which were paid for with an envelope of cash left on the porch. Those pizzas would ultimately help police identify the suspect through DNA recovered from a piece of uneaten pizza crust found inside the home (Figure 2.3).

The DNA matched that of 34-year-old Daron Wint, a man who was raised in Guyana and moved to Lanham, MD in 2000 and who had a

FIGURE 2.2 Bedroom where the body of Philip Savopoulos was found (Courtesy of U.S. Attorney's Office for DC).

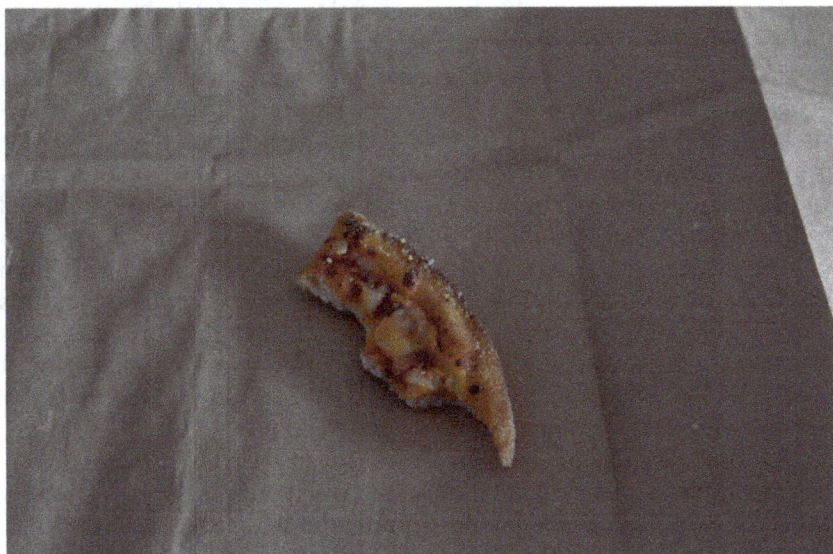

FIGURE 2.3 The piece of half-eaten pizza crust recovered from the crime scene (Courtesy of U.S. Attorney's Office for DC).

prior criminal history for theft, assault, sexual offenses, and burglary. Wint lived in an apartment complex close to where Mrs. Savopoulos' Porsche was abandoned. In October of 2018, Wint was convicted on 20 counts of murder, kidnapping, extortion, and arson, and sentenced to four consecutive life sentences in connection with the crime.[3]

QUESTIONS ABOUT THE MOTIVE

Even nearly ten years after the crime, unanswered questions remain. First, prosecutors were never able to provide clear proof of Wint's motive during his trial, and Wint himself has refused to discuss the case even after his sentencing. However, from the facts established by the investigation, we do know this was not a random crime.

According to police, from 2003 to 2005 Wint had been employed as a welder with American Iron Works, the company run by Mr. Savopoulos. He was reportedly fired after threatening a co-worker with a knife. After losing his job at American Iron Works, Wint had problems maintaining employment and contacted the company in 2008 and 2009 asking to be re-hired.

In 2010 Wint was arrested at a gas station across the street from the American Iron Works headquarters building, indicating his continued fixation on the company. At the time of that arrest, Wint was reportedly armed with a BB pistol and a machete. The weapons charges were reportedly dropped when Wint pleaded guilty to charges of possessing an open container of alcohol. However, based on the totality of these circumstances, it is not difficult to draw the conclusion that the 2015 home invasion and murders were connected to Wint's previous employment at American Iron Works. This was a case of workplace violence conducted by an aggrieved and unstable former employee.

That there was a period of ten years between Wint's firing from American Iron Works and the attack against Mr. Savopoulos and his family is somewhat unusual, but not unique in workplace violence cases involving "grievance collectors." There have been several examples of attackers who harbored grievances and who brooded over them for years, before finally lashing out in a violent action.

Another example of a workplace violence case with a long fuse was the June 2018 armed assault against the Annapolis Gazette Newspaper that left five people dead. Jarrod Ramos, the man who pleaded guilty to the attack, had sued the newspaper for defamation in 2012, but the lawsuit was dismissed in 2013. Ramos appealed the decision, but an appellate court eventually upheld the dismissal in 2015. Ramos made a series of threats against the newspaper via letters and on social media following the dismissal, but in 2016 he went silent, leading some at the newspaper to assume he had finally lost interest in them. Ramos broke his two-year silence with a vulgar tweet shortly before launching his deadly attack on the newspaper's office.[4]

In another case featuring a delay, Henry Bello conducted an armed assault against New York's Bronx-Lebanon Hospital in June 2017 after being fired by the hospital in 2015 for sexually harassing a colleague.[5] Nine days before the attack, Bello reportedly lost his job as a caseworker with New York's HIV/AIDS Services Administration, which appears to be the event that triggered his outburst of violence against the hospital. During his rampage, in which Bello killed one doctor and wounded six others, Bello was searching for a specific doctor, the one who forced him to resign amid the sexual harassment charges, and whom he blamed for his subsequent misfortune. That doctor was not working that day, and Bello's attack ended when he killed himself.

Coming back to the Savopoulos case, it's clear Wint did not just accidentally show up at the residence of the CEO of his former company and then kidnap, extort, torture, and murder the CEO and his family. Rather, this home invasion was the result of a decade-long process in which Wint had harbored and nurtured a grievance, thought about conducting an act of violence, and then planned and prepared for the attack. The process by which an aggrieved individual passes from holding a grievance to conducting an attack is known as the "pathway to violence."[6] (See Chapter 10 for a more detailed discussion of the Pathway to Violence.)

THE ATTACK CYCLE

Speaking of planning and preparing for the attack, one of the other still unanswered questions in this case is how Wint planned the attack against the Savopoulos' residence. A complex crime such as a home invasion kidnapping does not just happen. It is the result of a process we call the attack cycle.[7] We discuss the Attack Cycle in detail in Chapter 10.

Investigators obtained the results of searches Wint had conducted using his cell phone in the eight months prior to the murders, but there was no record that he had searched for the address of the Savopoulos family or for directions to the residence. This could have been a result of him conducting those searches using some other device; however, it could also indicate that he did not need to conduct the searches in the months leading up to the home invasion because he already had that information.

This is all pure conjecture, but it is important to remember that Wint was arrested in 2010 at a gas station across the street from American Iron Works. Such a location is a natural surveillance "perch," or place from which to watch a target.[8] Perches from which you can see a target's residence or office are critical locations for those conducting surveillance and should be carefully watched by those wanting to detect or deter hostile surveillance.

While it could be that Wint just coincidentally happened to be hanging out at a gas station across the street from American Iron Works in 2010 while armed—we believe it is far more likely that Wint was in that location with the intention of conducting surveillance on Mr. Savopoulos, or perhaps given the presence of weapons, even intending to attack him at the time of the arrest.

From Wint's perspective, the American Iron Works building was a location known to be associated with Mr. Savopoulos, and it would have been a logical point to begin surveillance if he didn't know the address of the Savopoulos residence. It is possible that Wint could have followed Mr. Savopoulos from American Iron Works to his residence—especially if Mr. Savopoulos was not practicing good situational awareness or looking for hostile surveillance.

Given the brutal nature of the murders and the 2010 arrest across the street from American Iron Works while armed, Mr. Wint appears to have wanted to attack Mr. Savopoulos for years.

Some of Wint's former co-workers from American Iron Works also noted in press interviews that they felt intimidated by Wint's behavior before he was let go[9]—a common occurrence in workplace violence attacks. In most cases like this, the aggrieved individual signals his grievance through threats and other communications. However, in this case, no evidence of any threats or other direct contact or communication with Mr. Savopoulos was produced during Wint's trial, and certainly prosecutors would have been searching for threatening communications as they sought to construct a motive for the attack.

PROTECTIVE INTELLIGENCE LESSONS

Despite the lack of clearly communicated threats, there are several things that a protective intelligence program could have done to prevent this attack.

First, it is important to recognize that communicated threats are not the only indicator of attack planning as a threat actor progresses through his attack cycle. As noted above, a complex crime such as a home invasion kidnapping requires extensive surveillance, and we can assert with some certainty that Wint must have conducted such surveillance prior to executing his attack. This surveillance would not only be required to identify the location of the Savopoulos residence, but also to ascertain the pattern of activity at the household, the pattern of activity in the neighborhood, judge the security measures in place, identify security vulnerabilities, and then use these observations to plot how and when to enter the residence and assert control over the occupants.

Furthermore, would-be attackers are vulnerable to detection as they progress through their attack cycle—and especially so during the surveillance phase of their cycle.[10] This is particularly true for threat actors like Mr. Wint who have not received training in surveillance tradecraft. Such actors tend to be awkward as they conduct their surveillance and are easy to identify—but only if someone is looking for them. As previously noted, we suspect Wint's 2010 arrest at the gas station across from American Iron Works likely occurred as he was attempting to conduct surveillance on Mr. Savopoulos, and at that time seemed sufficiently out of place that someone called the police on him.

One way to detect hostile surveillance is by deploying a protective intelligence "shadow" team tasked to watch for surveillance directed against company facilities, executives, and executives' residences. These teams are highly efficient at picking out poor criminal surveillance.

A secondary advantage of employing shadow team agents is that they are amorphous by nature, which makes them far more difficult for a potential assailant to detect than traditional security measures such as an executive protection detail. Even in cases involving a threat actor with very good surveillance tradecraft who is able to detect one of the shadow team members, the hostile actor's anxiety will increase because he will have difficulty identifying the entire team. In many cases this can cause him to make numerous false positive sightings and hopefully redirect him to another, easier to surveil target—even if he is not noticed by the countersurveillance team.

A second, less expensive way to increase the possibility of spotting hostile surveillance is to train corporate executives and staff in skills such as situational awareness and surveillance recognition. As noted above, criminal surveillance is generally poorly done and is not difficult to detect by an alert person.

THE IMPORTANCE OF RESIDENTIAL SECURITY

Like the office, the residence is a location where a person spends a significant portion of their time. Unless the residence is purchased through a non-descript limited liability corporation (LLC) or other vehicle and the executive is very careful to protect their home address, it can usually be identified by searching tax records, political donations, corporate filings, social media, and other sources. Because of this, for most executives the residence, like the office, should be considered a "known location," or a place where a hostile actor can reliably locate the executive at predictable times.

Because it is a known location, many attacks against executives happen as the victim is departing or arriving home, and executives should practice heightened situational awareness during those times.

The residence should also be assessed for vulnerabilities, and robust physical security measures should be implemented, including locks, alarms, etc. In the Savopoulos case, it appears the family was in the process of having a residential security system installed. They did have one security camera positioned to cover the front door, and glass-break sensors and carbon monoxide detectors both activated as the fire was starting, but there were gaps in the family's residential security measures that their attacker was able to identify and exploit.

There was no security camera coverage of the exterior of the residence except for the front door, and video from that camera was stored locally. This allowed the killer to take the hard drive after he realized he had been captured on video as he retrieved the pizzas from the front porch.

Investigators believe the killer launched his attack at the back door and gained entry to the residence after assaulting the housekeeper, Ms. Figueroa. It is believed he then went upstairs and restrained Philip, and then attacked, incapacitated, and restrained Amy and Savvas as they returned home, entering the home via the same back door.

The alarm system also does not appear to have featured panic buttons placed in locations where they could have been triggered to summon help as the killer launched his attack, or better yet wireless panic buttons that could have been carried.

The home also did not have a safe haven area where the family could have retreated to in the case of an intruder gaining entry to the residence.

In addition to solid physical security measures, security procedures must be established. The executive, their family, and household staff should be briefed and trained on potential threats, how to identify them, and what actions to take if a threat is spotted. Emergency plans should be created for fire, medical emergencies, natural disasters, and intruders. These plans should be practiced periodically and updated as necessary.

DURESS CODES

Another protective intelligence tool that could have been very useful in the Savopoulos case is a duress code, a seemingly innocuous word or phrase that is either inserted or withheld from a conversation to alert a contact that there is a serious problem. During the trial, evidence showed that Mr. Savopoulos either texted or made telephone calls to several people during the many hours he was held hostage to include his personal assistant, his company's chief financial officer, their alarm company, and their other housekeeper, who was asked not to come to the house for her scheduled shift. Had the family and staff been trained to use a duress code, it is very likely that the police could have been alerted to their danger and responded to the home before the family was killed.

KEY TAKEAWAYS

- The attack cycle can sometimes span years as a threat actor progresses along the pathway to violence toward an attack.
- Residential security is important. Many attacks against executives occur at or near their residences.
- In addition to physical security measures, residential security procedures and contingency plans are needed.
- Household staff and family members should receive situational awareness training and be trained on emergency contingency plans.
- Duress codes can be lifesavers and should be used.

NOTES

1 Much more detail on the background of this case, the investigation, and the trial can be found in the WTOP podcast *22 Hours: An American Nightmare*, https://wtop.com/22-hours-an-american-nightmare-podcast/.
2 Megan Cloherty, "Tortured and Killed in DC: Revisiting 2015 Mansion Murder Case as Trial Nears," *WTOP News*, September 5, 2018, https://wtop.com/dc/2018/09/tortured-and-killed-in-kalorama-revisiting-2015-mansion-murder-case-as-trial-nears/.
3 U.S. Attorney's Office, District of Columbia, "Darron Wint Sentenced to Life in Prison for Killing Four People in Northwest Washington Home Invasion," *Press Release*, January 31, 2019, https://www.justice.gov/usao-dc/pr/darron-wint-sentenced-prison-killing-four-people-northwest-washington-home-invasion.
4 Capital Gazette, "What to Know about the Capital Gazette Shooting Case," *Capital Gazette*, June 23, 2021, https://www.capitalgazette.com/2021/06/23/what-to-know-about-the-capital-gazette-shooting-case/.
5 ABC News, "Doctor Armed with Assault Rifle Kills 1, Injures 6 at New York City Hospital, Police Sources Say," *ABC News*, July 2017, https://abcnews.go.com/US/doctor-armed-assault-rifle-kills-injures-york-city/story?id=48378737.

6 Scott Stewart, "Where the Attack Cycle Intersects the Pathway to Violence," *TorchStone Global*, May 13, 2020, https://www.torch-stoneglobal.com/where-the-attack-cycle-intersects-the-pathway-to-violence/.

7 Scott Stewart, "Where the Attack Cycle Intersects the Pathway to Violence," *TorchStone Global*, May 13, 2020, https://www.torch-stoneglobal.com/where-the-attack-cycle-intersects-the-pathway-to-violence/.

8 Scott Stewart, "Detecting Hostile Surveillance," *TorchStone Global*, February 16, 2021, https://www.torchstoneglobal.com/detecting-hostile-surveillance/.

9 Erica Jones, "Who Is Daron Dylon Wint? History of Woodley Park Quadruple Murder Suspect," *NBC4 Washington*, May 22, 2015, https://www.nbcwashington.com/news/local/who-is-daron-dylon-wint/103818/.

10 Scott Stewart, "Exploiting Vulnerabilities in the Attack Cycle," *TorchStone Global*, May 4, 2020, https://www.torchstoneglobal.com/exploiting-vulnerabilities-in-the-attack-cycle/.

CHAPTER 3

A Rapid Attack
Cycle in Bel Air

Miguel Angel Aguiler was a self-made man—in more ways than one. Abandoned by his mother and left homeless as a teen when his father was sent to prison, he was able to beat the odds and graduate from high school after finding God, the sport of wrestling, and a mentor who invested in his life.[1] While many teens in his neighborhood joined a street gang and embarked on a life of crime, Miguel Angel went to work instead, first obtaining a real estate license and later establishing a personal training business, Self Made Family, Inc.[2]

Since its founding in 2014, Self Made Family has grown into a nationwide business empire with Self Made Training Facility (SMTF) gyms now operating in 21 locations across the United States. SMTF gyms have also become popular with the Hollywood elite, and this may have been helped by the fact that Miguel Angel's wife Priscilla is a Hollywood stylist who works with many "A list" celebrities.[3]

As a result of his success and celebrity contacts, Miguel Angel himself became a fitness and entrepreneurship influencer with tens of thousands of followers on social media. To maintain and grow his brand, Miguel Angel frequently posted photos of himself and his family on his various social media accounts.[4] While many of the social media posts pertained to entrepreneurship, he also posted many photos and videos of his family and their luxurious lifestyle, to include their home, their vacations, Miguel Angel's collection of custom cars, and expensive watches (Figure 3.1).[5]

Miguel Angel and Priscilla were living the influencer life on September 13, 2024. They had lunch at a trendy Los Angeles restaurant and then cruised around town in one of their customized classic cars before heading back to their home in Los Angeles' exclusive Bel Air neighborhood. What they hadn't realized though, was that their outing had drawn the attention of someone other than their social media fans. As Miguel Angel climbed out of his car, he was approached by a group of four armed men who demanded his watch and wallet.

DOI: 10.4324/9781003647744-4

FIGURE 3.1   Miguel Angel. Instagram profile (selfmadefamilyinc), fair use.

He refused to hand over his belongings, and a struggle ensued, during which several shots were fired.[6] Some media reports indicate Miguel Angel was also armed and fired back at the armed robbers.[7] One of the assailants was shot in the back during the encounter and would later die after being left at the hospital by the other three. Miguel Angel was shot in the face during the encounter, leaving him grievously wounded. He would die after spending three months in intensive care.[8]

Miguel Angel and Priscilla had become victims of one of the "follow home robbery" gangs that have plagued Los Angeles in recent years. In a similar deadly incident, Fashion Nova CEO Richard Saghian was victimized in a follow home robbery in June 2021 as he returned to his Hollywood Hills home in his Rolls Royce vehicle with two friends at 2:00 AM. Just as Mr. Saghian entered his home, three armed men approached his two friends and ordered them to the ground, relieving them of their watches and wallets.

In this case, Mr. Saghian had a security driver, a retired law enforcement officer, who drew his firearm to confront the robbers. The criminals opened fire, and in the ensuing firefight two of the suspects were shot by the security officer, one fatally, and the security officer suffered a serious wound to the abdomen. The two robbery victims were also injured during the incident,[9] but Mr. Saghian was not injured due to the intervention of his security officer.

In these follow home robberies, the criminals focus on high-end restaurants, stores, and clubs, and when they spot a victim who has a watch or other valuable item(s) they believe are worth stealing, they look for an opportunity to strike when they believe the victim is vulnerable. Sometimes the gangs set up on a high-end car and then follow the vehicle home, or to a place where they can steal the vehicle and rob the driver and passengers. Not all of these incidents occur at the victims' homes. Some robberies have been conducted in the middle of busy streets, even in broad daylight.[10]

Los Angeles is also not the only place such robberies are occurring. On the afternoon of August 31, 2024, San Francisco 49ers wide receiver rookie Ricky Pearsall was shot and seriously wounded during a robbery attempt as he was leaving a luxury store near San Francisco's Union Square. The teenage thief was after Pearsall's Rolex and expensive jewelry.[11]

New York has also been plagued by many similar robberies. Crypto entrepreneur Pierrick Jamaux was shot several times when he resisted an attempt to steal his $450,000 Richard Mille watch, as we mentioned in Chapter 1.[12] Brazen thieves in New York have even robbed victims at gunpoint who were sitting at tables in open-air restaurants.[13]

Another thief in New York would spot victims, follow them, and then sneak up behind them on the street and place them in a choke hold until they were rendered unconscious. Once the victims were incapacitated, he would steal their watches and other valuables. In one incident, he even attacked a victim on a subway platform and stole his $14,000 Rolex watch after disabling him.[14]

This is also not just an American problem. Watch thefts have been on the rise in a number of countries around the world. Even in London, a city considered to be "safer" there were some 6,800 watch thefts reported last year.[15] Of course watches are not the only valuables being stolen in this type of robbery; valuable rings, earrings, necklaces, and bracelets can also draw the attention of thieves.

Not all ambush criminals are watch and jewelry thieves. Express kidnappers[16] and some rapists also operate in this manner, as do bank "juggers" or criminals who wait outside a bank or near an ATM looking for a victim who appears to have withdrawn a lot of cash.[17] When Scott and his family lived in Guatemala City, there were gangs who staked out mall and supermarket parking lots, followed women home, and then followed them into their residence through their gates or garage doors to commit home invasion robberies (and often sexual assaults.)

Pava LePere, the CEO and co-founder of EcoMap Technologies, was a fast riser. The young entrepreneur had been featured on the Forbes "30 Under 30" list for 2023,[18] and her company's software, which collects and curates data about all the organizations, resources, and other assets within any ecosystem, was being used by a number of influential companies and organizations to include Meta, The Aspen Institute, the WXR Fund, and the T. Rowe Price Foundation.[19]

But on September 22, 2023, Pava's bright light was snuffed out when she was murdered on the rooftop of the building where her office is located by a follow home rapist. After her murder, police were able to use CCTV footage to piece together the events leading up to her death. That afternoon, as she walked home on the sidewalk, she was followed by a convicted rapist who Baltimore police were searching for in connection with a rape, double murder, and arson he had committed three days before.

The video showed the murderer following Pava at a distance and she appeared to be unaware of his presence. After Pava entered the lobby of the building, she saw the suspect standing outside the front door of the building waving to her and indicating he had forgotten his key and could not get into the building. She politely opened the door and let him into the building and the video showed him getting into the elevator with her. She was never seen alive again, and the suspect left the building some 40 minutes later. Her kind response to a stranger apparently in need was repaid with a violent death. Her body would not be discovered until the following Monday, after she was reported missing.[20]

This was a tragic example of how a criminal can use a ruse to launch a surprise attack upon an unsuspecting victim.

PROTECTIVE INTELLIGENCE LESSONS

As we will discuss in more detail in Chapter 10, not all criminal attack cycles progress in the same manner. While the criminals in most of the case studies we examine in Part I of this book are stalking criminals, who conduct longer, more deliberate attack cycles, the thieves and murderers we've described in the incidents in this chapter work more like "ambush predators." These are criminals who set up at a location such as a shopping area, restaurant, club, or hotel, and then once they spot a vulnerable victim, spring a surprise attack.

This type of criminal does not conduct the same amount of surveillance on their victim that a stalking predator does. In some cases, they may only watch a potential victim for a few seconds before selecting them as a target. Most of their pre-operational surveillance is focused on finding an area where they can locate a victim, and then safely deploy to conduct an attack. Once they identify and select a victim, they will usually deploy very quickly and launch their attack at the first opportunity.

While this type of attack cycle is condensed, the criminals are still vulnerable to detection as they progress through it, and quite often they can be diverted to an easier target if they believe they have been detected and could be caught. This is why we decided to dedicate this chapter to examining ambush criminals.

To illustrate the attack cycle of an ambush criminal, Scott likes to use an incident he was involved in while working as a member of a covert protection team in New York several years ago. The incident unfolded as the client left an upscale hotel in Midtown Manhattan while chatting on her cell phone and holding the phone to her ear. It just so happened that she was holding the phone to her ear with the same hand on which she was wearing a very expensive diamond bracelet. Holding her arm up to her head made her sleeve fall downward, making the valuable bauble on her wrist very easy to see as it sparkled in the sunlight.

As she exited the door and began to walk down the sidewalk, Scott and his partner noticed a man who had been standing next to a shop near the hotel entrance. The man saw the bracelet, and then began to follow their client, who was oblivious to the man. The suspect was intently focused on the client (and the bracelet) and did not notice as Scott and his partner maneuvered closer to the client to get between her and the would-be thief following her. After several steps, Scott's partner broke cover, waved a hand at the would-be thief to get his attention, wagged his finger, and while looking the man in the eyes, mouthed the word "no." Startled at having been spotted, the criminal quickly turned around and began to rapidly walk in the other direction, looking over his shoulder to see if he was being followed.

Scott and his partner reported the incident to the hotel's security director, who pulled video of the incident and passed it to NYPD. Scott and his partner did not see the man lurking outside the hotel for the remainder of that trip, or even during several subsequent trips, but they were certain that if they had not been there, the thief would have attempted to steal the bracelet from the client.

The first key to mitigating the threat posed by ambush criminals is to be aware of the threat they pose, and to practice a heightened level of situational awareness when you are in the sort of location ambush criminals typically set up on. This means paying attention to people who are on the street and who may be looking at you as you leave a high-end hotel, restaurant, or store. It also means carefully surveying the area around an ATM before you stop to use it, or the bank parking lot before you exit the doors. We will discuss how to practice good situational awareness and how to look for potential threat actors in later chapters. But typically, criminals prefer to prey on victims who are not aware of their presence so that they can gain an element of surprise when they launch an attack. This means they will typically shy away from an alert person who could spot them and call the police before they are ready to launch their attack.

Some criminals will behave quite brazenly if they believe the value of what they can steal is worth the risk of being caught. While they may not be conscious of it, all criminals run a cost/benefit analysis before conducting a crime. Criminals who see a big potential payday are more likely to conduct robberies on the street in broad daylight, at a sidewalk cafe, or on a subway platform with lots of witnesses. The best protection against this kind of brazen thief is to be careful not to flash valuables that will draw their attention to you as a potential victim, in addition to practicing good situational awareness.

We are not saying people should not wear a nice watch or other jewelry. What we are saying is that people must be conscious of when and where they do so and recognize the risk they are running of drawing hostile attention to themselves. They need to ask themselves if they really need to wear an item worth tens or hundreds of thousands of dollars every day as they take the subway or walk around town. Then, when they do decide to wear such an item, they should still use discretion to not consciously flash it, and again, they must be committed to practice an appropriate level of situational awareness. In such a situation it is also important to ensure that any valuables a person decides to wear in public are insured, so that they will not resist if someone attempts to steal them.

As a general rule, your belongings are not worth your life or even the risk of being seriously injured by an armed assailant. Because of this, we generally advise people not to resist economic crime. Even if the victim is armed themselves, like Miguel Angel was, they are highly unlikely to win a gunfight against multiple armed assailants. That only happens in Hollywood movies. If some item has enough monetary or sentimental value that a person would rather die than part with it, they really should not be carrying it in public.

The moment at which criminals launch their attack is very danger-ous. They are generally hyped up on adrenaline, which is sometimes amplified by drugs. They also generally have very little training in fire-arms safety and poor trigger discipline. The combination of these two factors produces a situation in which there is enormous potential for an incident to turn very bad very quickly. It is thus important for the victim to do their best to keep calm and not escalate the situation. This is far easier to do if the victim sees the situation developing, than if they are caught completely by surprise. We will talk more about what to do when things go sideways in later chapters.

KEY TAKEAWAYS

- Do not resist economic crime. Give the criminals your valuables and live to fight another day.
- It is always better to avoid an attack than it is to react to one. Situational awareness is a lifesaver.
- Avoid flashing valuables. When you do decide to wear or carry them, be aware of the hostile attention they can draw.
- Some attack cycles can progress very quickly, and an ambush predator may only surveil a target for a brief time.
- Be alert for ambush criminals when you are at the types of places they like to lurk and watch for victims.
- Be aware of the possibility that a criminal could use a ruse to launch a surprise attack.

NOTES

1   Miguel Angel Aguilar, "From Homelessness to Entrepreneurship: The Inspiring Story of Self Made Family Inc," *Self Made Training Facility*, May 9, 2023, https://selfmadetrainingfacility.com/from-homeless-ness-to-entrepreneurship-the-inspiring-story-of-self-made-family-inc/.
2   Miguel Angel Aguilar, "From Homelessness to Entrepreneurship: The Inspiring Story of Self Made Family Inc," *Self Made Training Facility*, May 9, 2023, https://selfmadetrainingfacility.com/from-homelessness-to-entrepreneurship-the-inspiring-story-of-self-made-family-inc/.
3   HOLA! USA, "Priscilla Valles," *HOLA! USA*, September 29, 2024, https://www.hola.com/us/latinapowerhouse/20240929714723/priscilla-valles/.
4   Miguel Angel Aguilar (@selfmadefamilyinc), Instagram Profile, accessed April 17, 2025, https://www.instagram.com/selfmadefamilyinc/?hl=en.
5   Miguel Angel Aguilar (@selfmadefamilyinc), "Building Your Ideal Car is Like Launching a Successful Business Venture from the Ground Up…" *Instagram Photo*, May 11, 2024, https://www.instagram.com/p/C6zuCmvvHX-/?hl=en.

6 Will Conybeare, "Popular Fitness Influencer in ICU after Being Shot during Attempted Robbery in Los Angeles," *KTLA*, September 15, 2024, https://ktla.com/news/local-news/popular-fitness-influencer-in-icu-after-being-shot-during-attempted-robbery-in-los-angeles/.

7 Nate Gartrell, "Ceasefire Raids Targeted Violent Oakland Gang Known as the 'Fein Team,'" *East Bay Times*, December 6, 2024, https://www.eastbaytimes.com/2024/12/06/ceasefire-raids-targeted-violent-oakland-gang-known-as-the-fein-team/.

8 Miranda Siwak, "Influencer Miguel Angel Aguilar Dead at 43 Months after He Was Shot," *Us Weekly*, December 22, 2024, https://www.usmagazine.com/celebrity-news/news/influencer-miguel-angel-aguilar-dead-at-43-months-after-he-was-shot/.

9 Leo Stallworth, "Botched Robbery near Hollywood Hills Home of Fashion Nova CEO Leaves 1 Dead, 4 Injured," *ABC7 Los Angeles*, June 26, 2021, https://abc7.com/hollywood-hills-deadly-shooting-richard-saghian-fashion-nova-ceo/10832481/.

10 FOX 11 Los Angeles, "'LA Is Literally GTA': Man Robbed over Rolex, Robbers Lead Police Chase," *YouTube*, June 21, 2024, https://www.youtube.com/watch?v=F4AyaUwbXVY.

11 CBS News, "Attorney: Teen Charged in Shooting of 49ers Rookie Ricky Pearsall Shouldn't Face Attempted Murder," *CBS San Francisco*, September 11, 2024, https://www.cbsnews.com/sanfrancisco/news/attorney-teen-charged-shooting-san-francisco-49ers-rookie-ricky-pearsall-attempted-murder/.

12 Jenny Stanton, "Crypto Expert, 33, Shot by Robber Targeting His $450k Watch Speaks Out," *Daily Mail*, March 29, 2022, https://www.dailymail.co.uk/news/article-10663677/Crypto-expert-33-shot-robber-targeting-450k-watch-speaks-out.html.

13 PIX11 News, "NYPD Investigate Armed Watch Thefts at NYC Restaurants," *YouTube*, June 28, 2024, https://www.youtube.com/watch?v=b0GM6kCwya0.

14 Eyewitness News, "NYPD Releases Footage of Suspect Wanted for Stealing Rolexes, High-End Watches in Manhattan," *ABC7 New York*, August 14, 2024, https://abc7ny.com/post/nypd-releases-footage-suspect-wanted-stealing-rolex-high-end-watches-manhattan/15183057/.

15 Ryan Hogg, "Billionaire Sir Jim Ratcliffe Says He Doesn't Wear a Watch in London Anymore amid Rolex Mugging Surge," *Fortune*, January 28, 2025, https://fortune.com/europe/article/billionaire-sir-jim-ratcliffe-doesnt-wear-watch-london-anymore-amid-rolex-mugging-surge/.

16 Scott Stewart, "Express Kidnapping," *TorchStone Global*, November 18, 2022, https://www.torchstoneglobal.com/express-kidnapping/.

17 FBI Baltimore, "Criminals Are Targeting Bank and ATM Customers in Maryland," *Federal Bureau of Investigation*, July 11, 2024, https://www.fbi.gov/contact-us/field-offices/baltimore/news/criminals-are-targeting-bank-and-atm-customers-in-maryland.

18 Forbes, "Pava LaPere," *Forbes*, 2023, https://www.forbes.com/profile/pava-lapere/.

19 Forbes, "Pava LaPere," *Forbes*, 2023, https://www.forbes.com/profile/pava-lapere/.

20 Holly Yan, Sara Smart, Raja Razek, Omar Jimenez, and Lauren Koenig, "Slain Baltimore CEO Died of Strangulation and Blunt Force Trauma, Court Documents Say," *CNN*, September 28, 2023, https://www.cnn.com/2023/09/28/us/baltimore-tech-ceo-killing-suspect-arrest-pava-lapere-thursday/index.html.

CHAPTER 4

Making a Deal with Kramer Kidnappers

Edward "Eddie" Lampert is a deal maker. After graduating from Yale University and then working for a few years at Goldman Sachs, Lampert established his own hedge fund, ESL Investments, and at age 25 began to make a name for himself on Wall Street.[1] After a string of highly successful investments that brought in billions of dollars, some even hailed Mr. Lampert as "the next Warren Buffett."[2]

By January 2003, Mr. Lampert was riding high in the investment world. He had experienced a great deal of success through his investments in AutoZone and AutoNation and was working long hours at his Greenwich, Connecticut office to put the final touches on his plans to acquire and reorganize Kmart. But when he left the office at 7:30 on the evening of January 10, 2003, his world suddenly turned upside down.

As Mr. Lampert walked to his car in the building's basement parking garage, two masked men suddenly accosted him, one brandishing a shotgun and the other a handgun. The men placed him in flex cuffs, blindfolded him, and shoved him into the back of a Ford Expedition being driven by a third man. There was a fourth man in the front passenger seat of the vehicle. As the Expedition raced out of the parking garage, the driver and the kidnapping gang's leader, Renaldo Rose, reportedly ordered the men in the back seat to throw Mr. Lampert's Blackberry device out of the vehicle.[3] They also relieved him of his wallet, but it was not discarded, because his captors later used his credit cards to make purchases.

As has been evidenced in many kidnappings, to include that of Exxon CEO Sidney Reso and Coors CEO Adolph Coors III,[4] the initial abduction phase of a kidnapping can be a dangerous and potentially deadly time, with both the kidnappers and victim hyped up on adrenaline.

In an interview published in Vanity Fair,[5] Rose told journalist William D. Cohan that as Mr. Lampert was being abducted, he "freaked out" and one of the gunmen in the backseat began punching him in the head. Rose claimed that he yelled at them both to calm down, and that

　　　　　　　　　DOI: 10.4324/9781003647744-5

he then promised Mr. Lampert that if he kept quiet, they would not hurt him, and Mr. Lampert complied with his request. Rose was obviously attempting to paint himself in the best light in the interview, and Mr. Lampert does not discuss the abduction, so it is unclear if they really calmed him down with kind words—or resorted to threats, but by whatever means, it appears they did somehow manage to calm him down and Mr. Lampert was not seriously injured during the abduction.

Mr. Lampert's captors drove him northeast to Hamden, CT, a small town just outside of New Haven. The 55-mile drive must have seemed interminably long to the stunned and frightened businessman, who had just been wrenched from his world of planning a multi-billion-dollar corporate reorganization and thrust cuffed and blindfolded into the gritty reality of being violently abducted at gunpoint.

Once the abductors reached Hamden, they drove to a Days Inn near Quinnipiac University. The Days Inn was an old-style "auto motel" where guests could park their vehicles right outside the door to their rooms. The motel was cheap and was also located in a quiet, isolated area on the north end of Hamden. It was the kind of place where lovers would meet for a clandestine tryst—it was also an ideal place for the kidnappers to quickly move their cuffed and blindfolded hostage into a room without anyone noticing. Once they got Mr. Lampert into the room, they forced him to lay in the bathtub, which is where they planned to hold him until the ransom was paid.[6]

According to court documents, once the gang got Mr. Lampert secured in the motel bathroom, Rose told him that he had been offered $1 million to murder him and demanded the payment of an equal ransom not to kill him.[7] Rose and one of the other kidnappers then compelled Mr. Lampert to record a message to his wife asking for her to raise the ransom. The pair then drove to New York where they used a pay phone to call Mrs. Lampert and play the recorded message to her and demanded a ransom for his release. They then returned to the motel and began to wait for the ransom to be rounded up and delivered.

At some point, the kidnappers learned the police had become involved in the case. According to court documents, this revelation sparked a disagreement between two of the kidnappers. Mr. Lampert reportedly heard one of them, later identified as Shemone Gordon, urging Rose to let him go. This caused Mr. Lampert to mentally label Gordon as the "let him go guy." Rose disagreed, and Mr. Lampert labeled him as the "bad day guy" because he heard Rose remark that he was having a bad day once he learned the police became involved.[8] In the Vanity Fair interview, Rose told Cohan that at this point he considered killing Mr. Lampert and two of his accomplices to avoid being caught, but noted that Gordon had become sympathetic to Mr. Lampert and talked him out of it.[9]

The painful impasse continued for many hours, as the kidnappers' frustration and disappointment grew. Early Sunday morning, over 24 hours after his initial abduction, Mr. Lampert pitched the deal of his life to his captors: if they would release him, he would gather $40,000 in cash and leave it at a Greenwich Wendy's on January 17 for them to collect.[10] Seeing their chance for a major payday gone, the kidnappers agreed to Mr. Lampert's cut-rate deal and drove him back to Greenwich. At 2:50 AM Sunday morning, Mr. Lampert was shoved out of the vehicle at an I-95 off-ramp and walked to the Greenwich Police Department.[11]

Police quickly rounded up Gordon and two of the other kidnappers, who were still at the motel room where they had held Mr. Lampert. Among the items recovered inside the room during the arrest were the shotgun and shells, and a microcassette recorder used to record Mr. Lampert's message to his wife. Amazingly, the group had used one of Mr. Lampert's credit cards to order a pizza that was delivered to their motel room, which allowed the police to quickly locate and arrest them.

Mr. Lampert's nightmare had ended, and he never delivered a dime of the money he had promised his kidnappers. Rose claimed in his Vanity Fair interview that he decided to let Mr. Lampert go due to the incompetence of his partners. He realized he was not going to get any ransom money but said he decided to use Mr. Lampert's offer as a way to call off what he saw had become a hopeless caper.[12] This rings somewhat true, because rather than remain at the hotel with his accomplices for the pizza party, Rose quickly left New Haven and fled to Canada in an effort to escape arrest. But, despite his best efforts, Rose was eventually detained by Canadian authorities and sent back to the United States where he was arrested, charged, and convicted.[13]

THE ATTACK CYCLE

Unlike the Savopoulos case where not much information about the attack cycle was available, investigators in the Lampert kidnapping were able to uncover a great deal of information about how Rose and his associates planned and executed their crime through the items seized during the arrest of the suspects as well as the result of a search warrant served on Rose's residence. Using these items, plus the testimony of Shemone Gordon, who cooperated with the authorities,[14] investigators pieced together the following chain of events.

Rose, a Jamaican-born 23-year-old, was discharged from the U.S. Marine Corps in September 2002. After his discharge from the Marines, Rose returned to Connecticut, and in October 2002 he was reunited with his longtime friend, Shemone Gordon, who was a small-time drug dealer in the New Haven area and a convicted felon. Rose told Gordon he had a plan to kidnap a wealthy individual for ransom and enlisted Gordon's help in the operation.[15]

From October through December 2002, an examination of Rose's electronics showed that Rose used the internet to compile a list of wealthy people who were potential targets for the kidnapping scheme—the target identification phase of the attack cycle. During the search of Rose's residence, investigators also found notes Rose had made that included the names and addresses of several wealthy Connecticut residents.[16]

As a result of this research, Rose eventually chose to focus on Mr. Lampert—target selection—and conducted additional research to obtain information regarding Mr. Lampert, his investments, his finances, and ESL Investments.[17] Authorities discovered that Rose initially intended to abduct Lampert's child in an effort to compel him to quickly pay a ransom without involving the authorities, but as they began to conduct surveillance on the family, they decided to focus on Mr. Lampert himself due to his predictable schedule.

As Rose and Gordon continued planning the abduction, they conducted additional surveillance of Mr. Lampert's home and office on several occasions to identify his pattern of life, select an attack site, and lay out the general flow of the operation. Material documenting this process was found in a notebook during the search of Rose's residence.

It's been our experience that in kidnapping and assassination cases, multiple targets are usually examined by a threat actor before the final target selection is made. The selection is usually based on a decision calculus to determine which of the potential targets will be the easiest to target. Which person is a creature of habit? Which person leaves their house or office at the exact time of the day and takes the same route? Which person parks in the same spot every day? Which person doesn't have security?[18]

While planning the kidnapping, Rose also purchased a Mossberg shotgun and an air pistol—the weapons acquisition phase of the attack cycle. The air pistol was the "handgun" used in the abduction, and Mr. Lampert did not realize it was just an air pistol at the time. But the shotgun was very real.

While acquiring the other items needed to conduct the kidnapping, Rose and Gordon approached a former girlfriend of Gordon's who worked as a desk clerk at a hotel and persuaded her to steal credit card numbers from hotel patrons. Rose and Gordon then used those credit card numbers to make online purchases of items used in the abduction, including flex cuffs, masks, and bulletproof tactical vests. Rose also reportedly used these credit cards to purchase information reports on potential kidnapping targets from internet data aggregator sites.[19]

In addition to conducting internet research, while planning the kidnapping Rose traveled to Greenwich on several occasions to surveil Mr. Lampert's residence and place of business. He rented several different minivans in preparation for the kidnapping. He did this presumably not only to change the profile of the vehicles he was using but also to avoid using his own car—demonstrating that he at least understood his vulnerability while conducting surveillance.

In December 2002, Rose and Gordon decided they needed additional help to abduct Lampert and then guard him after the kidnapping. They considered enlisting the help of two younger friends of Gordon, 19-year-old Devon Harris and 17-year-old Lorenzo Jones, who, like Gordon, were small-time drug dealers with criminal records. Jones reportedly accompanied Rose and Gordon on at least one occasion as they practiced firing the Mossberg shotgun.[20]

On December 24, 2022, the four men cruised Greenwich in Rose's car searching for a United Parcel Service truck. When they found a truck in a suitable place, Gordon, Harris, and Jones jumped out of the car and confronted the driver, with Jones pointing a .22 caliber revolver at the man. They demanded the keys to the truck but were ultimately unsuccessful. The demand for the keys may be an indication the group intended to use the truck in the Lampert kidnapping. Even though the group was not able to steal the truck, they did take money from the driver and four packages from the cargo area of the truck.

According to court records, the UPS robbery was also reportedly intended for Rose to test Harris and Jones to determine if they had the nerve for the Lampert kidnapping. Shortly after the robbery Rose and Gordon asked Harris if he wanted to participate in a kidnapping in exchange for $90,000. Rose also reportedly asked Jones if he was interested in participating, telling Jones that he "liked how Jones handled himself with the gun during the robbery."[21]

On at least one occasion prior to January 10, the group traveled to Mr. Lampert's office intending to abduct him but "aborted the plan when he left his office accompanied by another individual."[22] But on January 10, Mr. Lampert was not so lucky. The group rented the Ford Expedition and drove to the parking garage in Mr. Lampert's office building. Rose had Gordon and Jones exit the vehicle and hide in a position between the door and Mr. Lampert's vehicle. Rose then parked in a position where he could see people as they exited the building.

After a wait of several hours, Rose spotted Mr. Lampert leaving the building and walking to his car. Using a two-way radio, he ordered Gordon and Jones to grab him. Rose then put the Expedition into gear and pulled up beside them so they could bundle Mr. Lampert into the vehicle. The trap had been sprung on the unsuspecting financier.

PROTECTIVE INTELLIGENCE LESSONS

From the way this kidnapping progressed, it is quite clear that Rose and his crew of small-time street criminals were far more aspirational than they were operationally proficient. We often refer to this type of ama- teurish and inept criminal as a "Kramer" after the notoriously bungling character from the Seinfeld television series. However, this case is also a prime illustration of the fact that if allowed free rein to conduct surveil- lance at will, even a group of "Kramer kidnappers" can plan and execute a crime against a high-net-worth person even if the target lives in an exclusive neighborhood and works in a nice office building.

We have no doubt that Rose and his crew had very little in the way of surveillance tradecraft and even though they changed vehicles, we believe they would have appeared out of place as they lurked in Mr. Lampert's neighborhood or in the parking garage of his office building. They would not have had "cover for status," which tells a story to anyone seeing a person conducting surveillance that the surveillant belongs in that environment and they don't stand out. It simply would not have been difficult to spot the bungling crew as they conducted surveillance on Mr. Lampert's home and office, but only if someone had been looking for them. The reason they were able to get away with being sloppy and out of place is that nobody was paying attention.

In some ways, Kramer criminals are actually *more* dangerous than experienced professionals. They are more likely to be nervous and trigger- happy, and thus more apt to accidentally kill their target than a pro, as was seen in both the Coors and Reso kidnappings.

Criminals planning a targeted attack will usually begin their surveil- lance on a potential target at a known location, such as their residence or place of work, as Rose and his crew did in this case. Because of this, we encourage people to increase their level of situational awareness as they are leaving or returning to a known location, such as their home or office, to look for signs of possible surveillance. Family members and household staff can also be trained to spot and report potential sur- veillance activity. When Scott was posted in Guatemala City where the crime threat was critical and kidnapping had blossomed into a popular cottage industry, he not only practiced heightened situational awareness when he left home for the office each morning, but he would also peri- odically ask his wife to watch the street from a second floor window as he left the house for signs of surveillance he would not have been able to see from his vantage point in the car or after he left the area.

Rose's use of internet searches while planning the Lampert kidnap- ping, to include purchasing reports from data aggregator sites, is not unusual. Pre-operational surveillance of potential targets often begins with such searches. This highlights the importance of maintaining digital hygiene and limiting what information is posted on the internet that could aid potential attackers.[23]

We would also like to highlight how this case illustrates the value of a hostage establishing a rapport with their kidnappers and humanizing themself to them as much as possible. Once Rose learned the police were involved, he reportedly considered killing Mr. Lampert. But Mr. Lampert had formed a personal connection with Gordon, which caused Gordon to argue against killing him.

During the many hostage debriefings we have conducted over the years we learned that it is important for hostages not to close down or to display overt hostility toward their captors. By asking for basic human needs, such as food and water, or to use the bathroom, and then showing gratitude when those requests are granted, a hostage can become more than just an object to their kidnappers. It is also very useful to talk about your family when possible. Mr. Lampert's efforts to humanize himself likely saved his life, and by engaging with his captors, Mr. Lampert was able to eventually make a deal and talk his way out of danger.

KEY TAKEAWAYS

- Even "Kramer criminals" can pose a threat if they are allowed to conduct surveillance at will and plan their crime.
- As a "known location" the office is a key location for enhanced security coverage.
- Surveillance cameras may not stop a crime but can aid in the investigation of crime, and their presence can make criminals feel vulnerable.
- Heightened situational awareness is critical while walking between your office and vehicle, especially when doing so at a predictable time or when it is dark.
- Pay attention to people and things that seem out of place, such as lurkers or suspicious vehicles and report them to the appropriate entity.

NOTES

1 Edward S. Lampert, "About Eddie Lampert," *Eddie Lampert's Blog*, December 19, 2013, https://eddielampert.com/about/.
2 Hayley Peterson, "Inside Sears' Death Spiral: How an Iconic American Brand Has Been Driven to the Edge of Bankruptcy," *Yahoo Finance*, January 8, 2017, https://finance.yahoo.com/news/inside-sears-death-spiral-billionaire-134128865.html.

3 Edward S. Lampert, "About Eddie Lampert," *Eddie Lampert's Blog*, December 19, 2013, https://eddielampert.com/about/.
4 We examine the Coors kidnapping in Chapter 6.
5 William D. Cohan, "Inside the Strange Odyssey of Hedge-Fund King Eddie Lampert," *Vanity Fair*, March 25, 2018, https://www.vanityfair.com/news/2018/03/the-strange-odyssey-of-hedge-fund-king-eddie-lampert-sears-kmart.
6 The New York Times, "With Kidnapping of Executive, Security Has Become an Issue," *The New York Times*, January 19, 2003, https://www.nytimes.com/2003/01/19/nyregion/with-kidnapping-of-executive-security-has-become-an-issue.html.
7 United States District Court District of Connecticut, "Ruling on Defendant's Motions to Sever and to Suppress," January, 2004, https://www.ctd.uscourts.gov/sites/default/files/opinions/010904.EBB_.Rose1_.pdf.
8 United States District Court District of Connecticut, "Ruling on Defendant's Motions to Sever and to Suppress," January, 2004, https://www.ctd.uscourts.gov/sites/default/files/opinions/010904.EBB_.Rose1_.pdf.
9 William D. Cohan, "Inside the Strange Odyssey of Hedge-Fund King Eddie Lampert," *Vanity Fair*, March 25, 2018, https://www.vanityfair.com/news/2018/03/the-strange-odyssey-of-hedge-fund-king-eddie-lampert-sears-kmart.
10 United States District Court District of Connecticut, "Ruling on Defendant's Motions to Sever and to Suppress," January, 2004, https://www.ctd.uscourts.gov/sites/default/files/opinions/010904.EBB_.Rose1_.pdf.
11 CBS News, "Cops Hunt Millionaire Kidnap Ringleader," *Cbsnews.com*, January 13, 2003, https://www.cbsnews.com/news/cops-hunt-millionaire-kidnap-ringleader/.
12 CBS News, "Cops Hunt Millionaire Kidnap Ringleader," *Cbsnews.com*, January 13, 2003, https://www.cbsnews.com/news/cops-hunt-millionaire-kidnap-ringleader/.
13 United States District Court District of Connecticut, "Ruling on Defendant's Motions to Sever and to Suppress," January, 2004, https://www.ctd.uscourts.gov/sites/default/files/opinions/010904.EBB_.Rose1_.pdf.
14 Michelle Tuccitto, "Cooperative Kidnapper Gets Lighter Sentence," *New Haven Register*, June 11, 2004, https://www.nhregister.com/news/article/Cooperative-kidnapper-gets-lighter-sentence-11676406.php.
15 United States District Court District of Connecticut, "Ruling on Defendant's Motions to Sever and to Suppress," January, 2004, https://www.ctd.uscourts.gov/sites/default/files/opinions/010904.EBB_.Rose1_.pdf.

16 United States District Court District of Connecticut, "Ruling on Defendant's Motions to Sever and to Suppress," January, 2004, https://www.ctd.uscourts.gov/sites/default/files/opinions/010904.EBB_.Rose1_.pdf.

17 United States District Court District of Connecticut, "Ruling on Defendant's Motions to Sever and to Suppress," January, 2004, https://www.ctd.uscourts.gov/sites/default/files/opinions/010904.EBB_.Rose1_.pdf.

18 We have done security surveys at some major companies in which the executives names are listed in their parking spot. It's certainly a nice perk but makes it very easy to identify the executive's vehicle and where they park every day.

19 United States v. Rose, No. 05–5652 (2d Cir. 2007). We discuss the information available from data aggregators in Chapter 13.

20 United States v. Rose, No. 05–5652 (2d Cir. 2007

21 United States v. Rose, No. 05–5652 (2d Cir. 2007).

22 United States v. Rose, No. 05–5652 (2d Cir. 2007).

23 We discuss digital hygiene and protecting sensitive personal information in Chapter 13.

CHAPTER 5

An Inside Job in California

In the first four chapters we examined attacks by threat actors who were outsiders. Daron Wint had worked for American Iron Works, but was let go ten years before he attacked the Savopoulos family, so he wasn't a true insider with current knowledge of the company or the CEO. This meant he had to conduct his attack cycle in the same manner as an outside actor.

As former special agents and longtime protective intelligence practitioners, one thing we have noticed over the years is that many companies and organizations have insider threat programs focused on cyber threats such as theft and industrial espionage, but do not have a corresponding program that focuses on preventing insider physical threats. We believe this is a serious oversight and want to use this chapter to discuss the insider threat to executives and high-profile individuals. As we examine a case that provides a prime example of the insider threat, we are going to have to get into the weeds (pardon the pun).

THE ATTACK

Tushar Atre was living the American dream. Although he was born in Germany to Indian parents who had earned scholarships to study at the University of Heidelberg, Tushar became fully Americanized after his family moved to New York when he was a young child. After graduating from New York University with a degree in Political Science and German Literature, Tushar found his true niche in website creation.[1] In 1996 he moved to Santa Cruz and launched his own eponymous web hosting company, Atrenet.[2] The company was very successful, and Tushar was able to buy several homes in Santa Cruz, to include a multimillion-dollar home on Pleasant Point Drive that was perched on a cliff overlooking the ocean. Atre had always loved the water and became an avid surfer after moving to Santa Cruz. Living in a beautiful home on a cliff that looked over one of the best surf breaks in California was any surfer's dream.[3]

But that dream turned into a nightmare in the early morning hours of October 1, 2019, when guests staying in Tushar's home heard a

DOI: 10.4324/9781003647744-6

disturbance erupt in the house at about 3:00 AM. The guests reported that they heard loud voices and banging, with one of the house guests reporting they heard two unidentified male voices. Among other things, the guest reported that the men were asking about a safe. The guest then reportedly heard the commotion move outside and then the sound of cars driving rapidly away. One of the guests placed a 911 call at 3:34 AM—it is unclear why they did not place the call earlier.[4]

When police arrived, they found no sign of a forced entrance and noted that the home had not been ransacked, as was common in most home invasion robberies. They also learned that a safe in Tushar's bedroom still contained $80,000 that had not been stolen. However, they also learned that Tushar was missing, as was his girlfriend's white BMW sport utility vehicle. As officers canvased the neighborhood looking for evidence, they found a puddle of blood in the center of Pleasant Point Drive some 70 yards east of Tushar's home. Police called Tushar's girlfriend, who was visiting the East Coast, who did not know where Tushar or her car were.[5]

After an extensive search, the white BMW and Tushar's body were located at a rural property on Soquel San Jose Road in the Santa Cruz Mountains. Tushar had purchased the property as part of a legal cannabis business, Interstitial Systems, that he had started just months before his death.[6] Tushar had been stabbed repeatedly and then shot in the back of the head. He had been gagged and his hands had been bound behind his back with flex cuffs, and blood inside the BMW indicated he had been bleeding during the drive to the farm where he was murdered.

Although rumors circulated that Tushar had been murdered due to some sort of connection to the illegal black market cannabis trade,[7] those rumors led investigators to a dead end, and the investigation quickly went cold. A reward of $25,000 was offered for information leading to a resolution of the murder, but it produced no useful tips.

A neighborhood canvas by the police identified video footage from the security system at a neighbor's house of three suspects leaving an alley at 2:48 AM and heading west on Pleasant Point Drive in the direction of Tushar's residence. One of the men was seen in the video carrying an assault rifle–likely the rifle used to kill Tushar. Police released the video in mid-November 2019 and increased the reward amount offered for tips in the case to $150,000, but the investigation was still not making much headway (Figure 5.1).[8]

The neighbor's security system also recorded video footage of the horrific events that unfolded as the three men were leaving the house with Tushar. As they got out to the driveway, Tushar apparently saw an opportunity to escape, broke free from his captors, and sprinted down Pleasant Point Drive with his hands bound behind his back. One of the suspects ran him down, tackled him, and then stabbed him several times as he lay on the pavement. The gagged Tushar would not have been able

FIGURE 5.1 The three suspects observed approaching the Atre residence. CBS News, April 3, 2022, https://www.cbsnews.com/news/
tushar-atre-kidnapping-murder-timeline/.

to yell for help, and so his neighbors were unaware of the deadly drama
playing out in the middle of the street. The video also shows lights from
a neighbor's house reflecting off the blood pooling around Tushar's
body as he lay in the street after the stabbing—the puddle of blood the
police would later find. Wounded, Tushar struggled to his feet and again
attempted to run away, but he was once more tackled from behind,
stabbed several more times, and then forced into the white BMW, which
pulled up to where he was tackled. The vehicle then sped off, eventually
reaching the farm where Tushar was shot in the back of the head.[9]

As investigators continued to search for leads in Tushar's murder, they
interviewed the employees at both his web hosting and cannabis businesses.
Among the names of people who might have had a motive to attack Tushar
were two men who had briefly worked for Tushar's cannabis business in
August 2019, Kaleb Charters and Stephen Lindsay. Lindsay and Charters
were close friends who both served in the Army Reserve together and who
had moved to Las Vegas after the murder. Lindsay was also married to
Charters' sister. Santa Cruz detectives flew to Las Vegas in December 2019
to interview the two men. They admitted to the detectives they had a dispute
with Atre in August 2019 over pay he had withheld from them, and Lindsay
even admitted he was angry and had wanted to fight Tushar at the time,
but that they considered the matter settled. They also claimed they had not
returned to Santa Cruz since they stopped working for Tushar.[10]

The detectives returned from Las Vegas without arresting Lindsay
and Charters, but they had begun to focus on them as potential suspects. Their investigation of the pair received a big boost when cell phone

data revealed that Kaleb Charters' cell phone had pinged a tower near Tushar's home at the time of the abduction and had also pinged a tower near Tushar's cannabis farm at the time of the murder. Cell phone data further identified two other phones that matched the movement patterns of Kaleb Charters' phone: the phones of his brother, 22-year-old Kurtis Charters, and their friend, 23-year-old Joshua Camps. Detectives also learned that Stephen Lindsay's cell phone had been turned off on September 27 and was not turned back on again until October 5.

Having identified Camps as a possible suspect, they served a search warrant on his home, where they found numerous guns to include an AR-style rifle and ammunition that matched that used in the murder, but a forensic examination revealed the rifle was not the murder weapon. They also found flex cuffs of the same brand and manufacturing date as those found on Tushar's body. Detectives also learned that Kurtis Charter's palm print matched two latent palm prints recovered from the BMW after the murder (Figure 5.2).[11]

Based on this evidence, on May 19, 2020, over seven months after Tushar's murder, police arrested the four suspects. They announced that they believed the motive for the murder to be robbery, even though the four men gained very little from the abduction and crime.[12] The Charters brothers and Camps all gave statements to the police admitting to their roles in the abduction. Camps also told police where he had buried the murder weapon, which was recovered by police. Lindsay refused to talk.

FIGURE 5.2 Evidence photo of recovered SUV (Courtesy of Santa Cruz County court).

The four were charged with felony murder, that is, murder committed in the process of a felony, in this case armed robbery and kidnapping.[13]

After a long delay caused by legal wrangling over whether the men would be tried together or separately, it was decided they would receive separate trials. A jury found Stephen Lindsay guilty of home invasion robbery, kidnapping, and murder on March 10, 2025.[14] The trials for the other three suspects were scheduled to begin in March 2025 but have not yet begun as of the time of this writing.[15]

PROTECTIVE INTELLIGENCE LESSONS

The attack cycle for an inside threat actor will usually manifest itself differently from that of an outsider because an inside actor can begin their planning cycle while having access to the facility and executive. This access provides them with an opportunity to develop a thorough understanding of security procedures and protocols that can aid in planning the attack. In many cases access control can't stop an insider, because they either have access or know how to bypass access controls.

For example, in a 2006 workplace attack at a U.S. Postal Service facility in Goleta, CA, the murderer, a former employee, gained access to the parking lot by following another vehicle through the gate, and then took a building access badge from another employee at gunpoint which allowed her to gain access to the facility where she killed six postal employees.[16]

In the Atre case, when Tushar interviewed Kaleb Charters and Stephen Lindsay to work at his cannabis farm, he invited them to his home and even gave the pair a tour of the luxurious seaside residence. Kaleb Charters told detectives in an interview that the group was able to gain easy entry into Tushar's home because he had seen Tushar punch the door code into the lock on his front door, and Charters remembered the code. It is also believed that the two saw the large safe in Tushar's residence during that tour.[17]

One of the challenges facing cannabis entrepreneurs is that they are not able to use the banking system in the same manner as most other businesses due to federal banking and interstate commerce regulations.[18] Because of these regulatory challenges, cannabis businesses often keep large quantities of cash on hand, which makes them ripe targets for criminals. This reality could be one of the factors that helped influence the four to target Tushar for this crime.

In many cases, there is very little need for an inside actor to conduct additional pre-operational surveillance. Even if they do conduct additional surveillance, as insiders they belong in the area, and so they don't stick out as anomalous and are hard to detect as they do it. Because of this, in many insider threat cases, looking for surveillance is not the best way to detect an attack cycle in progress.

The Atre case, however, was a little different. Lindsay and Charters had been separated from Tushar's company for a month before they launched the assault on his home, and since they had worked at the farm, they had no reasonable excuse to be near the residence. Additionally, as people who had clashed with Tushar over the pay issue, they also would have stood out had Tushar seen them near his home. It is not known if the group conducted additional surveillance of the residence prior to the attack, but with Stephen Lindsay's phone turned off for four days prior to the abduction, it is possible he did conduct some final surveillance of the residence and was not detected.

In any case, despite the military training Lindsay and Kaleb Charters received, they did not have a very well-developed operations plan. Kaleb Charters told interviewing detectives the group was unsure if Tushar would be home that night. If he was, they planned to force him to open his safe and then steal what they could from the house. If he was not home, they would attempt to open the safe, and if they couldn't get it open, they would just steal whatever items of value they could find.[19] The yelling heard by the house guests about the safe would seem to indicate that the group did attempt to force him to open it and that he refused to do so.

Kaleb Charters also told the detectives interrogating him that the group had not planned to hurt Tushar,[20] but that claim seems to ring hollow. He and Lindsay were both known to Tushar, and he would have been able to identify them had they just obtained the money from the safe and left the residence while leaving him alive to be a witness. Even had the robbery succeeded, they would not have had enough money to leave the country and lay low somewhere beyond U.S. jurisdiction—especially after splitting the proceeds four ways. When combined with the grievance they held against Tushar, and the fact that they brought flex cuffs, were armed, approached on foot, and left the residence in the white BMW, it appears more likely that they intended all along to abduct and kill him if they encountered him in the residence.

Since insiders are known actors, which places them in jeopardy of being caught, it is not unusual in insider theft cases for the thief to kill the victim in an attempt to cover up their crime. In June 2010, retired bio-tech CEO John Watson was murdered by his friend and financial advisor, Kent Keigwin, who hit Watson with a stun gun and then strangled him to death. Watson's death was initially ruled natural, and before the body was discovered, Keigwin impersonated Watson to transfer $8.9 million from one of Watson's accounts to his own.[21]

In a more recent case, in July 2020, tech entrepreneur Fahim Saleh was murdered by his former personal assistant, Tyrese Haspil, who had embezzled hundreds of thousands of dollars from him and who feared being caught. Haspil, dressed in black and with his face covered, waited in a stairwell and ambushed Saleh when he returned to his apartment. Haspil hit Saleh with a stun gun and then stabbed him to death. Haspil then began to dismember Saleh's body with a Sawzall to dispose of it, but was interrupted when Saleh's cousin, who was concerned since she had not heard from him, stopped by the apartment to make a welfare check and discovered the partially dismembered body of her cousin.[22]

These cases all illustrate the need for the proper vetting of employees, as well as robust financial controls. In Tushar's case, inviting unknown laborers who wanted to work for his cannabis farm to his home for their employment interviews was simply not wise. It would have been far better to have held the interviews at a neutral site and maintained more distance between his personal and professional lives. While Tushar did not give the door code to Lindsay and Charters, this case also demonstrates the importance of being careful when entering codes in front of others. It is also critical to change entry codes when an employee is let go.

As previously mentioned, many times the attack planning cycle of an insider is hard to detect. Because of this, it is really important to focus on the pathway to violence model when considering insider threats. Indications that an employee or former employee is harboring a grievance, making threats or beginning to exhibit other signs of violent ideation are important signals that must be watched for.

In the Atre case, although Lindsay and Charters only worked for Tushar for a short period of time, they built up a great deal of animosity toward him. Media reports noted that Lindsay and Charters apparently lost a set of Atre's car keys, and that after they were let go because of it, they learned he had stopped payment on their paychecks. The keys were apparently found later, and Tushar then paid the men some, but not all of what he owed them, making them angry. This grievance is part of what caused investigators to focus on the pair as potential suspects. Other employees at the farm also told investigators that on one occasion Tushar punished Lindsay and Charters by making them perform pushups in front of other employees—humiliating them in front of their peers.[23] It could have been the accumulation of grievances, humiliation, and frustration at being unable to get into the safe that led the group to attack Tushar so savagely when he attempted to run away.

Treating employees poorly and terminating their employment in a way that makes them feel cheated is a surefire recipe for generating grievances.

The Atre abduction and murder is also another example of the need for robust residential security. It is noteworthy that all the security camera footage police obtained in this case came from neighbors' homes and not Tushar's, which would seem to indicate he did not have a camera system installed at his residence. In this case an alarm system with hidden panic buttons could also have allowed him to signal for help. An alarm system set in "home" mode or a secondary deadbolt on his front door could have helped prevent the three attackers from simply walking into Tushar's home and catching him while he was asleep.

In the years we've spent investigating and analyzing kidnappings, we've learned that once the kidnappers have the victim's hands bound and secure, it's difficult to escape. This means a potential victim may only have seconds to decide to comply, fight back, or attempt to escape. If the victim does decide to fight back or escape, the risks are very high. The risks are also high once the bad guys have the victim secured, so there is no simple answer. Ordinarily, our advice is not to resist economic crime, but we believe in general precepts to guide decisions and not iron-clad rules that must be followed in every situation. As seen by this case, the killers may not have let Tushar live even if he had opened the safe. Tushar may have realized they intended to kill him, which is what prompted him to attempt to escape from them. It likely also explains why they stabbed him so quickly and furiously when they caught up to him.

We believe it is important for people to think about various scenarios and consider what they would do ahead of time. In some situations, there simply are no right answers, just a choice between two or three difficult choices. But it is still better to have some sort of mental plan to begin with and then alter it according to circumstances, rather than to have no plan at all and have to make things up on the fly.

KEY TAKEAWAYS

- Residential security is critically important. It's generally the first place a threat actor seeks to find their target. We will discuss residential security in more detail later, but proper locks and doors and a residential alarm system are a must. Panic alarms placed in strategic locations around the house can be a lifesaver.
- People should consider defending their home with whatever weapons they are comfortable using, from non-lethal sprays, to the good old Louisville Slugger, to firearms. *However, if someone decides to use a weapon for home defense, they must receive proper training on using it.*
- Insiders can easily obtain knowledge of an executive's environment and daily routine.
- Efforts should be made to minimize the access of random employees and other insiders to an executive's residence. Privacy should be maintained to the greatest extent possible.

NOTES

1 Santa Cruz Sentinel, "Tushar Atre Obituary," *Santa Cruz Sentinel*, November 28, 2019, https://www.santacruzsentinel.com/obituaries/tushar-atre/.

2 AtreNet, "Our Mission - AtreNet," *AtreNet*, July 21, 2023, https://www.atre.net/our-mission/.

3 CBS News, "Tushar Atre Murder: Surveillance Video Captures the Brutal Kidnapping of a Tech Executive — but What Happened off Camera?" *Cbsnews.com*, August 20, 2023, https://www.cbsnews.com/news/tushar-atre-tech-executive-kidnapping-murder-surveillance-video-48-hours/.

4 Lauren Turner Dunn, "Tushar Atre Case: Inside the Kidnapping and Murder of the Tech Executive," *Cbsnews.com*, April 3, 2022, https://www.cbsnews.com/news/tushar-atre-kidnapping-murder-timeline/.

5 Lauren Turner Dunn, "Tushar Atre Case: Inside the Kidnapping and Murder of the Tech Executive," *Cbsnews.com*, April 3, 2022, https://www.cbsnews.com/news/tushar-atre-kidnapping-murder-timeline/.

6 Max Chun, "Opening Statements in Trial for Murder of Pleasure Point Tech Executive Tushar Atre to Begin This Week," *Lookout Santa Cruz*, January 21, 2025, https://lookout.co/tushar-atre-trial-opening-statements-murder-of-pleasure-point-tech-executive-to-begin-this-week/.

7 Marlene Lenthang, "Murdered Tech Boss Tushar Atre May Have Been Involved in 'Black Market Deals' in Cannabis Company," *Mail Online*, October 3, 2019, https://www.dailymail.co.uk/news/article-7533599/Murdered-tech-boss-Tushar-Atre-involved-black-market-deals-cannabis-company.html.

8 Lauren Turner Dunn, "Tushar Atre Case: Inside the Kidnapping and Murder of the Tech Executive," *Cbsnews.com*, April 3, 2022, https://www.cbsnews.com/news/tushar-atre-kidnapping-murder-timeline/.

9 CBS News, "Tushar Atre Murder: Surveillance Video Captures the Brutal Kidnapping of a Tech Executive — but What Happened off Camera?" *Cbsnews.com*, August 20, 2023, https://www.cbsnews.com/news/tushar-atre-tech-executive-kidnapping-murder-surveillance-video-48-hours/.

10 CBS News, "Tushar Atre Murder: Surveillance Video Captures the Brutal Kidnapping of a Tech Executive — But What Happened off Camera?" *Cbsnews.com*, August 20, 2023, https://www.cbsnews.com/news/tushar-atre-tech-executive-kidnapping-murder-surveillance-video-48-hours/.

11 CBS News, "Tushar Atre Murder: Surveillance Video Captures the Brutal Kidnapping of a Tech Executive — But What Happened off Camera?" *Cbsnews.com*, August 20, 2023, https://www.cbsnews.com/news/tushar-atre-tech-executive-kidnapping-murder-surveillance-video-48-hours/.

12 Jim Hart, "Arrests Made in Tushar Atre Murder," *Press Release*, May 21, 2020, https://shf.santacruzcountyca.gov/Portals/1/PRESS%20RELEASE%20ARRESTS%20IN%20ATRE%20CASE.pdf.

13 CBS News, "Tushar Atre Murder: Surveillance Video Captures the Brutal Kidnapping of a Tech Executive — But What Happened off Camera?" *Cbsnews.com*, August 20, 2023, https://www.cbsnews.com/news/tushar-atre-tech-executive-kidnapping-murder-surveillance-video-48-hours/.

14 Ricardo Tovar, "Man Found Guilty of Murdering Santa Cruz County Tech Executive, 3 Others Face Trial," *KSBW*, March 11, 2025, https://www.ksbw.com/article/guilty-murdering-santa-cruz-county-tech-executive/64135398.

15 Zoe Hunt, "Trial Begins for Man Accused of Santa Cruz County Tech Executives Murder," *KSBW*, January 22, 2025, https://www.ksbw.com/article/trial-santa-cruz-county-tech-executives-murder/63501150.

16 Barney Brantingham, "The Goleta Postal Murders," *The Santa Barbara Independent*, January 31, 2013, https://www.independent.com/2013/01/31/goleta-postal-murders/.

17 CBS News, "Tushar Atre Murder: Surveillance Video Captures the Brutal Kidnapping of a Tech Executive — But What Happened off Camera?" *Cbsnews.com*, August 20, 2023, https://www.cbsnews.com/news/tushar-atre-tech-executive-kidnapping-murder-surveillance-video-48-hours/.

18 https://www.securityinfowatch.com/cannabis-security/article/21269162/commercial-security-meets-the-needs-of-evolving-cannabis-industry.

19 CBS News, "Tushar Atre Murder: Surveillance Video Captures the Brutal Kidnapping of a Tech Executive — But What Happened off Camera?" *Cbsnews.com*, August 20, 2023, https://www.cbsnews.com/news/tushar-atre-tech-executive-kidnapping-murder-surveillance-video-48-hours/.

20 CBS News, "Tushar Atre Murder: Surveillance Video Captures the Brutal Kidnapping of a Tech Executive — But What Happened off Camera?" *Cbsnews.com*, August 20, 2023, https://www.cbsnews.com/news/tushar-atre-tech-executive-kidnapping-murder-surveillance-video-48-hours/.

21 Rebecca Stickney, "Man Guilty in La Jolla Millionaire's Murder," *NBC 7 San Diego*, November 21, 2011, https://www.nbcsandiego.com/news/local/man-guilty-in-la-jolla-millionaires-murder/1911850/.

22 Maia Coleman, "He Stole from His Tech Boss and Killed Him to Conceal the Crime," *The New York Times*, June 25, 2024, https://www.nytimes.com/2024/06/24/nyregion/fahim-saleh-murder-dismemberment-trial.html.

23 Richard Fetzer, "Did Push-ups and Disrespect Lead to Murder? *Cbsnews.com*, August 16, 2023, https://www.cbsnews.com/news/tushar-atre-death-did-pushups-and-disrespect-lead-to-murder/.

CHAPTER 6

Missing the Signs of Danger in Colorado

On a steamy late August day in 2009, a reclusive 80-year-old man with cancer shot and killed himself inside room 307 of the Royal Chateau Apartments in Denver.[1] Despite the regal name, the apartments at the Royal Chateau are not quite fit for a king—but the small one-bedroom apartment on the top floor of the building was ideal for someone like Joseph Corbett, who wanted to keep a low profile and avoid the judgment of his fellow citizens due to the deeds of his notorious past.

Very few of Corbett's neighbors knew that he had once been a Fulbright scholar bound for medical school, with a genius-level IQ, or that he had also been a cold-blooded murderer, an escaped convict, and one of the most notorious kidnappers of all time.[2]

The apartment suited his reclusive nature so much that he lived there for some 25 years before he took his life. The seclusion of the small apartment even helped conceal his final deed: a self-inflicted gunshot to the head. Nobody heard the shot that ended Corbett's life, and his body was only discovered after the apartment manager noted that he had not collected the newspaper that had been left in front of his door. Perhaps the shot was muffled somewhat by the contact with his head, or maybe the street noise created by the heavy traffic on South Federal Boulevard served to conceal the sound of the pistol's report.

But the shot he fired that took his own life generated far less attention than the two shots he fired some four decades earlier that took the life of Adolph Coors III during a botched kidnapping attempt. According to our friend Phillip Jett, who wrote the definitive book on the Coors kidnapping: *The Death of an Heir: Adolph Coors III and the Murder That Rocked an American Brewing Dynasty,*[3] the search for Corbett was the largest manhunt in the United States since the kidnapping of the Lindberg baby in 1932.[4]

DOI: 10.4324/9781003647744-7

THE ATTACK

Adolph Coors III (most people called him Ad) was the chairman and CEO of the eponymous brewing company founded by his Grandfather Adolph Herman Joseph Coors in 1873 in Golden, Colorado. Although the 45-year-old father of four was brought up in a life of privilege, attending the exclusive Phillips Exeter Academy in New Hampshire before graduating with a degree in engineering from Cornell, most people considered Ad to be humble and relatable.[5] Unlike his father, who wore a suit to work every day, Ad was usually dressed in chinos and a button-down shirt. He was frequently seen wearing a tan baseball cap, which was perhaps a nod to his passion for baseball, but it was also far less formal than the fedoras worn by his father and many other businessmen at that time. Even his vehicle was humble. Rather than drive or be driven around in a Cadillac or Lincoln limousine, Ad drove an International Harvester Travelall,[6] a rugged station wagon built on a truck chassis. The Travelall was the forerunner of today's large sport utility vehicles but was very utilitarian, and far less flashy than a modern-day Escalade or Yukon Denali.

Perhaps Ad's biggest indulgence was his ranch. In addition to being an excellent athlete, Ad was an outdoorsman who loved to hike and ride horses. In the summer of 1958, he and his family moved from their home in Denver to a new home they had built on 480 acres of ranchland lying at the foot of the Rockies just outside the small town of Morrison, located some 15 miles southwest of Denver. Morrison is perhaps best known for being the home of the famous Red Rocks Amphitheater. Making the move to the ranch gave Ad the space and solitude he sought while still being close enough to Denver for his wife and family to be able visit their friends.[7]

Living in Morrison also provided Ad with an easy commute to his office at the brewery in Golden. He was able to take roads that bypassed Denver to the west and avoided all the traffic and lights in downtown Denver. In February 1960, though, Ad's commute had been lengthened a bit by construction that closed off the gravel road he normally took for a mile to get to U.S. Highway 285. In fact, construction had dragged on for a month, forcing Ad to take a narrow, winding dirt road for four miles to get to the highway. That road forded Turkey Creek via a narrow, wooden bridge aptly named the Turkey Creek Bridge.[8]

Turkey Creek Bridge was a choke point, a physical feature that served to funnel traffic into a narrow point that had to be traversed if one hoped to get from point A to point B. With the other road closed for construction, to get to the highway, and then on to work from his ranch, Ad had to pass over the Turkey Creek Bridge. To someone planning an ambush for an assassination or abduction, a choke point can become an attack site if it has features that permit the attacker to deploy and launch the attack without being detected. Another consideration is whether the site offers a quick escape route after the attack. Turkey Creek Bridge was remote, and on a sparsely traveled road. Corbett could deploy and prepare to launch his ambush without being detected by Ad or others. It was also located not too far from the highway, providing an easy escape route and thus provided Corbett with an ideal attack site.

On the morning of February 9, 1960, Corbett parked his canary yellow 1951 Mercury at the end of the bridge at about 8:00 in the morning, the time he knew Ad would be leaving his home for his morning commute to the Coors brewery. Corbett propped the vehicle's hood open, feigning car trouble. As Ad approached the bridge in his Travelall, he saw the stranded vehicle and slowed to a stop, placing his still running vehicle in park in the middle of the bridge. Ad opened the door and exited his vehicle to see if he could help the stranded motorist. The exact sequence of events that transpired after Ad approached Corbett is murky, but from the evidence later found at the bridge, Corbett apparently drew his firearm and attempted to abduct Ad, who resisted, resulting in a struggle. At some point in the struggle, Corbett shot Ad twice, wounding him. Corbett then evidently placed the wounded Ad into his vehicle—it is unclear if he applied the handcuffs and leg irons he had purchased by mail to a still conscious victim, or if he simply threw an unconscious Ad into the trunk. Corbett then sped away from the scene and Ad was never seen alive again.[9]

The attack site was so isolated that Ad's Travelall sat on the bridge idling for over two hours after the attack. At 10:20 AM a milkman making his rounds approached the bridge and found the Travelall running with the driver's door window open and the radio on. Thinking the vehicle's owner must be close by, the milkman honked the horn and waited for the owner to return and move the vehicle off the bridge so he could finish his deliveries. After some 15 minutes and several other annoyed horn blasts, the perturbed milkman backed the vehicle off the bridge and parked it on the side of the road, turning the ignition off and leaving the keys inside the vehicle. When the milkman returned down the road after making a delivery, he noticed the Travelall was still parked where he had left it. Thinking it odd, he called the State Police when he got to a phone, and at 11:35 AM, a State Police patrolman arrived at the scene and radioed in the vehicle license plate and description. Learning the vehicle belonged to the Coors brewery, the State Police contacted the company and learned from Ad's brothers that he had not shown up at work as expected that morning.[10]

A thorough search of the bridge and the surrounding area found a baseball hat belonging to Ad and a fedora hat belonging to an unknown person on the creek bank just below the bridge. Blood was found on the wood planks of the bridge and on the left side of the Travelall's front bumper. Police also noticed spatters of blood on the driver's side of the Travelall. Later that afternoon, the police were able to divert the flow of the creek to conduct a more thorough search. After the water level subsided, they located a pair of glasses with a broken left lens that they suspected belonged to Ad. The glasses were later confirmed to be Ad's by his eye doctor.[11]

The police also noted a set of skid marks in the gravel just south of the bridge which indicated a vehicle had departed the scene at a high rate of speed.[12] This evidence all pointed to a struggle and an abduction, but there was no sign of Ad and no communication from whoever kidnapped him (Figure 6.1).

The following day brought confirmation of what everyone had feared when a ransom letter was received by the post office in Morrison. The letter was addressed to Mrs. Adolph Coors III, Morrison, Colorado, and marked "special delivery" and "personal." The letter, which was post-marked at 3:00 PM on February 9, in Denver, demanded a ransom of $500,000: $200,000 in ten-dollar bills and $300,000 in twenty-dollar bills, noting there would be no negotiation and threatening to kill Ad if the police or FBI were called.[13] The letter further demanded that the bills be "used / non-consecutive / unrecorded / unmarked" and that a classified ad be placed in *The Denver Post* when the money was ready (Figure 6.2).

As the results of the crime scene investigation came in, it became clear that the amount of blood discovered at the scene was much greater than initially thought, and that if the blood was Ad's, it was unlikely he survived the abduction attempt. Despite the family's doubts that Ad was still alive, at the direction of the FBI, they gathered the requested ransom money, posted the classified ad in *The Denver Post* and waited for the kidnapper to make contact. The call never came.[14]

A massive investigation into the kidnapping was launched, with dozens of FBI agents pouring into Denver to augment the efforts of the state and local police. While forensic examinations of blood and soil samples and the ransom letter were being conducted at the FBI laboratory, investigators fanned out across the area searching for leads and interviewing hundreds of people. They soon focused on a canary yellow 1951 Mercury that witnesses noted had been seen in the area (pre-operational surveillance) on several occasions, to include at approximately 8:00 AM the morning before the incident, as well as several mornings the previous week.[15]

One witness provided the FBI with a partial license plate number, which led them to the only yellow 1951 Mercury, which was registered to a man named Walter Osborne. The FBI learned that Osborne had left his apartment in a hurry on the morning of February 10, telling his landlady

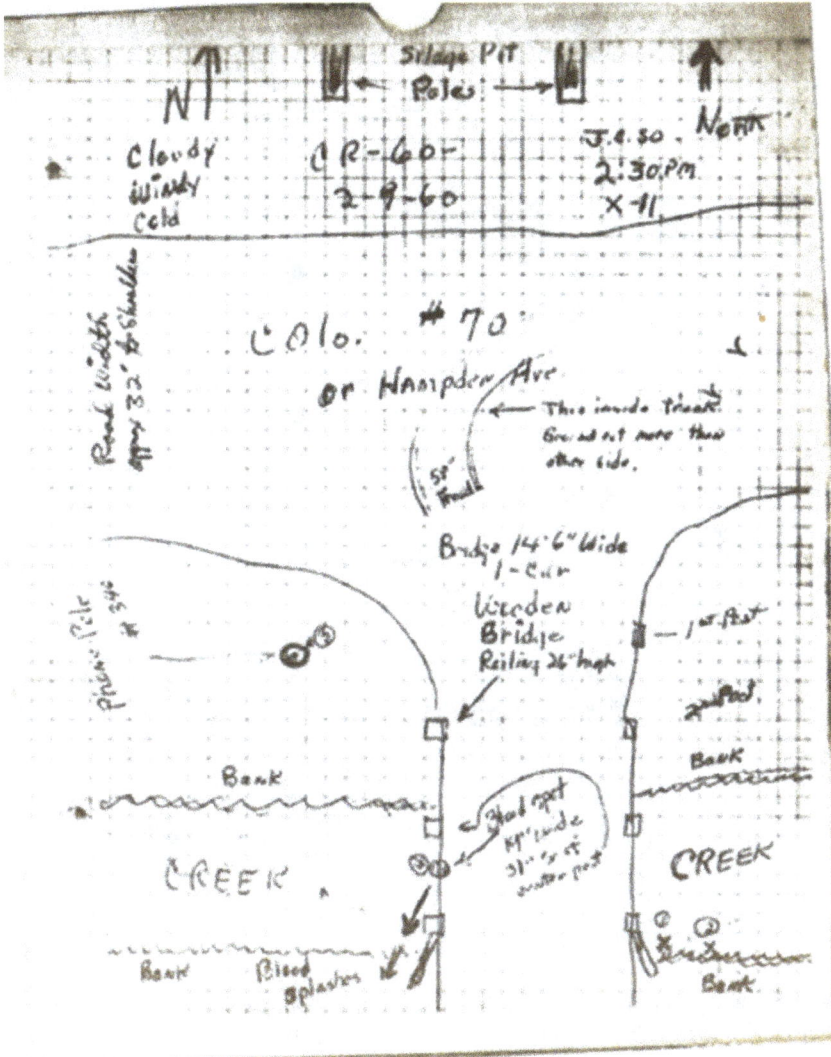

FIGURE 6.1   Crime scene sketch from a Jefferson county Sheriff's depart
ment report.

that he was moving out to go back to college. A week later, Osborne's
vehicle was found burning in a garbage dump in Atlantic City, New
Jersey, on February 17, but investigators were able to learn very little
about Osborne. The discovery of the car in Atlantic City explained why
there had been no follow-up call by the kidnapper to the family. The man
who attempted to abduct Ad had fled Denver and had very little interest
in collecting the ransom because Ad was likely dead.[16]

Mrs. Adolph Coors III

Morrison, Colorado

PERSONAL

SPECIAL DELIVERY

Mrs. Coors:

Your husband has been kidnaped. His car is by Turkey Creek.

Call the police or F.B.I.: he dies.

Cooperate: he lives.

Ransom: $200,000 in tens and $300,000 in twenties.

There will be no negotiating.

Bills: used / non-consecutive / unrecorded / unmarked.

Warning: we will know if you call the police or record the serial numbers.

Directions: Place money & this letter & envelope in one suitcase or bag.

Have two men with a car ready to make the delivery.

When all set, advertise a tractor for sale in Denver Post section 69. Sign ad King Ranch, Fort Lupton.

Wait at NA 9-4455 for instructions after ad appears.

Deliver immediately after receiving call. Any delay will be regarded as a stall to set up a stake-out.

Understand this: Adolph's life is in your hands. We have no desire to commit murder. All we want is that money. If you follow the instructions, he will be released unharmed within 48 hours after the money is received.

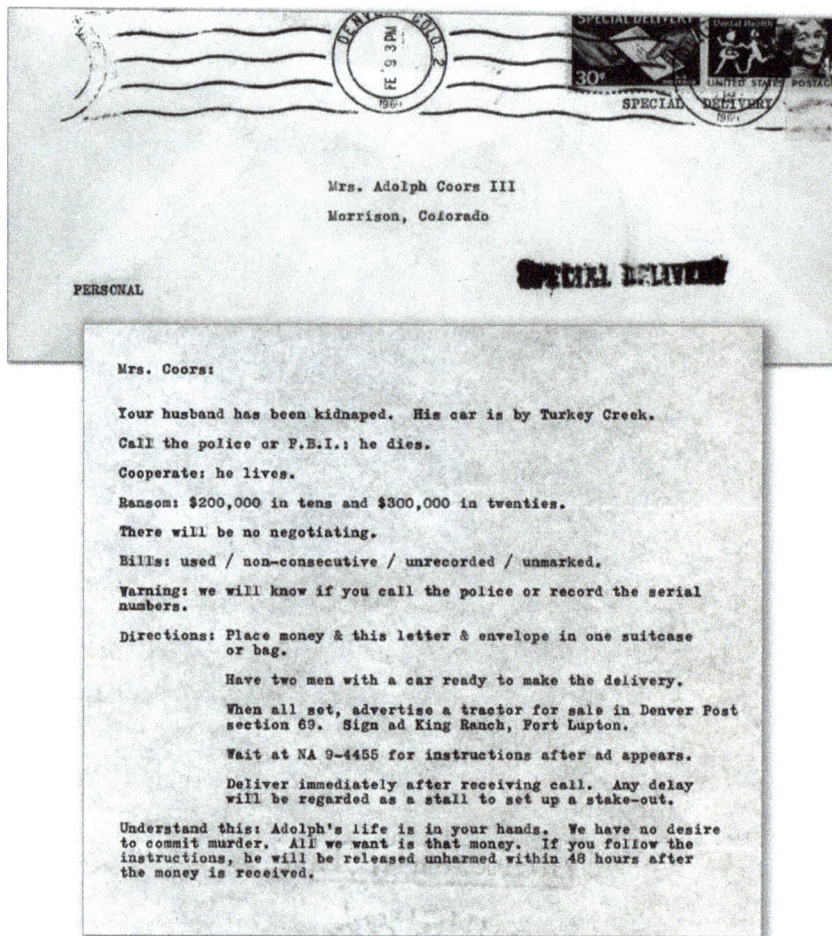

FIGURE 6.2   A copy of the ransom letter. Federal Bureau of Investigation, accessed April 29, 2025, https://www.fbi.gov/history/artifacts/coors-kidnapping-ransom-note.

The big break in the case came on March 5, when the FBI was able to match fingerprints found at the apartment and on Osborne's driver's license application to an escaped murderer named Joseph Corbett.[17] The FBI now knew who they were chasing. Corbett became the chief suspect in the Coors case and the FBI obtained a fugitive warrant for him and soon placed him on the FBI's Ten Most Wanted Fugitives list.

Throughout the summer of 1960, Corbett's trail remained cold. But tragically, the trail leading to Ad Coors ended on September 11, 1960, when hikers came across a pair of trousers in the woods near a dump about 12 miles southwest of Sedalia, a town south of Denver. The pants had a key ring in them, and a penknife attached to the key ring bore the initials AC III. A more thorough search of the site found other items of clothing consistent with those worn by Ad the day of his disappearance, to include a ski-shaped tie clasp also inscribed with AC III. A watch bearing the inscription A. Coors III was also found at the site. Searches of the dump on subsequent days found bones belonging to a man approximately six feet tall. On September 15, a human skull was found that was positively identified as Ad's through dental records. An examination of the clothing revealed that the jacket and shirt had bullet holes in them indicating Ad had been shot in the back. Forensic analysis of a shoulder bone found at the site confirmed this. After being shot and killed, Ad had been wrapped in a green blanket and thrown in the dump, his remains scattered by animal predation.[18]

The story of Ad Coors' disappearance remained in the public eye and was featured in various publications, including *Reader's Digest*. Corbett's wanted photo sparked interest and leads across America, but it was the magazine's readers in Canada who would break the case. One reader pointed the Royal Canadian Mounted Police to an apartment rented by a man who resembled Corbett, but the man had recently moved. The next day, the manager of a rooming house in Winnipeg called local police to report that a man who looked like the fugitive had recently stayed at her establishment. She also noted that the suspect had been driving a fire engine red Pontiac. That new information went out across Canada, and on October 29, 1960, a Vancouver police officer reported a similar vehicle parked outside of local motor inn. Soon, police—with the assistance of the FBI's Toronto legal attaché office—were knocking on the door of the hotel room. The man who answered said, "I give up. I'm the man you want."

Corbett was returned to Colorado, where he was tried by the state for Coors' murder (because Coors' remains were found within the state, he wasn't tried on federal kidnapping charges). Especially compelling was the ransom note believed to have been typed on Corbett's typewriter, and damning evidence taken from his burned-out canary yellow Mercury, which was recovered by law enforcement in New Jersey shortly after Coors' disappearance.

On March 19, 1961, Joseph Corbett, was convicted and sentenced to life in prison.[19] However, he would only spend 18 years in jail, before being released, working for a manufacturing company and driving a truck for the Salvation Army, in Denver, Colorado. He lived as a recluse and took his life at the Royal Chateau Apartments on that hot August day in 2009.

THE ATTACK CYCLE

An FBI interview of one of Corbett's co-workers who had a criminal history for petty crimes provided some interesting insight into Corbett's attack cycle. The man told the agents that Corbett had cased some banks in Denver for a potential robbery, and identified their delivery schedules, but calculated that such a robbery would likely only net him $5,00–$10,000 dollars and that he wanted to pull "one big job" that would net him $500,00 to a million dollars. The co-worker added that Corbett had boasted that he had spent two and a half years planning for the big job and planned to conduct it in the summer of 1958, but that something had happened that caused him to postpone it. The Bureau noted in their report that Ad Coors had moved during this timeframe from a house in Denver to his home in Morrison.[20] This move apparently disrupted Corbett's original abduction plan and forced him to begin a new attack planning cycle.

Due to the complexity involved in a kidnapping for ransom, this crime requires a much more thorough attack cycle than those for most crimes. Once a target has been selected from the potential targets identified, more intensive surveillance is then conducted to determine when and where the target is most vulnerable for a successful abduction attempt. As noted above, kidnappers usually choose an abduction site that offers them the ability to deploy without detection, control the target's movement, and allows for a quick escape.

While other crimes such as a bank robbery also require the criminal to conduct research on their target, perform pre-operational surveillance, and make escape plans, kidnappers must take the additional steps of planning for a secure place to hold the victim, establishing secure communications with the family, and planning for a safe ransom drop.

Generally, the safe house or other location where the hostage is detained during the kidnapping is located in an area the criminal can easily control and where they can operate with relative freedom and without fear of detection. In some locales, this may be a remote rural area, while in others, it may be in a congested urban neighborhood or slum. For a prolonged kidnapping, the safe house must be stocked with some sort of cell or restraints to hold the victim, as well as provisions to feed them. The criminal must also find a way to provide around-the-clock security at the detention site to ensure the hostage does not escape.

In the Coors case it appears Corbett planned to hold Ad in a cave or other remote area, as his co-worker told the FBI that he had spent considerable time exploring mines, caves, and abandoned mining towns in the Colorado back country. He had also purchased a lot of camping gear in an after Christmas sale in late December 1959. The FBI investigation also determined that Corbett had purchased four pairs of hand and leg irons by mail in February 1959 and four sets of handcuffs in April 1959. It would appear he intended to use these to restrain Ad during and after the abduction.[21]

In addition to the safe house, kidnappers must make plans for secure communications with the victim's representatives when negotiating the ransom and arranging for the ransom drop and the victim's release. Despite Corbett's demand in the ransom letter not to involve police, the disruptions caused by the abduction and the concerning evidence left behind at the bridge ensured that police became involved well before the family received the ransom note in the mail with his demand the following day. The involvement of the police and FBI would have complicated the situation for Corbett even if he had not killed Ad during the bungled abduction attempt. Corbett may have had a genius-level IQ, but he did not do a very good job of planning the kidnaping.

While Corbett did identify a good attack site, the abduction itself was not well planned out, and Ad resisted, rather than comply with Corbett. As we've noted in previous chapters, the initial abduction is a very dangerous time for both the criminals and the victim, and they each experience a great deal of adrenaline. Quite often, kidnappers will attempt to use the elements of surprise and overwhelming force to compel the victim to surrender and comply with their demands like the multiple armed assailants involved in the Lampert abduction. Other times they will use a drug, stun gun, or some other means to incapacitate the victim. When overwhelming force is not present, the victim might decide to resist. This can sometimes result in the victim's escape, but in other cases, like that of Ad Coors, or the botched kidnapping of Exxon CEO Sidney Reso in 1992,[22] the victim can be shot, wounded, or killed, while resisting.

Planning for the ransom-victim exchange often requires the abductors to make elaborate arrangements to ensure their security and maximize their chances of escape. These arrangements may include surveillance of the area to check for law enforcement and ensure that the victim's representatives comply with instructions. In many cases, the operational plan will also include a pre-established rendezvous point where the criminals will meet after the ransom drop. The ransom drop itself is a delicate operation. Things can often go wrong if the criminals get spooked or there is some other sort of misunderstanding. In such cases, situations can go bad quickly, resulting in either the capture of abductors or the abandonment or death of the victim.

As the attack cycle demanded, Corbett conducted a great deal of surveillance prior to attempting to kidnap Ad, and this surveillance spanned months. Two men working in a mine near the Turkey Creek Bridge told the FBI that they had seen Corbett on December 9, while driving the vehicle he previously owned, a gray and white 1957 Ford. Corbett sold the Ford on December 23, 1959 and bought the canary yellow Mercury on January 8, 1960. The bright yellow Mercury stood out, and many people interviewed by the FBI reported seeing the vehicle in the vicinity of the Turkey Creek Bridge in January and February 1960. On January 25, the Colorado State Highway Patrol issued a speeding ticket to Corbett on Highway 285, just three miles east of Morrison.

Corbett's penchant for flashy cars was ultimately his undoing. Not only did the canary yellow Mercury stand out in the Colorado country roads around Ad's home, causing many people in the area to recall seeing it, including one who remembered a partial license plate number, but it was also the only yellow Mercury registered in the Denver area. This led the FBI to discover the Osborne identity which subsequently allowed them to match the fingerprints on his driver's license with those of Joseph Corbett, the escaped fugitive. His bright red Pontiac also made him stand out while he was attempting to evade justice in Canada.

PROTECTIVE INTELLIGENCE LESSONS

The botched Coors kidnapping again illustrates how prominent people without executive protection must take responsibility for their own security. This includes practicing proper situational awareness to detect pre-operational surveillance—especially when the executive is passing through a choke point at a predictable time, such as during their morning commute to work.

If possible, executives should make the effort to vary the routes they take and the time they take them, to make it more difficult for anyone seeking to plan an attack to identify an attack site. Furthermore, we advise executives to conduct an analysis of their routes and schedule to identify places and times when they are vulnerable.

Choke points are not difficult to identify, and executives who do not have security should take the time to identify them. Once these choke points are identified, whether they are a bridge, the entrance to a subdivision, or a highway on-ramp, an evaluation should then be made to determine which choke point(s) could make ideal attack sites based on the ability to deploy without detection and escape after an attack.

Once choke points and possible attack sites are identified, the next step is to establish an environmental baseline, that is, gaining an understanding of who is normally around the choke points at the time the executive passes through. Once a baseline is established, the executive should pay attention to anomalous people and activities occurring around a choke point.

Corbett also stuck out to people he encountered while conducting surveillance because he was an outsider who had no discernable reason to be where he was and was lurking rather than doing something that fit in with the location. It is not unusual for criminals to have such poor surveillance tradecraft, and they often stick out. This means that criminals can be spotted as they progress through points in the attack cycle when they are vulnerable to detection, such as when they are conducting surveillance at a potential attack site. *But they are only vulnerable to detection if someone is watching for them!* Sadly, it is often only in retrospect that victims or witnesses recall anomalous people and incidents that were the signs of impending danger, even when the anomaly is a flashy yellow car that does not belong in the area parked near an obvious choke point that would make an ideal attack site.

In 1960, the world was a much simpler place, and there were far less distractions to divert people's attention away from practicing good situational awareness. In today's busy world it is critical that people exercise the self-control needed to pay attention to the environment around them, especially if they are potential targets for an attack. If an executive is too busy to practice situational awareness or identify choke points on their daily route, perhaps it is time to delegate that responsibility to a security team.

KEY TAKEAWAYS

- Routines can make anyone an easy target. Varying routes and times can make anyone a harder target.
- Choke points and potential attack sites along a regularly traveled route should be identified, and heightened situational awareness should be practiced while passing through them—especially at predictable times.
- Anomalous incidents should be viewed as potential ruses—especially those that occur at choke points and at predicable times.
- People should game out what they would do if they spotted a suspicious person at a potential attack site, noticed if someone was following them, or if they were being confronted by an armed kidnapper. There are no easy answers.

NOTES

1 Kevin Vaughan, "Adolph Coors Murder: Notorious Killer's Quiet End," *The Denver Post*, August 29, 2009, https://www.denverpost.com/2009/08/29/adolph-coors-murder-notorious-killers-quiet-end/.
2 History.com Editors, "Coors Brewery Heir Is Kidnapped," *History*, November 13, 2009, https://www.history.com/this-day-in-history/coors-brewery-heir-is-kidnapped.
3 Philip Jett, *The Death of an Heir: Adolph Coors III and the Murder That Rocked an American Brewing Dynasty* (New York: St. Martin's Press, 2017).
4 "Lindbergh Kidnapping," *Federal Bureau of Investigation*, 2019, https://www.fbi.gov/history/famous-cases/lindbergh-kidnapping.

5 Philip Jett, *The Death of an Heir: Adolph Coors III and the Murder That Rocked an American Brewing Dynasty* (New York: St. Martin's Press, 2017).

6 Robert Sanchez, "Anatomy of a Murder," *5280*, August 28, 2010, https://www.5280.com/anatomy-of-a-murder/.

7 Philip Jett, *The Death of an Heir: Adolph Coors III and the Murder That Rocked an American Brewing Dynasty* (New York: St. Martin's Press, 2017).

8 Philip Jett, *The Death of an Heir: Adolph Coors III and the Murder That Rocked an American Brewing Dynasty* (New York: St. Martin's Press, 2017).

9 Jefferson County Sheriff's Department, *Documents from the Adolph Coors Murder Investigation Records*, 1960, 4, https://cdm17197. contentdm.oclc.org/digital/collection/documents/id/265/rec/1.

10 Jefferson County Sheriff's Department, *Documents from the Adolph Coors Murder Investigation Records*, 1960, 4, https://cdm17197. contentdm.oclc.org/digital/collection/documents/id/265/rec/1.

11 Jefferson County Sheriff's Department, *Documents from the Adolph Coors Murder Investigation Records*, 1960, 4, https://cdm17197. contentdm.oclc.org/digital/collection/documents/id/265/rec/1.

12 Jefferson County Sheriff's Department, *Documents from the Adolph Coors Murder Investigation Records*, 1960, 4, https://cdm17197. contentdm.oclc.org/digital/collection/documents/id/265/rec/1.

13 Jefferson County Sheriff's Department, *Documents from the Adolph Coors Murder Investigation Records*, 1960, 20–36, https://cdm17197. contentdm.oclc.org/digital/collection/documents/id/265/rec/1.

14 Philip Jett, *The Death of an Heir: Adolph Coors III and the Murder That Rocked an American Brewing Dynasty* (New York: St. Martin's Press, 2017).

15 Jefferson County Sheriff's Department, *Documents from the Adolph Coors Murder Investigation Records*, 1960, 20–36, https://cdm17197. contentdm.oclc.org/digital/collection/documents/id/265/rec/1.

16 Jefferson County Sheriff's Department, *Documents from the Adolph Coors Murder Investigation Records*, 1960, 20–36, https:// cdm17197.contentdm.oclc.org/digital/collection/documents/ id/265/rec/1.

17 Jefferson County Sheriff's Department, *Documents from the Adolph Coors Murder Investigation Records*, 1960, 20–36, https:// cdm17197.contentdm.oclc.org/digital/collection/documents/ id/265/rec/1.

18 Jefferson County Sheriff's Department, *Documents from the Adolph Coors Murder Investigation Records*, 1960, 20–36, https:// cdm17197.contentdm.oclc.org/digital/collection/documents/ id/265/rec/1.

19 Federal Bureau of Investigation, "Coors Kidnapping Ransom Note," *Federal Bureau of Investigation*, 2022, https://www.fbi. gov/history/artifacts/coors-kidnapping-ransom-note.

20 Jefferson County Sheriff's Department, *Documents from the Adolph Coors Murder Investigation Records*, 1960, 20–36, https:// cdm17197.contentdm.oclc.org/digital/collection/documents/ id/265/rec/1.

21 Jefferson County Sheriff's Department, *Documents from the Adolph Coors Murder Investigation Records*, 1960, 20–36, https:// cdm17197.contentdm.oclc.org/digital/collection/documents/ id/265/rec/1.

22 Philip Jett also wrote an excellent book on the botched Reso kidnapping: Philip Jett, *Taking Mr. Exxon* (Chronos Books, 2021).

CHAPTER 7

A Game Changing Attack in Germany

During the Cold War era, an array of Marxist terrorist groups conducted attacks across the globe as part of an anti-capitalist collective. These groups were trained, armed, and funded by the Soviet Union and its communist allies and used as a tool against the United States and its coalition partners. Terrorist training camps in places like South Yemen, Iraq, Libya, and Lebanon were packed with militants from a variety of countries receiving high-level instruction in terrorist tradecraft skills such as attack planning, bomb making, clandestine communications, and surveillance. It was not unusual in these classes to find terrorist operatives from the Middle East being trained alongside Europeans, Asians, and South Americans. Many of the instructors at these camps were intelligence professionals from the Soviet KGB, Soviet military intelligence (GRU), the East German Stasi, and other aligned agencies.

The training provided in these camps was thorough, in depth, and effective. It equipped Marxist terrorist groups to conduct an array of spectacular, made for television attacks such as the Black September Organization's attack against Israeli athletes at the 1972 Olympic Games,[1] the Popular Front for the Liberation of Palestine's 1975 seizure of the OPEC headquarters in Vienna,[2] the Japanese Red Army's 1972 attack against Lod airport in Israel,[3] and a long list of airline hijackings and bombings.

Among the attacks conducted by these Marxist terrorist groups was a campaign of kidnappings and assassinations of high-profile political and business leaders, to include the likes of former Italian Prime Minister Aldo Moro,[4] British Lord Louis Mountbatten,[5] Spanish Prime Minister Luis Carrero Blanco,[6] Greek Industrialist Dimitrios Aggelopoulos,[7] and Spanish industrialist Javier de Ybarra y Bergé,[8] among others.

One of the Marxist terrorist groups that stands out to us for the sophisticated capabilities demonstrated in their targeted attacks against high-profile people, as well as the sheer number of these attacks, was

DOI: 10.4324/9781003647744-8

the German Red Army Faction (RAF).[9] The RAF, frequently referred to as the "Baader-Meinhof Gang" in West German newspapers, operated throughout Europe and much of the Middle East.[10]

In addition to killing numerous police officers and American soldiers in attacks in Germany, two German Diplomats during the 1975 seizure of the German Embassy in Stockholm,[11] and nearly assassinating the commander in chief of NATO forces, General Alexander Haig, in an attack in Belgium,[12] the RAF also murdered influential Germany business figures such as Juergen Ponto, the CEO of Dresdner Bank,[13] Industrialist Hanns Martin Schleyer,[14] Ernst Zimmermann, the CEO of MTU Aero,[15] and Siemens Chief Technology Officer Karl Heinz Beckurts.[16]

From a counterterrorism perspective, the RAF had shown themselves to be very capable of attacking "hard," protected targets, conducting in-depth surveillance, and carrying out sophisticated attack plans.[17] But among all the RAF attacks, the one that stood out as a watershed moment for security teams in both the public and private sectors was the November 30, 1989 assassination of German banker Alfred Herrhausen in Bad Homburg, Germany.[18]

When we served as special agents with the Diplomatic Security Service, we were frequently reminded of the Herrhausen killing in threat assessments while serving on protective details, especially when traveling in Europe with the Secretary of State. The "Herrhausen hit" quickly became *the* attack of the decade and served as a vivid reminder of what highly trained and committed adversaries are capable of doing—even against a target with a protective detail. We decided to include this case study in this book as a reminder that not all threat actors are amateurish Kramers. We have learned over the years that the past is indeed prelude to the future, so the details of this attack and the lessons learned remain relevant today.

THE ATTACK

Alfred Herrhausen was the 59-year-old Chairman of Deutsche Bank, which at the time was the fifth largest bank in Europe. His position at the largest financial institution in West Germany, and his personal friendship with then-Chancellor Helmut Kohl, made him one of the most influential economic figures in the country. His influence was even felt beyond Germany's borders due to his advocacy of European economic integration.[19] Mr. Herrhausen served on the boards of several influential German companies, to include Daimler Benz AG, Xerox, and Continental AG. While on the board of Daimler Benz, he helped drive the merger of the company with aerospace company Messerschmitt-Bolkow-Blohm to create the biggest arms manufacturing company in West Germany.

Due to his position at the pinnacle of the West German capitalist system, his role in the West German defense industry, his efforts to promote the reunification of Germany, and his plans to expand Deutsche Bank into formerly communist parts of Eastern Europe, Mr. Herrhausen was considered a prime target by the RAF in their campaign against what they termed the "military-industrial complex."[20]

Although there had been no direct threats or past attacks directed against Mr. Herrhausen, due to his profile, and the RAF's history of attacks against other high-profile "military-industrial complex" figures, Mr. Herrhausen and his family were afforded a very high level of security. Their residence in an exclusive area of the Frankfurt suburb of Bad Homberg was afforded 24-hour police protection and was protected by a high wall and other physical security measures commensurate to the threat. People walking by the residence were subject to being stopped and interviewed by the police officers posted outside the residence. Mr. Herrhausen typically traveled in a three-car motorcade consisting of a security lead, a fully armored Mercedes limousine, and a security follow car.[21] [22]

This level of security illustrates the threat environment in West Germany at that time and the fear the RAF assassination campaign generated among the West Germany financial and industrial elite. It has been our experience that few executives ever travel in a motorcade with this level of security unless they are operating in a high-threat environment. While armored limousines and heavy protection details are not unusual in Mexico City or Lagos, Nigeria, at the present time few, if any, protection details inside the United States and Europe operate with that level of security except for heads of state and other high-level government officials. Many executives and CEOs view that level of security as bad for business, unless they are facing a specific threat.

While Mr. Herrhausen was security conscious, he was also a creature of habit. He departed his residence promptly at 8:30 AM each morning for his office, and due to the layout of his neighborhood, the security team had very few options to vary his route. The result was that the motorcade took a route most mornings that passed through a park near the residence. The narrow, tree-lined road through the park had a pedestrian crossing and a bus stop that served to restrict the speed at which the motorcade could travel.[23] Because of these characteristics, the park was the attack site chosen by the RAF.

On the morning of November 30, 1989, Mr. Herrhausen left his house on time, with the security lead car departing before the limo and follow car so the agents could scan the route for threats. As the lead car passed through the attack site, they would have seen a man down the street before the park wearing a set of Walkman-like headphones over his ears and dressed in a jogging outfit. They then would have passed a child's bicycle leaning on a white post next to the park, with a small package on a rack over the bike's rear wheel.[24]

What they did not see was a second man dressed in jogging gear wearing headphones, who was kneeling down in the bushes around the corner from the park. After the lead car passed, the first "jogger" sent a signal to the second "jogger" indicating that the limousine was approaching. Upon receiving the signal, the second man flipped a toggle switch that activated an infrared (IR) beam affixed to one of the white posts that was aimed across the street at a small reflector attached to a post on the opposite side.[25]

As the armored Mercedes broke the IR beam, the 10 kg (22 pound) shaped charge of military-grade high explosive contained in the package resting on the back of the bicycle detonated, collapsing the metal cone contained at the front of the device, which formed an explosively formed penetrator (EFP), a high speed jet of molten metal, that ripped through the armored right rear door of the limousine—the place where Mr. Herrhausen always sat. The device is estimated to have detonated when it was only three feet from the rear door of the vehicle. The force of the explosion was strong enough to spin the moving 2.8-ton armored vehicle, which came to rest perpendicular to the narrow road. The EFP struck Mr. Herrhausen directly, severing his legs and he quickly bled to death. Because of the focused nature of the device, however, his driver was only slightly injured in the attack (Figure 7.1).[26]

FIGURE 7.1 The damage to Mr. Herrhausen's armored limousine. Bundes kriminalamt, accessed April 24, 2025, https://www.bka.de/DE/Unsere Aufgaben/Ermittlungsunterstuetzung/Kriminaltechnik/Spektakulaeres/ spektakulaeres.html.

FIGURE 7.2   RAF logo.

When the police inspected the scene, they recovered a piece of paper in a protective plastic cover bearing the RAF logo that had been intentionally placed underneath the detonating device. Underneath the logo were the words: "Kommando Wolfgang Beer." Wolfgang Beer was an RAF terrorist who had died in a car accident in July 1980 (Figure 7.2).[27]

The German Federal Police Bundeskriminalamt (BKA) lists the investigation of the assassination of Alfred Herrhausen as "one of their historical spectacular cases in the history of their Forensic Sciences Institute."[28]

PROTECTIVE INTELLIGENCE LESSONS

As agents assigned to the Diplomatic Security Service Counterterrorism Investigations Division, the authors received specialized bomb training by various U.S. Government agencies and were dispatched to investigate numerous attacks as post-blast investigators.[29] Based on our training and experience, the degree of terrorist tradecraft and discipline required to carry out such a precise bombing assassination against a protected target was truly remarkable.

The first lesson we can draw from this case is that if a threat actor is given a free hand to conduct pre-operational surveillance, they will be able to identify life and travel patterns they can use to plan an attack. Unhindered surveillance also allows a hostile actor the opportunity to observe and quantify the security measures protecting the target. This knowledge provides them with the opportunity to craft and execute an attack plan designed to exploit identified security vulnerabilities and to deploy sufficient force to overwhelm the security team and physical security measures. A robust program to detect and countersurveillance by hostile actors must be employed to deny them the opportunity to conduct surveillance at will.

On a related note, being driven in an armored vehicle itself is also not a guarantee of security. Armored vehicles are fantastic security tools, but they have their limitations. Like Mr. Herrhausen, coalition forces in Iraq learned that even well-armored M1 Abrams tanks and M2 Bradley fighting vehicles were vulnerable to EFP devices and large mines buried in the road.[30] But even in criminal scenarios, we have seen businessmen in Mexico extracted from armored vehicles by heavily armed gangs[31] and even government officials attacked with sufficient firepower (to include .50 caliber Barrett rifles) to breech their fully armored vehicles.[32]

Many people, including some security professionals, hold the mistaken belief that guns and armor alone are enough to protect them against threats. This is a form of "not me" denial and can lead to complacency in things like efforts to counter surveillance and varying routes and times. Other tactics, such as running dummy motorcades, or occasionally using low-profile vehicles can also help throw off attack planners and hopefully divert them to a target that is easier to predict and plan an attack against.

The RAF conducted ten attacks directed against prominent government and private sector targets. Six of the ten victims had been afforded some degree of protection and three were attacked while traveling in three-car motorcades like that utilized to transport Mr. Herrhausen.[33]

The training the RAF received from the KGB, the Stasi, and other intelligence agencies resulted in them having excellent surveillance tradecraft. While it is possible they located Mr. Herrhausen's residence through a human intelligence source, or perhaps even through some media report, it is more likely that they simply followed his motorcade home after it left the bank. The RAF cell that conducted the attack against Mr. Herrhausen employed at least five operatives on the morning of the attack, three on foot and two in separate cars. It is also believed that one of the operatives on foot was a woman.[34] It is likely, therefore, that they used at least that many during the surveillance conducted during various phases of their attack cycle as they watched Mr. Herrhausen's movements and residence.

Detecting surveillance conducted by a team of operatives trained in surveillance is obviously far more difficult than detecting surveillance conducted by an untrained solo actor. Women surveillants are especially effective, because security personnel typically do not view them as a threat. However, detecting surveillance conducted by a group of trained operatives is not impossible, and security personnel should be provided with training in surveillance techniques and surveillance detection. We will discuss detecting and countering surveillance in more detail later in this book, but the bottom line is that Mr. Herrhausen's security detail did not detect the surveillance directed against them. This permitted the RAF cell to establish Mr. Herrhausen's morning pattern and select their attack site.

The attack site the cell chose was ideal due to several factors. First, the street was a narrow, single-lane road, meaning that the limousine would have to pass next to the post where the device was to be placed. There was no parking on the street, which meant a bystander could not park a vehicle between the device and the road to hinder the attack. The bus stop and the crosswalk at the attack site also meant that the motorcade would pass through the area at a slow speed. The bus stop, a pool, a parking garage, and a running path running through the park allowed the attack team to deploy without being detected by the lead car sweeping the route for threats by fading in with the normal pedestrian traffic. Wearing running gear near the park provided the deployed operatives with both cover for status and cover for action—they did not appear out of place. The bushes in the area provided concealment to the operative who armed the device. The street's location also afforded the team a quick escape route once they made their way to the waiting vehicles.

As far as weapons acquisition, it is believed that the RAF cell received the explosives used in the attack from the Stasi, and we believe it is even likely that they received the completed shaped charge device from them. But the cell nevertheless showed a remarkable amount of patience in deploying the device. First, six weeks prior to the attack members of the cell dressed as workmen dug a trench across the sidewalk so they could run the activation wire from the device to the hiding place in the bushes. Again, the cell did this in plain sight, using good cover for status and cover for action. Amazingly, a municipal work crew came and repaired the trench in the sidewalk after the first wire was laid, forcing the cell to dig it again, replace the wire, and then patch the sidewalk.[35]

Additionally, the child's bicycle had been left next to the white post in the park for several days prior to the attack, albeit without the backpack containing the device. This permitted the security agents in the advance car to become accustomed to seeing the bike at that spot, and even had they stopped to check the bike the first time they noticed it, it would not have stood out an anomalous on the morning of the attack aside from the fact that there was a child's backpack on the back rack that morning.[36] Again, this demonstrated the patience and foresight of the attack planners (Figure 7.3).

The rack on the back of the child's bike situated the device at the ideal height to hit Mr. Herrhausen as he sat in the right rear seat of his limousine. The attackers also needed to accurately calculate the speed the vehicle would be traveling as it broke the IR beam as well as account for the length of the vehicle, so that they could place the bike and the IR beam in the precise locations to ensure the narrow path of the EFP would strike the victim and not miss. The complexity and precision involved in planning and executing the attack were unprecedented and caught the attention of security agencies around the globe.

The attack cell escaped from the attack site and has never been identified. German authorities have never charged anyone in connection with the murder. The RAF exploited the attack by leaving the paper with their logo under the detonator, and then followed up that claim by sending a rambling communique to several news outlets on December 5 that again claimed the attack in the name of the Wolfgang Beer Commando.[37]

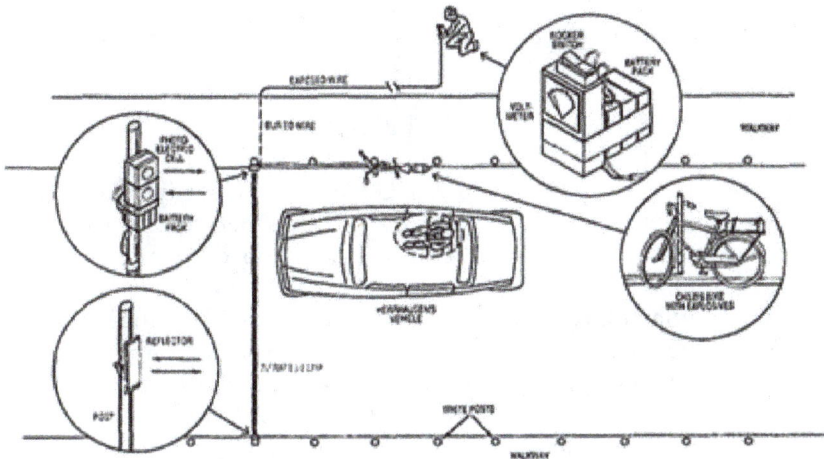

FIGURE 7.3 State Department Diplomatic Security Service schematic of the Herrhausen attack site. United States Department of State, Bureau of Diplomatic Security, accessed April 24, 2025, https://www.ojp.gov/pdffiles1/Digitization/153346NCJRS.pdf.

It was well known in intelligence circles that the RAF and other Marxist terrorist groups received training from the Soviet KGB and the Stasi, but after the collapse of East Germany, it was learned that the relationship between the Stasi and the RAF went much deeper than previously known. The RAF not only received training and logistical support from the East German intelligence service, but also safe haven and intelligence support.[38] Because of the depth of this relationship, it has also been speculated that the Stasi may have been directly involved in the murder of Mr. Herrhausen, but the degree of their participation remains unknown to this day.[39]

KEY TAKEAWAYS

- Not all threat actors are unsophisticated "Kramers" like those featured in some of our other case studies.
- Threat actors must not be permitted to conduct surveillance at will.
- Route analysis is critical. Attention should be paid to anomalous items and actions, especially at possible attack sites.
- No matter what level of security is afforded to a principal, varying the times and routes of predictable moves, such as the home-to-office morning move, is key to becoming a much harder target.
- Armored vehicles can be defeated with the right degree of planning and expertise. Guns and armor alone are not a guarantee of safety.

NOTES

1 Sean McManus, "'They're All Gone': The Tragedy of the 1972 Munich Olympics," *Cbsnews.com*, December 8, 2024, https:// www.cbsnews.com/news/sean-mcmanus-on-the-tragedy-of-the-1972-munich-olympics/.

2 Aaya Al-Shamahi, A Alaa, and Hossam Sarhan, "Turning Point: The Siege of Opec," *Middle East Eye*, 2024, https://www.middleeasteye. net/video/turning-point-siege-opec-21-december-1975.

3 "26 Killed in Lod Airport Massacre," *Center for Israel Education*, May 30, 2020, https://israeled.org/26-killed-in-lod-airport-massacre/.

4 "The Kidnapping and Assassination of Aldo Moro," *Wanted in Rome*, December 14, 2021, https://www.wantedinrome.com/news/ the-kidnapping-and-assassination-of-aldo-moro.html.

5 Lesley Kennedy, "The IRA Assassination of Lord Mountbatten: Facts and Fallout," *History*, November 13, 2020, https://www.history. com/news/mountbatten-assassination-ira-thatcher.

6 Office of the Historian, *196. Memorandum From the President's Assistant for National Security Affairs (Kissinger) to President Nixon,* accessed April 30, 2025, https://history.state.gov/historical documents/frus1969-76v02/d1.

7 UPI Archive, "Gunman Kills Top Greek Businessman," *United Press International,* April 8, 1986, https://www.upi.com/Archives/ 1986/04/08/Gunman-kills-top-Greek-businessman/65175 13320400/.

8 James M. Markham, "Kidnapping of Basque Industrialist Heightens Tension," *The New York Times,* May 21, 1977, https://www.nytimes. com/1977/05/21/archives/kidnaping-of-basque-industrialist-heightens-tension.html.

9 BBC, "Who Were Germany's Red Army Faction Militants?" *BBC News,* January 19, 2016, https://www.bbc.com/news/world-europe-35354812.

10 Two members of the Baader-Meinhoff group also were involved in the infamous Palestinian hijacking of an Air France aircraft taken to Entebbe, Uganda in 1976, which resulted in the raid by Israeli commandos.

11 The New York Times, "3 Die as Guerrillas Seize and Blow up West German Embassy in Stockholm," *The New York Times,* April 25, 1975, https://www.nytimes.com/1975/04/25/archives/3-die-as-guerrillas-seize-and-blow-up-west-german-embassy-in.html.

12 John Vinocur, "Gen. Haig Unhurt as Car Is Target of Bomb on Road to NATO Office," *The New York Times,* June 26, 1979, https:// www.nytimes.com/1979/06/26/archives/gen-haig-unhurt-as-car-is-target-of-bomb-on-road-to-nato-office-gen.html.

13 Paul Hofmann, "Four Women Sought as German's Killers," *The New York Times,* August 1, 1977, https://www.nytimes.com/1977/08/01/ archives/four-women-sought-as-germans-killers-four-women-are-hunted-in.html.

14 Michael Getler, "Kidnapers Slay Schleyer," *The Washington Post,* October 19, 1977, https://www.washingtonpost.com/archive/politics/ 1977/10/20/kidnapers-slay-schleyer/dce95731-26f9-4e8d-93e4-f163 047d6476/.

15 James M. Markham, "Top West German Arms Executive Is Assassinated," *The New York Times,* February 2, 1985, https://www. nytimes.com/1985/02/02/world/top-west-german-arms-executive-is-assassinated.html.

16 Siemens, "Siemens Pays Tribute to Karl Heinz Beckurts and Eckhard Groppler," *Siemens.com,* July 8, 2011, https://press.siemens.com/ global/en/pressrelease/siemens-pays-tribute-karl-heinz-beckurts-and-eckhard-groppler.

17 John Pike, "Red Army Faction (RAF)," *irp.fas.org,* August 8, 1998, https://irp.fas.org/world/para/raf.htm.

18 Ferdinand Protzman, "Head of Top West German Bank Is Killed in Bombing by Terrorists," *The New York Times*, December 1, 1989, https://www.nytimes.com/1989/12/01/world/head-of-top-west-german-bank-is-killed-in-bombing-by-terrorists.html.

19 Ferdinand Protzman, "Head of Top West German Bank Is Killed in Bombing by Terrorists," *The New York Times*, December 1, 1989, https://www.nytimes.com/1989/12/01/world/head-of-top-west-german-bank-is-killed-in-bombing-by-terrorists.html.

20 Ari Weil, "The Red Army Faction: Understanding a Measured Government Response to an Adaptive Terrorist Threat," *Cornell International Affairs Review* 10, no. 2 (2017), http://www.inquiriesjournal.com/articles/1646/the-red-army-faction-understanding-a-measured-government-response-to-an-adaptive-terrorist-threat.

21 The best unclassified analysis of the Herrhausen assassination we are aware of was conducted by our friend Dennis Pluchinsky from the Diplomatic Security Service Office of Intelligence and Threat Analysis and was published in the 1994 publication *Terrorist Tactics and Security Practices*. We relied heavily on Dennis' excellent analysis while writing this chapter.

22 Office of Intelligence and Threat Analysis, Bureau of Diplomatic Security, "Terrorist Tactics and Security Practices," *Ojp.gov* (United States Department of State Bureau of Diplomatic Security, February 1994), https://www.ojp.gov/pdffiles1/Digitization/153346NCJRS.pdf.

23 Office of Intelligence and Threat Analysis, Bureau of Diplomatic Security, "Terrorist Tactics and Security Practices," *Ojp.gov* (United States Department of State Bureau of Diplomatic Security, February 1994), https://www.ojp.gov/pdffiles1/Digitization/153346NCJRS.pdf.

24 Office of Intelligence and Threat Analysis, Bureau of Diplomatic Security, "Terrorist Tactics and Security Practices," *Ojp.gov* (United States Department of State Bureau of Diplomatic Security, February 1994), https://www.ojp.gov/pdffiles1/Digitization/153346NCJRS.pdf.

25 Office of Intelligence and Threat Analysis, Bureau of Diplomatic Security, "Terrorist Tactics and Security Practices," *Ojp.gov* (United States Department of State Bureau of Diplomatic Security, February 1994), https://www.ojp.gov/pdffiles1/Digitization/153346NCJRS.pdf.

26 Office of Intelligence and Threat Analysis, Bureau of Diplomatic Security, "Terrorist Tactics and Security Practices," *Ojp.gov* (United States Department of State Bureau of Diplomatic Security, February 1994), https://www.ojp.gov/pdffiles1/Digitization/153346NCJRS.pdf.

27 Office of Intelligence and Threat Analysis, Bureau of Diplomatic Security, "Terrorist Tactics and Security Practices," *Ojp.gov* (United States Department of State Bureau of Diplomatic Security, February 1994), https://www.ojp.gov/pdffiles1/Digitization/153346NCJRS.pdf.

28   Bundeskriminalamt, "History," *bka.de*, accessed April 24, 2025, https://www.bka.de/EN/OurTasks/SupportOfInvestigationAndPrevention/ForensicScience/History/history_node.html.

29   State Department, FBI, BATF, CIA, Department of Defense.

30   Clay Wilson, "Improved Explosives Becoming More Deadly in Iraq: Effects and Countermeasures" (Congressional Research Services, February 10, 2006), https://www2.law.umaryland.edu/marshall/crsreports/crsdocuments/RS22330_02102006.pdf.

31   The Nayarit Post, "Kidnapped Businessman from Puerto Vallarta Found Dead in Nayarit," *The Mazatlan Post*, November 25, 2020, https://themazatlanpost.com/2020/11/25/kidnapped-businessman-from-puerto-vallarta-found-dead-in-nayarit/.

32   Scott Stewart, "Protective Intelligence Lessons from a Failed Assassination in Mexico - TorchStone Global," *TorchStone Global*, June 30, 2020, https://www.torchstoneglobal.com/protective-intelligence-lessons-failed-assassination-mexico/.

33   Office of Intelligence and Threat Analysis, Bureau of Diplomatic Security, "Terrorist Tactics and Security Practices," *Ojp.gov* (United States Department of State Bureau of Diplomatic Security, February 1994), https://www.ojp.gov/pdffiles1/Digitization/153346NCJRS.pdf.

34   Office of Intelligence and Threat Analysis, Bureau of Diplomatic Security, "Terrorist Tactics and Security Practices," *Ojp.gov* (United States Department of State Bureau of Diplomatic Security, February 1994), https://www.ojp.gov/pdffiles1/Digitization/153346NCJRS.pdf.

35   TrapWire, "A Well-Planned Assassination," *TrapWire*, January 6, 2017, https://trapwire.com/blog/well-planned-assassination/.

36   TrapWire, "A Well-Planned Assassination," *TrapWire*, January 6, 2017, https://trapwire.com/blog/well-planned-assassination/.

37   Marc Fisher, "W. German Terrorists Say They Killed Banker," *The Washington Post*, December 6, 1989, https://www.washingtonpost.com/archive/politics/1989/12/06/w-german-terrorists-say-they-killed-banker/6c947d62-5cc9-4f7a-ad77-1299b530d407/

38   John Philip Jenkins, "Red Army Faction," *Encyclopedia Britannica*, March 25, 2025, https://www.britannica.com/topic/Red-Army-Faction.

39   David Crawford, "The Murder of a CEO," *The Washington Post*, September 15, 2007, https://www.wsj.com/articles/SB118981435771628219.

CHAPTER 8

The Butler Did It

Really, the butler *did* do it—and what's even crazier is that he actually "did it" on a dark and stormy night! Some crimes affecting high-profile people can seem like they came right out of a blockbuster movie or a thriller novel, and the home invasion that targeted Anne Bass at her Connecticut estate is one of those cases. But beyond being an interesting story, as a case study, it also provides us with some priceless protective intelligence lessons regarding insider threats and residential security.

Anne Bass was a well-known member of America's social elite. She was also a contributing editor at Vogue, a generous patron of the arts, and a significant art collector. When she divorced billionaire oilman Sid Bass in 1988, she received a settlement that was reportedly somewhere between $200–$500 million, one of the largest in Texas history.[1] The settlement not only enabled her philanthropy, but it also gave her the freedom to live the life she wanted.

Although Anne owned a palatial co-op on Fifth Avenue in Manhattan,[2] which was decorated with priceless works of art by masters such as Picasso, Monet, and Degas,[3] she also yearned for solitude, which she found on Rock Cobble Farm, her 1,000-acre estate in South Kent, Connecticut. Anne poured herself into every element of the estate, which she painstakingly transformed into a peaceful re-creation of the eighteenth-century New England pastoral countryside. The rolling hills of her estate were lined with fieldstone walls, orchards of heirloom fruit trees, and lush green pastures dotted with herds of Randall Lineback cattle, among the oldest livestock breeds in North America. Anne was also a devoted gardener, and the estate featured extensive gardens and greenhouses in which she preserved hundreds of varieties of heirloom vegetables and flowers.[4]

Located in South Kent, Rock Cobble Farm was remote enough to provide Anne the opportunity to spend time meticulously planning and tending the extensive gardens she so loved, and yet close enough to Manhattan that she and her boyfriend, the British abstract painter Julian Lethbridge, could also enjoy the New York social and arts scene.[5] Ann and Julian were not the only high-profile people who found the Kent area

DOI: 10.4324/9781003647744-9

to be an idyllic place to live. Many other luminaries lived there, including actors, news anchors, business leaders, and even former Secretary of State and DSS protectee Dr. Henry Kissinger and his wife Nancy.[6]

Anne's home on the Rock Cobble Farm estate was a pair of vintage barns joined at right angles that had been transformed into a spacious and luxurious country home. It was peaceful, but it was also isolated, and while the residence did reportedly have a state-of-the-art security system,[7] there were no security personnel posted on the 1,000-acre estate, which was a half-hour drive from the closest Connecticut State Police barracks in Litchfield. From a security standpoint, it was a very different environment from Anne's Fifth Avenue co-op which had an excellent security system that was backed up by a 24/7 doorman and a constant NYPD presence in the neighborhood.

Anne had previously experienced a home invasion robbery in 1980, when she and her then-husband, Sid, were ambushed by armed men as they returned home from a social outing and forced to open the safe in their home.[8] Despite this incident, Anne apparently felt safe enough at Rock Cobble Farm to not have any security officers guarding the estate. And this brings us back to the butler on that dark and stormy night.

The middle of April 2007 was wet and windy on Rock Cobble Farm, as the area was hit for four days by a surprise Spring nor'easter.[9] The storm, which began on April 15, caused flooding and power outages throughout much of Connecticut. After a late dinner prepared by their cook, who had then gone home at around 10:30 PM, Anne went upstairs to take a shower while Julian watched television on the main floor of the residence. Anne came downstairs to check on Julian sometime between 11:00 and 11:30 PM, and as she passed by the main staircase, she saw three masked men running up the stairs from the ground floor to the main floor.[10]

In her court testimony she described the encounter: "I heard war cries, a terrifying sound. I saw three men, dressed in black, charging up the stairs, almost like they were in military formation."[11] Startled by the three masked intruders, who were armed with knives and handguns, Anne screamed and ran into the kitchen. She attempted to block the door leading from the living room into the kitchen, but the three intruders quickly overpowered her, opening the door and pulling her back into the living room. The men forced Anne to the floor where they bound her hands with zip ties. She then heard the men confront Julian, whom they also ordered to the ground in the living room and restrained.[12]

The armed men then led the bound and terrified couple upstairs to the bedroom level. They were taken to the bathroom in the master suite where they were forced to sit in chairs, were blindfolded, and then had hoods placed over their heads. One man stayed in the bathroom to guard the couple while the other two went back downstairs, where they were heard ransacking the home in search of valuables.[13]

Before being blindfolded, Anne and Julian had been able to see that the men had brought some large cases with them. As they sat in the bathroom blindfolded and hooded, they could hear snaps, clicks, and zips that seemed to indicate the men were accessing items they had brought in the cases. The terrified Anne conjectured that the cases might have contained explosives and feared the men intended to kill her and blow up her house.[14]

Once the two men were finished searching the downstairs, they returned to the bathroom and demanded to know the location and combination to the safe. The safe was located in Anne's dressing room, and after opening it, the men were disappointed to find it only contained few hundred dollars in cash and some jewelry.[15]

After the group finished cleaning out the safe, one of the men removed Anne's blindfold. This allowed her to see that the strange sounds she heard were not the men wiring her home with explosives but rather setting up some sort of makeshift medical laboratory on a small table in the room. She watched in horror as one of the men snapped a pair of green rubber gloves on his hands and picked up a syringe filled with a strange-looking blue liquid. The man then walked over to Julian, slashed his shirt sleeve open with a knife, rubbed his arm with an alcohol wipe, and injected the substance into him. He then cut the sleeve of Anne's bathrobe with the knife and injected a syringe of blue liquid into her arm.[16]

Then, like something out of a Hollywood thriller, the intruder told Anne and Julian that they had been injected with a sophisticated, deadly virus, one that would kill them in 24 hours if they did not receive the antidote that only the intruders possessed. The price for the antidote was $8.5 million. Anne told the men that she didn't have ready access to that kind of cash because her money was tied up in investments, and that her accountant in Texas handled all her finances.[17]

After an interminable argument over how to get access to the money the intruders were demanding for the antidote, it was finally agreed that in the morning Anne would call her accountant in Texas and have him wire $250,000 to Julian's bank account—$8.5 million would simply raise too many flags and endanger everyone. Julian would then drive into Manhattan and withdraw the money from the bank along with $50,000 of his own money.[18]

By that point the night was waning, and the captors cut Anne and Julian's hands free and allowed them to change into street clothes so that Julian would not look suspicious when he went to the bank after it opened. After Anne and Julian dressed, their hands were bound again. After some time, and a conversation among the captors that Anne and Julian could not hear, the men returned and told the couple that the plan to get the money from the bank had been scrapped and that they wanted $8 million for the antidote.[19]

The intruders then forced Anne and Julian to drink a bitter-tasting liquid that was later determined to be sleeping pills. The intruders then also bound their feet and made the couple lay face down on the floor. Anne could not get comfortable, and was complaining, so the men hauled her off the floor, moved her into the bedroom and placed her on the bed. Sometime between 4:00 and 6:00 AM Anne fell asleep.[20]

When Anne awoke, she heard the noise of her dog's collar. She listened for indications that her captors were still there, but when she was sure they were not in her room, she quietly rose up out of bed and used a pair of scissors to cut herself free. Still not seeing any sign of the intruders, she then roused Julian and cut him free.[21]

During the entire ordeal, Anne's grandson, Jasper had been asleep in one of the bedrooms. Anne became concerned that the men might have kidnapped the child when they left. Too terrified and traumatized to go to the bedroom and check on Jasper herself, she asked Julian to do so. Much to Anne's relief, Julian quickly returned with the sleepy child in his arms.[22]

Julian then quickly called Anne's private security company, who alerted the police. Anne, Julian, and Jasper were all transported to a hospital by ambulance on the morning of April 16, where it was determined the substance they had been injected with was harmless, and that they would not die in 24 hours from a mystery virus.[23]

It was learned that in addition to the cash and jewelry taken from the safe, the intruders stole Anne's 2006 black Jeep Cherokee when they left Rock Cobble Farm.[24]

THE INVESTIGATION

Even as the nor'easter continued, police launched a massive investigation into the dramatic home invasion and extortion attempt. In addition to processing the residence for forensic evidence, they also fanned out and began to canvas the neighborhood searching for leads.

A pair of Anne's neighbors reported that on the night of the attack, they had seen a silver two-door car with a Pennsylvania license plate parked on the road near Rock Cobble Farm. Thinking the vehicle appeared suspicious, they stopped their vehicle to ask the driver what he was doing. The driver responded that he was "just taking a piss." Not satisfied with that explanation, the neighbors wrote down a partial license plate number when they returned home, "PA-5057."[25]

A major break in the investigation came on April 21, when a woman living on the shore of Jamaica Bay in New York City found an accordion case that had washed up on her property. It was not unusual to find things washed up on the shore after a big storm, but finding an accordion case was a novelty. Upon opening the case she found it contained a small crowbar, an airsoft gun, a stun gun, a laminated white card, sleeping pills, latex gloves, a large knife, and three silver cylinders that had hypodermic needles in them. One of the needles had a bluish liquid in it. The laminated card had phone numbers on it, and when the woman searched the numbers online, she found they corresponded to the name Bass. Having seen news reports about the Anne Bass home invasion, she called police to report the find and an NYPD detective came to her residence and took custody of the case.[26]

The next day, April 22, a loss prevention investigator at a Home Depot in New Rochelle, NY contacted the police to report a Jeep Cherokee that had been abandoned in the store's parking lot for about a week. The keys were left in the ignition, and the front windows had been left rolled down. It was Anne's Jeep. Video footage from the parking lot showed the Jeep had entered the Home Depot parking lot at 7:06 AM on April 16, and a tan Cadillac Escalade had pulled into the parking lot and stopped next to the Jeep at 7:09 AM.[27]

It took years, and thousands of hours of painstaking work, but investigators were eventually able to piece all the evidence together and identify a prime suspect, Emanuel Nicolescu. Nicolescu had been hired to work as a butler for Anne on March 2, 2006, and worked in that capacity until being terminated for cause on May 8, 2006. As a butler, Nicolescu was permitted to use one of Anne's Jeep Cherokee vehicles to complete his tasks, which sometimes involved running errands. He was, however, prohibited from driving the vehicle into New York on personal business. Ignoring this restriction, Nicolescu had decided to take the vehicle into New York and was involved in a traffic accident that left the Jeep totaled. This resulted in Nicolescu losing his job.[28] As a member of the staff, Nicolescu was issued a laminated staff phone directory card for the Rock Cobble Farm, like the one that was found in the accordion case.

On September 23, 2010, law enforcement officers took a DNA sample from Nicolescu after obtaining a grand jury subpoena. Realizing that the authorities were closing in on him as a suspect in the Anne Bass case, Nicolescu purchased a one-way ticket to Frankfurt and left the United States on October 4, 2010. He was later arrested when he attempted to re-enter the United States at Chicago's O'Hare airport on January 23, 2011, to visit his girlfriend.[29] On August 17, 2012, Nicolescu was sentenced in federal court to serve 20 years for his involvement in the home invasion.[30]

Investigators also subsequently identified three other suspects in the case: Emanuel Nicolescu's brother, Alexandru, Stefan Barabas, and Michael Kennedy. Kennedy, a former roommate of Emanuel Nicolescu, and his best friend, owned a gray 2001 Honda registered in Pennsylvania which had a license plate reading GNV5057, matching the partial license plate number recorded by Anne's neighbors. Kennedy's father was a professional accordion player who had given him an accordion with a case.[31]

Investigators determined that Emanuel Nicolescu and Kennedy worked with Barabas and Alexandru Nicolescu to plan the invasion, and the group researched and purchased two-way radios, stun guns, and imitation pistols to prepare for the attack. On the night of the invasion, Kennedy drove Barabas, Emanuel Nicolescu, and Alexandru Nicolescu to a location near the estate and then picked them up at the Home Depot in New Rochelle after they abandoned Anne's Jeep.[32]

Like Emanuel Nicolescu, the other three suspects fled the United States during the investigation to avoid arrest. Kennedy was charged in an indictment with Emanuel Nicolescu in February 2011, and Barabas and Alexandru Nicolescu were charged by indictment in November 2012. Michael Kennedy was arrested on October 23, 2012, after voluntarily returning to the United States from Romania to face the charges. He pleaded guilty on November 4, 2012,[33] and on May 4, 2016, was sentenced to serve four years. Alexandru Nicolescu was arrested in the United Kingdom on November 14, 2013, and pleaded guilty on January 8, 2016. On May 15, 2019, he was sentenced to serve ten years.[34]

Barabas remained a fugitive until his arrest in Hungary on August 16, 2022. On June 18, 2024, he pleaded guilty to the charges against him, and on December 6, 2024, he was sentenced to seven years for his participation in the crime.[35]

PROTECTIVE INTELLIGENCE LESSONS

Unfortunately, the court documents in this case do not shine much light on the attack cycle the group followed as they planned this crime. However, during his two months of employment as a butler on the estate, Emanuel Nicolescu would have been in a position to amass a great deal of knowledge about the layout of the property, Anne and Julian's life patterns, security measures and procedures, and daily staff operations. This detailed knowledge would have been very useful in planning the attack. For example, Nicolescu would have known that there were no security personnel guarding the estate and that the alarm system was never armed when Anne was on the premises.[36]

Despite the home invasion robbery Anne had experienced at her home in Fort Worth in 1980, she apparently felt secure at Rock Cobble Farm. In court testimony, she noted: "Before the home invasion, I felt quite comfortable being there by myself. I can't stay there by myself anymore."[37] She may have also reckoned that the earlier incident was really aimed at Sid and not her and did not consider herself to be a potential target. It does appear that for whatever reason, the "not here" and "not me" forms of denial created a sense of complacency that led to her decision not to have security on the estate and not to arm the alarm when she was home.

It's also possible she considered the alarm system to be too complex, or simply too cumbersome for her to feel comfortable operating it. While conducting residential security assessments, Scott has frequently encountered people who do not use their residential security alarms for this very reason. Because of this, it is important that residential security system integrators design systems that are simple to use, and that they take the time to train the residents in the operation of the system. Naturally, it is also incumbent on the residents to learn how to operate their alarm system with confidence and then use it, even while they are home. Had Anne's alarm system been activated in the home mode after the cook left on the night of the attack, the home invasion would likely have been thwarted.

If the alarm had tripped when the entry door was opened, Anne and Julian would have had time to retreat to a hardened shelter to wait for a law enforcement response, assuming the residence had one or more secure shelter areas. Additionally, if Anne's alarm system had a panic button in the living room or kitchen that she could have reached before the intruders restrained her, or even a portable panic button in her robe pocket, they very likely would have fled the premises when the alarm sounded. We are big proponents of both panic alarms and properly constructed and stocked shelters.

Emanuel Nicolescu would also have known from his time working at the residence that the cell reception at Rock Cobble Farm was very bad and the attackers could not rely on cell phones to communicate. Anne reported to investigators and during court testimony that she heard the distinct sound of a walkie-talkie as she was being held captive.[38] Court documents showed that on April 4, eleven days before the attack, Michael Kennedy purchased a set of two-way radios at a Sports Authority store in Queens. Kennedy also reportedly researched self-defense items on the Internet, which could include items such as the stun gun and the flex cuffs used in the attack. A realistic-looking airsoft gun was found in the recovered accordion case. It is unclear if the group also had a real gun on the night of the attack.

Because of Nicolescu's inside knowledge of Rock Cobble Farm, perhaps the only pre-operational surveillance the group would have needed to conduct was to drive by the residence after dark to see if the lights were on, which would confirm that Anne and Julian were home as they usually were on weekends. The attackers could then deploy by getting out of Kennedy's car and walking up to the house.

It is not clear how Nicolescu and his crew entered the residence, but it may have been as easy as just using a key to open the staff door. In court testimony, the estate manager testified that he could not recall if he had taken the keys to the property back from Nicolescu when he terminated him in May of 2006.[39] Since Nicolescu had retained a laminated staff phone directory card after being terminated, the one found in the accordion case, it is also possible that he still had a key.

This highlights the importance of establishing a formal employee exit procedure for household staff like that used when off-boarding a corporate employee. This should include collecting the employee's keys and access badges, any other issued equipment like phones or computers, and sensitive information like staff directories. The employee should not receive their final pay until all accountable items are returned. If the employee was issued an individual access code for the alarm, gate, or entry doors, those codes should be disabled. If there are general codes used by the staff to open doors, gates, etc., those must also be changed. Wi-Fi passwords should likewise be disabled or changed.

Court documents also noted that Nicolescu's familiarity with residential procedures and household patterns could also have permitted the group to gain access to the residence on the night of the attack. For example, they note he would have known that the staff door on the ground floor was normally unlocked until the staff left at the end of the night and that the staff would typically all be on the second floor in the kitchen and dining room around dinnertime. He would have also known that there are a number of large closets on the entry level in which multiple people could secrete themselves and then wait until the staff left.[40] However, if this is how they gained entry, it seems unlikely to us that the men would have waited in one of the closets for over an hour after the cook left before beginning their attack.

From the description of the attack above, it is not difficult to see that this was a poorly conceived operation conducted by amateurs. Simple mistakes such as having Kennedy's vehicle remain in the area after dropping the team, failing to properly dispose of the accordion case and its contents, and abandoning Anne's Jeep in a parking lot with surveillance cameras ultimately proved to be the group's undoing.

The entire concept of the operation—viruses don't have antidotes— and the group's demand for $8.5 million in cash also demonstrated their lack of sophistication. They clearly didn't understand how wealth works and appeared to believe affluent people maintain vaults of cash like the cartoon character Scrooge McDuck. More sophisticated criminals would have recognized the opportunity to make a substantial haul of valuable artwork from the home of a serious collector like Anne and would have pre-arranged a way to sell it.

In the end, Anne, Julian, and Jasper are fortunate they were not seriously injured in this half-baked plot.

KEY TAKEAWAYS

- Insiders such as household staff pose a unique security challenge for executives and high-net-worth families.
- A formal off-boarding process should be established for when a member of the household staff departs or is let go. The process should be carefully followed.
- Alarm systems should be easy to use, and the residents must feel comfortable using them.
- Panic buttons and safe havens are important features of a solid residential security program.
- Setting the alarm system in the "home" mode can alert residents to an intrusion and provide critical time to get to a protected shelter where they can call for help.
- Background checks on staff, both pre-hire and periodic updates, should be conducted and can be easily written into personal service contracts.

NOTES

1 Deborah Solomon, "Anne Bass, 78, Arts Patron and Peerless Gardener, Dies," *The New York Times*, April 8, 2020, https://www.nytimes.com/2020/04/08/arts/dance/anne-bass-78-arts-patron-and-peerless-gardener-dies.html.

2 Kim Velsey, "The 960 Fifth Co-Op That Belonged to Anne Bass Has Sold," *Curbed*, January 17, 2025, https://www.curbed.com/article/960-fifth-avenue-co-op-anne-bass-sold.html.

3 Christie's, "The Collection of Anne H. Bass," *Christies.com* (Christie's, 2022), https://www.christies.com/auction/the-collection-of-anne-h--bass-21517-nyr.

4 Linda Tuccio-Koonz, "Rock Cobble Farm," *Litchfield Magazine*, August 19, 2021, https://litchfieldmagazine.com/onourradar/rock-cobble-farm/.

5 Artnet News, "Anne Bass, the Philanthropist and Art Collector Who Captivated New York's High Society, Has Died at 79," *Artnet News*, April 3, 2020, https://news.artnet.com/art-world/anne-bass-obituary-1825035.

6 Peter Yankowski, Kaitlin Keane, and Rob Ryser, "In Henry Kissinger's CT Town, Residents 'Knew a Whole Different Face,'" *CT Insider*, November 30, 2023, https://www.ctinsider.com/news/article/henry-kissinger-dies-kent-ct-secretary-of-state-18523917.php.

7 Michael Shnayerson, "Something Happened at Anne's!" *Vanity Fair*, August 13, 2007, https://www.vanityfair.com/culture/2007/08/michael-shnayerson-anne-bass-attack-200708.

8 Eric Konigsberg, "The Reclusive Rich Neighbor and Her Report of Intruders," *The New York Times*, May 18, 2007, https://www.nytimes.com/2007/05/18/nyregion/18bass.html.

9 Elizabeth A. Ahearn, "Prepared in Cooperation with the Federal Emergency Management Agency Flood of April 2007 and Flood-Frequency Estimates at Streamflow-Gaging Stations in Western Connecticut" (U.S. Geological Survey and Federal Emergency Management Agency, 2009), https://pubs.usgs.gov/sir/2009/5108/

10 United States of America v. Michael N. Kennedy, 12–3446 (Conn. 2014).

11 Randall Beach, "Anne Bass Testifies She Heard 'War Cries' during South Kent Home Invasion," *New Haven Register*, March 20, 2012, https://www.nhregister.com/news/article/Anne-Bass-testifies-she-heard-war-cries-during-11460798.php.

12 United States of America v. Michael N. Kennedy, 12–3446 (Conn.2014).

13 Emanuel Nicolescu v. United States of America, No. 3:15-cv-756-VLB (Conn.2021).

14 Emanuel Nicolescu v. United States of America, No. 3:15-cv-756-VLB (Conn.2021).

15 Michael Shnayerson, "Something Happened at Anne's!" *Vanity Fair*, August 13, 2007, https://www.vanityfair.com/culture/2007/08/michael-shnayerson-anne-bass-attack-200708.

16 Emanuel Nicolescu v. United States of America, No. 3:15-cv-756-VLB (Conn.2021).

17 Emanuel Nicolescu v. United States of America, No. 3:15-cv-756-VLB (Conn.2021).

18 United States of America v. Michael N. Kennedy aka Nicolae Helera, No. 12–3446 (Conn.2013).

19 United States of America v. Michael N. Kennedy aka Nicolae Helera, No. 12–3446 (Conn.2013).

20 Emanuel Nicolescu v. United States of America, No. 3:15-cv-756-VLB (Conn.2021).

21 Emanuel Nicolescu v. United States of America, No. 3:15-cv-756-VLB (Conn.2021).

22 Michael Shnayerson, "Something Happened at Anne's!" *Vanity Fair*, August 13, 2007, https://www.vanityfair.com/culture/2007/08/michael-shnayerson-anne-bass-attack-200708.

23 Emanuel Nicolescu v. United States of America, No. 3:15-cv-756-VLB (Conn.2021).

24 Emanuel Nicolescu v. United States of America, No. 3:15-cv-756-VLB (Conn. 2021).

25 Emanuel Nicolescu v. United States of America, No. 3:15-cv-756-VLB (Conn. 2021).

26 Emanuel Nicolescu v. United States of America, No. 3:15-cv-756-VLB (Conn. 2021).

27 Emanuel Nicolescu v. United States of America, No. 3:15-cv-756-VLB (Conn. 2021).

28 Emanuel Nicolescu v. United States of America, No. 3:15-cv-756-VLB (Conn. 2021).

29 Emanuel Nicolescu v. United States of America, No. 3:15-cv-756-VLB (Conn. 2021).

30 U.S. Attorney's Office, "New York Man Sentenced to 20 Years in Federal Prison for Role in 2007 Connecticut Home Invasion," *Press Release*, August 17, 2012, https://archives.fbi.gov/archives/chicago/press-releases/2012/new-york-man-sentenced-to-20-years-in-federal-prison-for-role-in-2007-connecticut-home-invasion.

31 Emanuel Nicolescu v. United States of America, No. 3:15-cv-756-VLB (Conn. 2021).

32 Emanuel Nicolescu v. United States of America, No. 3:15-cv-756-VLB (Conn. 2021).

33 U.S. Attorney's Office, "Co-Conspirator in 2007 Connecticut Home Invasion Pleads Guilty," *Press Release*, November 5, 2012, https://archives.fbi.gov/archives/newhaven/press-releases/2012/co-conspirator-in-2007-connecticut-home-invasion-pleads-guilty.

34 U.S. Attorney's Office, "Romanian National Involved in 2007 Connecticut Home Invasion Sentenced to 7 Years in Federal Prison," *Press Release*, December 6, 2024, https://www.justice.gov/usao-ct/pr/romanian-national-involved-2007-connecticut-home-invasion-sentenced-7-years-federal.

35 U.S. Attorney's Office, "Romanian National Involved in 2007 Connecticut Home Invasion Sentenced to 7 Years in Federal Prison," *Press Release*, December 6, 2024, https://www.justice.gov/usao-ct/pr/romanian-national-involved-2007-connecticut-home-invasion-sentenced-7-years-federal.

36 United States of America v. Michael N. Kennedy, 12–3446 (Conn. 2014).

37 Randall Beach, "Anne Bass Testifies She Heard 'War Cries' during South Kent Home Invasion," *New Haven Register*, March 20, 2012, https://www.nhregister.com/news/article/Anne-Bass-testifies-she-heard-war-cries-during-11460798.php.

38 United States of America v. Michael N. Kennedy, 12–3446 (Conn. 2014).

39 United States of America v. Michael N. Kennedy, 12–3446 (Conn. 2014).

40 United States of America v. Michael N. Kennedy, 12–3446 (Conn. 2014).

CHAPTER 9

Mindset

Beginning in this chapter, we will shift gears away from the case studies and provide readers with an assortment of mutually supportive tools they can use to keep themselves and their families safe. People won't—and perhaps can't—properly utilize these tools, however, unless they first possess the proper mindset. Mindset, therefore, serves as the foundation upon which every effective personal and collective security effort is built.

From our perspective the proper security mindset consists of three elements: recognition of the threat, accepting responsibility for one's own security, and the will and determination to use the available tools.

RECOGNIZING THE THREAT

The first thing someone must understand is that the world is, and has always been, a dangerous place. We included a series of case studies in the first eight chapters of this book that were intended to drive home the point that there are bad people in the world who are looking for people to victimize for a wide range of motives. Anyone who pays attention to the news or spends much time on social media should be well aware of this reality.

Violence and terror have been a significant element of the human condition since the beginning of mankind. The Chinese began building the Great Wall in the seventh century B.C. for reasons other than Twenty-First century tourism. While today's terrorists strike fear into the hearts of their targeted populations, they are far less dangerous to society as a whole than were the Viking berserkers and barbarian tribes who terrorized the population of Europe for many centuries. That said, even though we live in an overall "safer" society today, we still face an array of potential threats daily. These threats emanate from a variety of threat actors, with some motivated by greed, others by ideology and still others by retribution and grievance, either real or imagined.

Personal and collective security are built upon the recognition that threats exist. Before someone can establish an effective security program,

DOI: 10.4324/9781003647744-10

they must accept the reality that there are evil people in the world who seek to rob, rape, kidnap, and kill. Ignoring or denying this reality will not make the threat go away. Indeed, as we highlighted in the case studies contained in the previous eight chapters, ignorance and denial work to ensure that a person's chances of recognizing a threat in time to avoid it are very slim.

Quite frankly, many victims of violence become victims because they are either oblivious to the threat or because they have somehow denied the fact that they can be victimized.

A prime example of denial endangering security is the case of Terry Anderson, the Associated Press bureau chief in Lebanon who was kidnapped on March 16, 1985.[1] The office in Diplomatic Security that we served in was intricately involved in the efforts to investigate the kidnapping of the Americans in Beirut in the 1980s. The FBI called the investigation of these abductions "LEBNAP,"[2] and agents from our office worked on the Hostage Location Task Force (HLTF) inside the CIA Counterterrorism Center (CIA/CTC) that was formed to investigate the kidnappings and attempt to locate the hostages while they were being held in captivity and bring their captors to justice. Fred was the first DSS special agent to participate in the investigation and in the debriefing of the released hostages. Scott joined the effort a couple of years later. Fred provides more detail on these efforts in his book *Ghost: Confessions of a Counterterrorism Agent*.[3]

On the day before his abduction, Anderson was driving in Beirut when a car pulled in front of his vehicle, nearly blocking him in. Due to the traffic situation—and perhaps a bit of luck—Anderson was able to avoid what he thought was just an automobile accident and went on his way without giving the incident much thought. Even though there had been a long list of American citizens and other Westerners kidnapped in Beirut, including journalists like CNN Beirut bureau chief Jerry Levin, Anderson did not think he would be targeted, and therefore did not see the near-miss for what it really was: a failed kidnapping attempt.

Anderson's luck ran out the next day when the same vehicle successfully blocked him in at the same location. Anderson was abducted at gunpoint and held hostage for the next six years and nine months. He paid a steep price for his denial, the horrific details of which were detailed in his memoir, *Den of Lions: Memoirs of Seven Years*.[4]

Many victims who survive abductions and other attacks are often able to look back and describe in detail how they were surveilled, recalling how their assailants planned and executed the attacks against them. They also acknowledge having indications that they were about to be attacked, such as ominous feelings about particular people or situations or a subtle suspicion that things were not quite "right." Because of their mindset at the time, however, they failed to heed the warning signs and take action to avoid the perceived threat. We have interviewed many victims who expressed regret for failing to heed their observations and intuition.

In many cases, like Terry Anderson's, people such as journalists, missionaries, and aid workers fail to protect themselves by choosing to forgo the necessary physical security measures for the sake of accomplishing their mission. In such cases, these individuals and their organizations need to establish tripwires to alert them when their mission becomes too risky. People in this type of work also need to avoid the form of denial that says they cannot be targeted because of the altruism of their mission or their ties to the local community. History clearly shows that neither can protect them from criminals or terrorists who decide to target them.

Setting tripwires for action, and then heeding them, can help people from becoming victimized by succumbing to the "frog in the pot" syndrome. Like the story of the frog in the pot of water, people can become accustomed to the gradual deterioration of the threat environment and fail to understand the true extent of the danger they are facing, which is in effect a form of denial.

People will also often adopt a mindset of denial because they believe they are not a significant enough target to warrant an attack, so they ignore the signs of an impending attack directed against them, believing some suspicious person or action they see is directed against another, more substantial target. This is the "not me" form of denial. It is not until after the attack that they realize the activity they observed was indeed directed at them.

When Scott was assigned as the Deputy Regional Security Officer at the U.S. Embassy in Guatemala City, he investigated the kidnapping of an American businessman who resided in an upscale neighborhood that was also the home to many American diplomats—including Scott and his family. The man was released from captivity after the payment of a ransom, and Scott had the opportunity to debrief him regarding his ordeal, hoping to gather information to help the Guatemalan authorities catch the perpetrators, as well as information he could use to help prevent other Americans from being kidnapped.

The victim recounted that he had noticed a man and a woman who suddenly appeared in a park down the block from his home a couple of weeks before his abduction. He said he saw them sitting on the same bench every morning as he left home for work. The couple were not from the neighborhood, and the victim said he felt there was something "not right" about them and got a bad feeling from them, but he decided to ignore his intuition since he did not consider himself to be rich enough to be a kidnapping target. When his vehicle was boxed in and he was abducted as he passed that park on his way to work one morning, he immediately knew that the couple was part of the kidnapping crew and that they had been conducting surveillance of his predictable morning routine to plan his abduction. Unsurprisingly, he never saw the couple sitting on that park bench again after his release.

Two years earlier, the American businessman likely would not have been targeted for kidnapping, since only members of the richest Guatemalan families were being victimized at that time. However, kidnapping had become something of a cottage industry in Guatemala, and while there were still gangs that targeted the wealthiest tier of society for very large ransoms, an array of less sophisticated gangs had emerged that were victimizing lower-profile victims for smaller ransoms. He was targeted by one of them. The wealthiest families had also reduced their exposure by sending family members abroad or had hired armed security, making them harder targets. These actions also resulted in some of the more established kidnapping gangs to select less affluent, but easier targets.

The American businessman had established a solid baseline for what was normal in his environment and was able to notice when people who did not belong in his neighborhood appeared, but like our frog in the pot, he lacked an understanding of how the criminal dynamics in the city had changed. That lack of situational understanding resulted in a "not me" form of denial that caused him to decide to ignore the suspicious couple in the park, and resulted in a terrifying experience, and the loss of tens of thousands of dollars in ransom. We will talk more about developing an environmental baseline and the importance of situational understanding in Chapter 11.

YOU ARE RESPONSIBLE FOR YOU OWN SECURITY

Once people recognize they are facing threats and that they can be victimized, they must then accept the reality that they are ultimately responsible for their own security. Unfortunately, too many people mistakenly believe that security is somebody else's job. It is something the police and other government agencies are responsible for, or maybe the corporate security department. The truth, however, is that governments and security teams lack the resources to protect everyone and everything from every potential threat. This is especially true in an open and free society. Even authoritarian regimes wielding an iron fist have proved incapable of protecting everything all the time.

It is totally unrealistic to expect the government to uncover and thwart every terrorist plot or criminal act. There are simply too many potential threat actors and too many vulnerable targets to prevent them all. Because of this, individuals need to assume responsibility for their own security and the security of their families and homes. This responsibility can be shouldered individually, or it can be shared with trusted partners to provide additional security services as needed.

The need to take responsibility for one's own security is not something that only applies to people living in high-threat environments such as Lagos or Mexico City. As illustrated by the case studies examined in this book, people are regularly victimized in cities and neighborhoods that are generally considered "safe." In the United States, the security situation is currently being exacerbated by the political environment in which the actions of police officers and departments are being highly scrutinized, resulting in poor police morale and a reluctance to act. In many jurisdictions, the police departments are desperately underfunded, understaffed, and have not been expanded to match the growth of the population. This results in increased response times, and in some cases, there are simply not enough officers to respond to every call for assistance.[5]

Political decisions to institute bail reform in some jurisdictions have also resulted in many hardened criminals being released back onto the street while they await trial for previous offenses. In some cases, criminals are released from custody even though they have been charged with several serious crimes that have not yet been adjudicated.

One of Scott's clients experienced a traumatic home invasion burglary in 2024 involving a suspect who had been released from custody due to a bail reform law. The family owned a beautiful home in a very exclusive neighborhood of a major city. They noticed when a mentally unstable and belligerent homeless man began hanging around the neighborhood near their home. They even called the police twice to report him for aggressively confronting pedestrians as he panhandled on a street corner near their residence. The police responded to the home and identified the man, a violent "frequent flyer" who had to be tased repeatedly after assaulting police officers the last time he had been arrested. However, the officers told the homeowners there was nothing they could do to remove the man from the neighborhood due to the district attorney's refusal to charge such cases, and the man was allowed to continue haranguing and frightening the residents.

The morning after the second time the client called the police to report his erratic behavior, the husband left home to go to the gym. He saw the man still on the street, but figured it was broad daylight, and the unstable man posed no threat to his family. After the husband left, however, the man removed a hammer and crowbar from his bag, approached the residence, and used the tools to pry open a window and enter the home. Fortunately, the family was able to retreat to a safe place and await the arrival of police, so they were unhurt in the incident, but this case illustrates how "not here and not now" denial can be dangerous. Even people living in exclusive neighborhoods can be targeted by criminals in broad daylight and must be prepared to act.

As we will discuss in more detail in Chapter 12, effective residential security measures—like good window locks and shatterproof films—will provide a delay, but they are simply not designed to withstand a prolonged assault by a person armed with tools. In many residential burglaries, thieves simply smash through a sliding glass door or window at the back of the house using a glass punch, or a heavy object such as a rock or cement block, and then easily walk into the home.

As seen in the video of the October 2022 attack on then-House Speaker Nancy Pelosi's San Francisco home,[6] even heavy, forced entry ballistic resistant windows and doors can be defeated by a person with tools if he is given enough time. With police response times sometimes long, layered residential security is needed (more on this in Chapter 12).

Part of taking responsibility for one's security is being prepared to act as Scott's client's family did in the daylight home invasion case, quickly retreating to a secure place until the police arrived. And this takes us to the third facet of mindset, having the will and discipline to use the available security tools.

JUST DO IT

Another important foundational truth we want to impart to our readers is that you don't have to be the super-skilled former SEAL hero in a Brad Thor or Jack Carr thriller to practice good security. Anyone with the will and discipline to do so can use the tools contained in this book. Indeed, almost everything we discuss in the last eight chapters of this book is more a matter of will and discipline than skill and ability.

Even the best residential security alarm system is useless if it is not activated, and a door is left unlocked. Locking the door and arming the system is a simple matter of discipline,[7] but we have done residential security assessments on high-end homes where the residents lacked the will and discipline to take those simple steps. We've even surveyed homes containing valuable pieces of art that did not have a residential alarm system to activate because of "not here, not me" denial. "We don't need it because we live in a gated community." We're not sure their insurance company would agree with that sentiment.

The same principle applies to street skills. Paying attention to what is happening around you (situational awareness) is just a matter of willing yourself to do so. It is not some esoteric, secret skill. Yet many people lack the discipline to pay attention to their surroundings, and as seen in Chapter 1 and some of the previous examples cited in this chapter, not paying attention can lead to tragedy.

A prime example of having security training and skills and not using them due to "not here" denial is former Exxon CEO Sidney Reso, who was shot during a bungled kidnapping in April of 1992, and subsequently died from his wound while being held captive. Reso had received security training before being sent to work in Colombia for Exxon,[8] and he had access to a company car and security driver, but he did not use his situational awareness training, and he chose not to use the car and driver since he did not believe he was in danger in the exclusive New Jersey neighborhood where he resided.[9]

Closely related to paying attention is having the will and discipline to do something when you notice something amiss, rather than just ignoring your observation. We will discuss reacting to danger in more detail later, but doing something, almost anything, is often a better solution than continuing on without acting—and becoming a victim.

The world is a dangerous place, and you are responsible for your own security, but the good news is that criminals and other threat actors are not all-powerful. As we outlined in the case studies contained in the earlier chapters of this book, many, if not most, criminals are unsophisticated, and even inept. For the most part bad actors are only able to succeed in their crimes because their victims don't possess the proper mindset. When people take responsibility for their own security and use the security tools at their disposal, they can prevent themselves from becoming victims.

KEY TAKEAWAYS

- The world is, and has always been, a dangerous place. Denying threats exist, or that one can be targeted, can be deadly.
- Don't be a frog in the pot.
- People are responsible for their own security. They cannot totally rely on the police and government to protect them from every threat.
- If someone has the will and discipline to use the security tools at their disposal, they can protect themselves and their family.

NOTES

1 VOA News, "This Day in History: Journalist Terry Anderson Abducted in Beirut," *Voice of America*, March 16, 2017, https://www. voanews.com/a/ap-journalist-terry-anderson-abducted-in-beirut-this-day-in-history/3768836.html.
2 LEBNAP was the FBI code name for the Lebanese kidnappings by the Islamic Jihad Organization (IJO). For more on those abductions also see *Beirut Rules: The Kidnapping of a CIA Station Chief and Hezbollah's War on America*, by Fred Burton and Samuel L. Katz.

3 Fred Burton, *Ghost* (Random House Trade Paperbacks, 2009).
4 Terry A. Anderson, *Den of Lions* (Macmillan Reference USA, 1993).
5 Joanna Putman, "NYPD Hits Longest Response Times in Decades as Officer Numbers Drop," *Police1*, September 17, 2024, https://www.police1.com/911-and-dispatch/nypd-hits-longest-response-times-in-decades-as-as-officer-numbers-drop.
6 KPIX | CBS NEWS BAY AREA, "Paul Pelosi Attack: Security Camera Video Shows Break-in by David DePape," *YouTube*, January 27, 2023, https://www.youtube.com/watch?v=xwLbJveUgvs.
7 TMZ Staff, "'Selling Sunset' Stars Mary & Romain Bonnet's L.A. Home Burglarized for Bling," *TMZ*, January 21, 2025, https://www.tmz.com/2025/01/21/selling-sunset-mary-romain-bonnet-los-angeles-home-burglarized/.
8 Philip Jett, *Taking Mr. Exxon: The Kidnapping of an Oil Giant's President* (Chronos Books, 2021).
9 Katie Banahan, "How the Kidnapping of Exxon's President Forever Changed Executive Protection," *Ontic* (The Connected Intelligence Podcast, October 7, 2020), https://ontic.co/resources/podcast/how-the-kidnapping-of-exxons-president-forever-changed-executive-protection/.

CHAPTER 10

Understanding Predators

While a road rage incident or a bar fight can escalate quickly, targeted attacks don't just happen in a flash. They are the result of distinct actions that can be observed and detected. This means they can also be prevented. In this chapter, we want to outline three frameworks that can help understand the actions preceding a targeted attack and place them in context: they are the attack cycle, the pathway to violence, and the social media threat continuum.

Once an attack is initiated, it is impossible to put the bullets back into the gun or to reverse the thrust of a knife. It is always far better to avoid or prevent an attack than it is to react to one. When it comes to attacks, an ounce of prevention is worth a ton of cure not just a pound, which is what makes frameworks that allow one to proactively recognize and understand criminal activity so valuable. While all frameworks are imperfect to some extent—no model can ever fully represent every possible sequence of events in the real world—nonetheless, frameworks are helpful for those seeking to proactively place behaviors and communications into context in order to determine if they are indicators of a threat.

We want to share three frameworks that are different, but complimentary, and are useful for identifying threats that can manifest themselves in different ways. The attack cycle model is focused on identifying outward actions and behaviors and is therefore the best tool to help identify signs of a pending attack being planned by an unknown assailant who has not indicated a threat or grievance.

The pathway to violence model allows a potential attacker to be identified before they progress to the attack cycle,[1] and can hopefully lead to an intervention before an attack, but this model requires communication or interactions with the potential attacker to identify the grievance(s) they hold, and to observe indications of violent ideation—internal thoughts and feelings that may or may not be displayed by outward behavior.

The social media threat continuum plays out in public on social media and can be observed by monitoring social media for grievances, denunciation, and doxing. It does not require direct contact with the

DOI: 10.4324/9781003647744-11

threat actor like the pathway to violence but it also focuses upon public communications from the threat actor rather than their actions.

Let's examine these three models in more detail.

THE ATTACK CYCLE

We referenced the attack cycle many times while examining the case studies contained in the first eight chapters of this book because it provides a useful reference for investigating or analyzing past attacks. Indeed, it's the framework we used when we were investigating terrorist attacks against American diplomats and embassies while assigned to the Diplomatic Security Service's Counterterrorism Investigations Branch.

However, we believe the most important function of the attack cycle is providing a framework people can use to proactively understand, identify, and detect behaviors associated with a pending attack to prevent the attack from being launched.

There are several variations of the attack cycle model, and these variations tend to highlight different aspects of the cycle. Some insert multiple surveillance phases into the cycle or a final target selection phase, while others add a separate rehearsal or dry run phase. There is nothing wrong with those models and they all have merit; however, for our purposes here, the graphic below depicts how we prefer to conceptualize the attack cycle (Figure 10.1).

Many people refer to this model as the "terrorist attack cycle" but in our experience, it applies to targeted attacks conducted for any motivation, so we refer to it simply as the attack cycle.

When it comes to applying the theoretical attack cycle model to real-life events, one of the mistakes we frequently observe is that people attempt to apply the model too rigidly. When the attack cycle is applied in an inflexible manner, there is a tendency to jump to the conclusion that the model does not work and then abandon it. To avoid this trap, it is important to think of the attack cycle as an elastic and general guideline rather than an inflexible law.

In practice, there is a great deal of variation in how the attack cycle is completed for a particular attack depending on the threat actor(s) involved, the target, the assailant's level of training and skill, and the environmental factors present at the specific time and place of the attack. A sophisticated terrorist organization with professional planners and dedicated surveillance and logistics cells like the Red Army Faction operatives responsible for the assassination of Alfred Herrhausen will progress through the attack cycle in a far different manner than a lone assailant like Daron Wint. Additionally, the attack cycle of a criminal who operates like a stalking criminal will differ from that of a criminal who operates like an ambush criminal.

The Attack Cycle

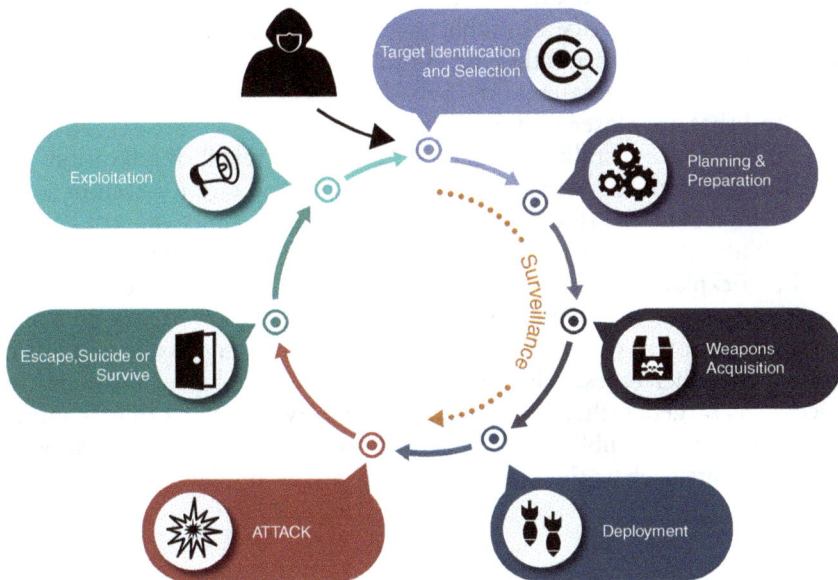

©2022 TorchStone Global, LLC | www.torchstoneglobal.com

FIGURE 10.1   The attack cycle. Used with permission of TouchStone Global, accessed April 24, 2025, https://www.torchstoneglobal.com/attack-cycle-remains-relevant/.

However, despite the differences in *how* they accomplish the activities associated with the attack cycle, all threat actors are nevertheless bound to follow these general steps when conducting an attack. Therefore, the attack cycle model still provides a useful reference point for helping understand the steps required to plan and execute an attack, as well as a helpful guide for identifying, contextualizing, and critically—recognizing—pre-attack behaviors.

With that introduction, let's now examine the different steps of the cycle.

Target Identification and Selection

By definition, a targeted attack must involve a pre-selected target, and this is the step in the attack cycle where the type of target to be attacked is identified, and then a specific target is selected from a list of potential targets. There can be a great deal of variation in how target identification and selection is accomplished depending on the type of threat actor involved. In the case of a sophisticated terrorist organization with highly trained cadres, they may search extensively across a country or even region to identify a suitable target once the group's leadership has selected the type of target they would like to attack. On the other end of the spectrum, lone assailants tend to hit targets they are more familiar with and that are closer to home.

In the case of a stalker, target selection is the result of a fixation the attacker has with the target, and oftentimes this fixation develops long before the would-be attacker develops a specific grievance or even begins to think about conducting an act of violence against the target.

In workplace violence cases, attackers often select specific people or groups of people they have a grievance against as their targets. In some cases, the shooters will even spare employees they don't have a grievance against. In other cases, a business itself and the employees inside it are selected as targets rather than specific people. We see this same dynamic play out in mass public attacks such as vehicular assaults or attacks against events such as the New Year's Day attack in New Orleans.[2]

Surveillance

As we mentioned above, some attack cycle models delineate specific surveillance phases. However, surveillance can and does occur throughout several phases of the attack cycle from target selection and identification through deployment and the execution of the attack. Because of this, we believe models that indicate surveillance only occurs during certain phases of the cycle can be misleading and potentially dangerous.

Surveillance is a critical element of the attack cycle and is something that must be done to conduct an attack. While many phases of the attack cycle can be conducted covertly and out of sight, those conducting surveillance must expose themselves to detection while they do it. Surveillance therefore is a major vulnerability in the attack cycle. We will talk more about detecting surveillance in the next chapter.

The amount of surveillance required to select a target, plan an attack, and launch the attack can vary greatly depending on the type of attacker, the type of attack, and the nature of the target itself. In some cases, the surveillance can take weeks or even months, and like the surveillance of Brian Thompson, as we highlighted in Chapter 1, can even include surveillance conducted in different geographic locations.

The amount of research and surveillance required during the attack cycle will also be different for an internal threat actor as opposed to an external assailant. As we noted in Chapters 5 and 8, insiders have intimate knowledge of the layout of the targeted facility, as well as the security programs, policies and procedures in place. If they still have access to the location as they plan their attack, they also have natural cover for status and action as they conduct any additional surveillance, giving them a distinct advantage over an outside attacker.

In addition to conducting physical surveillance of potential targets during the target selection and planning phases, attackers will often also conduct surveillance using the internet, as Renaldo Rose did as he was planning the kidnapping of Eddie Lampert. This electronic surveillance or "cyber stalking" can be as basic as compiling a list of potential targets in a city, or as detailed as obtaining building blueprints, geolocating the photos posted by a target on social media to identify their home address, or even combing through the social media of employees at a targeted facility to find photos of building access passes to make a counterfeit.

As we will discuss in more detail in Chapter 13, not posting sensitive information on the internet is one way people can make themselves more difficult targets. However, while cyber stalking can greatly assist in planning an attack and can sometimes help a threat actor shorten the amount of physical surveillance they need to conduct, by itself cyber stalking simply cannot provide enough information to conduct an attack, and physical surveillance will always be conducted during the attack cycle.

The good news is that criminals, terrorists, and other attackers often have very little in the way of surveillance training and tend to exhibit poor tradecraft and demeanor when conducting physical surveillance. They tend to lurk and stand out like Luigi Mangione did as he was waiting across the street and watching for Brian Thompson to approach the attack site he had selected. Due to their bad surveillance tradecraft, most attackers are vulnerable to detection while conducting surveillance prior to an attack—but they can only be seen if someone is looking for them.

Planning and Preparation

The planning and preparation phase of the attack cycle can also vary considerably depending on the actor involved and the type of attack being planned. Again, however, it is simply not possible to have a targeted attack without at least some degree of pre-attack planning and preparation. This phase not only includes developing the attack plan, but also a number of other preparatory steps such as acquiring information and materials required for the attack, training, rehearsals or dry runs, etc.

This stage can also include additional surveillance if that is required to establish the pattern of life for the target for an assassination or kidnapping, or to answer specific questions the planner may have about security measures at the target. For example, the number of guards, their deterrent capability, types of locks on doors, CCTV coverage, etc.

In some past attacks, the planning and preparation stage has been quite elaborate. Consider 9/11 where some of the attackers were sent to the United States many months in advance to attend pilot training and the elaborate dry runs the attackers conducted that included taking the exact same flights from the same airports and sitting in first class so they could better observe cabin crew procedures. The 9/11 Commission Report provides a detailed account of this planning process.[3]

At the other end of the spectrum, a lone attacker who decides to conduct an armed assault against the management of the company where he works may be able to plan such an attack in only a few hours and may already possess the gun he intends to use for the attack.

Weapons Acquisition

The weapons acquisition phase is just that: acquiring the weapons required for the attack. In the case of the Herrhausen assassination, this meant assembling a sophisticated explosive device containing military-grade high explosives, electronics, and a metal cone to create the EFP. In the Thompson murder, Mangione had to acquire a "ghost Glock" kit, use a 3D printer to fabricate the lower receiver and suppressor, and then assemble and test the weapon. In some cases, the attacker already owns a gun or has the materials required to construct a pipe bomb in their garage or basement.

Deployment

The deployment stage involves getting the attacker(s) and weapons to the selected attack site so the assault can be launched. For some attacks, this can be a complex process, like placing the bomb and dispatching the surveillance operatives to arm the device in the Herrhausen assassination we examined in Chapter 7.

In the case of the unstable stalker who stabbed twenty-year-old Japanese pop music star Mayu Tomita 61 times, deployment consisted of taking the subway to the venue where she was scheduled to perform while carrying the kitchen knife he used to attack her and then waiting for her to arrive at the known location he had chosen as the attack site.[4]

Escape, Suicide, or Survive

Some have argued that the escape step in the attack cycle is no longer relevant in the post-9/11 world, but we disagree. Even in cases where a suicide attack is conducted, often those who dispatched the suicide attackers, or in the case of leaderless resistance, the ideological influencers responsible for radicalizing and operationalizing the lone attacker, do seek to survive themselves.

Many homegrown violent extremists, school and workplace shooters do, however, commit suicide after their attacks like the Bronx Lebanon Hospital shooter.[5] Other times the attacker will commit "suicide by cop," shooting it out with responding police until they are killed, like the Virginia Beach shooter.[6]

Not all attackers, however, are suicidal. Rather than confront responding police, Luigi Mangione and Daron Wint both escaped from the scene after their attacks. Other assailants such as the shooter at the Capital Gazette in Annapolis in June 2018[7] simply surrender without a struggle when confronted by police. For some of these attackers this step is simply about survival, for others, like the shooter at a supermarket in Buffalo in 2022,[8] it is survival for the purpose of spreading propaganda, which takes us to the exploitation phase of the attack cycle.

Exploitation

In cases such as the Lampert kidnapping, or the 2010 murder of Tech CEO John Watson,[9] the exploitation phase of an attack is focused on spending the ill-gotten proceeds of the violent crime. The Unabomber's attacks against business executives and academic researchers were conducted to publicize his anti-technological ideology in an ill-conceived effort to change the nature of society. In the case of John Hinckley,[10] he delusionally believed that by assassinating President Ronald Reagan, he could gain the attention and affection of the actress he had become fixated on.

Even in cases where the attacker commits suicide or is killed by police, they often leave written or video statements they intend to be used to promote the cause that motivated them to conduct their attacks and inspire future assailants.

THE PATHWAY TO VIOLENCE

The concept of the "Pathway to Violence" was developed by Frederick Calhoun and Steve Weston in 2003. As we noted above, people don't "just snap" and conduct an act of targeted violence. Targeted attacks are the result of discernible processes. Calhoun and Weston's model involves six steps, two of which occur before the attack cycle commences. Because of this, the pathway to violence model is very useful for those hoping

The Pathway to Violence

©2022 TorchStone Global, LLC | www.torchstoneglobal.com

FIGURE 10.2   The pathway to violence. Used with permission of Touch Stone Global, accessed April 24, 2025, https://www.torchstoneglobal.com/where-the-attack-cycle-intersects-the-pathway-to-violence/.

to prevent attacks, but the downside of this model is that it can only be applied when there is contact or communication with the potential attacker (Figure 10.2).

Grievance

According to this model, the pathway leading to violence—an attack—begins with a grievance. Some grievances are personal in nature, such as the termination of employment, workplace bullying, or romantic rejection. Other grievances can be more general in nature, such as the climate extremist narrative that fossil fuels are killing the earth, or Mangione's criticism of the American health care system. In many cases, assailants embrace these general narratives, resulting in them becoming quite personal. Grievances can also start out as a personal issue that festers and later becomes part of a more general grievance narrative. For example, someone who loses their job for performance reasons, but then begins to view their dismissal through the prism of some larger grievance such as the white supremacist replacement theory.[11]

Grievances can be exhibited by hostile, sarcastic, or bitter speech directed toward the person's perceived enemies, inappropriate jokes, sketches and drawings, writings, and other means of expression. The types of books read, websites visited, and social media channels and feeds participated in can also be signs that a person is harboring a grievance. Other indicators can include hard looks and other nonverbal body language and hostile demeanor directed toward members of "out-group(s)"—those they blame for being the root cause of their grievance. The person holding a grievance may also attempt to recruit other people they perceive to be members of their "in-group" to embrace their ideology. These recruitment attempts can be either overt or subtle depending on the person and grievance narrative.

In cases involving mentally unstable individuals, grievances can sometimes appear irrational or unreasonable. For example, a belief that another person or organization is controlling the aggrieved person's mind, or that the person is the "real partner or spouse" of a celebrity. Sometimes a grievance can be born from some incident or event that an outsider may consider a minor issue. But even when a grievance appears irrational or inconsequential, to an outsider, it can be very real and very significant to the individual holding it, and it must be taken seriously.

Violent Ideation

The second step in the pathway to violence is violent ideation, in which the person holding a grievance begins to have thoughts or fantasies of hurting or killing the person(s) they have a grievance against, or members of the out-group(s). For example, a person may hold a grievance against their former employer for being dismissed from a job. When that person begins to think about hurting or killing those they hold responsible for their dismissal, such as their manager or the company president, they have moved on to the ideation phase. Sometimes this ideation starts indirectly, e.g., "someone should kill them all," and then later progresses to a more direct form such as "I should kill them all."

It is not unusual for a potential attacker to share these thoughts, fantasies, and attitudes with friends, colleagues, or in online forums. Sometimes they even share their violent ideation in communications with the target of their grievance. When a person shares violent ideation that may signal an impending violent act, it is called "leakage." Such leakage can occur in many forms, including conversations, utterances, threats, letters, emails, voice mails, manifestos, diaries, videos, etc.

A fixation on, or admiration of, past attackers can also be a sign of violent ideation. This has been seen in many school shootings, where the attackers have studied the 1999 Columbine attack. There are entire "Columbiner" communities on social media sites where the attack is discussed in detail, and the attackers have generated a cult-like following.[12] These communities have inspired attacks across the globe, and in some instances, the attackers have even attempted to dress like the Columbine killers.[13]

In addition to a fixation on attacks and attackers, a sudden interest and fixation on weapons and violence can also be a sign that a person has progressed to the violent ideation step along the pathway to violence.

Like the attack cycle, the pathway to violence model must be considered an elastic rather than a rigid guide. People move along the pathway at different paces, and in fact, most people do not progress through all the steps and conduct an attack. Many people with grievances never progress to violent ideation, and not everyone who fantasizes about conducting a violent act progresses to planning and preparing for one. Furthermore, the pathway is not a one-way street. Not everyone who begins to plan an attack follows through by executing the plan. People can de-escalate, either through outside intervention or due to internal factors. The goal of workplace violence prevention programs is to spot people early as they enter the pathway to violence and then guide them to employee assistance programs or other places where they can receive help to move back down the pathway.

Once a potential attacker goes beyond mere ideation and decides to act, the pathway to violence then begins to intersect with the activities and behaviors associated with the attack cycle, to include target identification and selection, planning and preparation (training, weapons acquisition, etc.), and finally, deployment and attack. During these three phases of the pathway to violence model, planning and research, preparation and probing, and breaching, those planning an attack are again vulnerable to detection because of their external actions—but only if someone is watching for them.

While the pathway to violence model is most often associated with workplace violence, intimate partner violence, and school shootings, it also clearly applies to ideologically motivated terrorists. Human resources professionals, mental health practitioners, religious leaders, family members, and others are becoming increasingly aware of the importance of spotting and reporting people holding grievances or who have begun to fantasize about conducting an attack. This realization is one of the big reasons the "see something, say something" approach has been successful in thwarting so many attacks.

Investigations into ideologically motivated attacks also frequently provided ample evidence of grievances and violent ideation after an attack, as seen in the Mangione investigation. But in most terrorist cases, the victim doesn't have visibility into the grievances and ideation driving the attacker. Because of this, the victim's first chance to detect attack-related activity is when the planning phase of the pathway to violence begins—which is roughly analogous to the beginning of the attack cycle.

In most cases, the victim or target of an attack will only be aware of the assailant's grievance and violent ideation if they have contact with them. This contact can be in person or by letter, email, etc. The pathway to violence model is thus widely used for assessing threats related to cases like workplace violence, stalkers, and school shooters. People holding onto grievances must be taken seriously and carefully assessed and investigated to determine if they pose a potential threat. Monitoring the contacts or communications from an aggrieved person can provide useful insight into where the aggrieved subject is on the pathway to violence. If possible, their communications should also be kept for later reference. If communications indicate the person is progressing along the pathway, strategies to protect the potential target or otherwise mitigate the threat should be developed and implemented.

THE SOCIAL MEDIA THREAT CONTINUUM

Over the past several years, we've been tasked to conduct assessments of the threat posed to individuals, companies, and organizations by extremist organizations or movements that are operating under the principles of leaderless resistance. Extremists of all stripes are currently using the leaderless resistance model to recruit and radicalize individuals and then operationalize them to conduct acts of targeted violence. Those using this approach include jihadists, white supremacists, incels, anarchists, and climate change extremists. Their primary communication tool is social media.

Leaderless Resistance and Social Media

While the practice of leaderless resistance is actually quite old, perhaps one of the clearest modern descriptions of the operational model was penned in 1983 by Louis Beam and published in a Ku Klux Klan newsletter.[14] In Beam's conceptualization of leaderless resistance, the violent extremist movement should be divided into two tiers.

The first element is the legal and above-ground "organs of information," who would "distribute information using newspapers, leaflets, computers, etc."

The ideologues who comprised the organs of information were encouraged to use the protection of First Amendment free speech to shield their operations and were advised not to conduct any illegal acts. Instead, their role was to articulate grievances, provide direction for those conducting attacks, identify enemies of the movement, and issue propaganda for recruitment purposes.

The second tier of the extremist movement would be made up of individual operators and small "phantom" cells that would conduct attacks and other illegal activities.

These people were to remain low-key and anonymous, with no connections to, or communications with, the above-ground activists. In today's parlance, we often refer to this violent, operational tier of the extremist movement as "self-initiated terrorists" or "grassroots terrorists."

This strict separation between the segments of the ideological movement is meant to prevent government agencies from being able to prosecute the ideologues for the crimes they encourage. It is also intended to make it more difficult for the government to identify individual actors and infiltrate or compromise the small cells.

When Beam penned his description of the leaderless resistance model, the main channels of communication extremists were using were somewhat limited in reach and consisted primarily of underground newspapers, pamphlets, a few shortwave and pirate radio stations, and in some cases cable TV public access channels. But by the time Beam's essay was reprinted in 1992, extremists had begun to adopt internet relay chat channels, computer bulletin board services, and email lists to transmit propaganda.

By the mid-1990s, extremists of all stripes had adopted the internet and websites for jihadists, white supremacists, and anarchists rapidly propagated in cyberspace. Fast-forward to today and social media has become a huge game changer in terms of propagating extremist material. The internet has supplanted print and broadcast media in reach; and social media applications have become an important, if not the primary, source of news and other information for most people. Social media applications have also served to democratize the media and have allowed extremists and extremist movements to become their own media—even to the point where they can live broadcast terrorist attacks.[15]

Some social media applications are also encrypted, thus further complicating the efforts of law enforcement and security agencies to monitor their communications.

As has been widely reported by a variety of academic and governmental organizations,[16] social media algorithms allow people to rapidly become inundated by extremist material. Extremist ideologues who are essentially "ideological social media influencers" can reach a wide audience of like-minded individuals.

While mainstream social media influencers use their celebrity to hawk yoga pants, cosmetics, and vacation destinations, their extremist counterparts use their platforms to recruit, radicalize, and operationalize their grassroots followers to conduct attacks.

The wide array of movements employing social media-fueled leaderless resistance has created a need to develop a framework that can help understand and contextualize the threats emanating from them, which is why Scott developed the social media threat continuum model.

Social Media Threat Continuum (Figure 10.3)

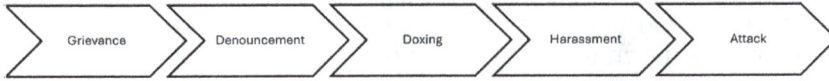

FIGURE 10.3   Social media threat continuum.

Grievance

As noted in the pathway to violence, targeted violence is always fueled by some sort of grievance, and these grievances can be either real or imagined. As noted above, just because a grievance appears delusional or fantastical to an outside observer doesn't mean that it is not very real to the person holding it. A grievance is not really a threat but rather serves as a starting point for the continuum. Since the threats on the continuum flow from the grievance, it is important to identify and monitor people holding grievances, individuals we often refer to as grievance collectors, as well as communities of such people.

Public Denouncement

Denouncement involves publicly ridiculing or criticizing an individual who is part of the "out group" in order to clearly identify them as an enemy of the ideology/movement and its supporters. Denouncement is a form of intimidation and can generate a great deal of fear in the target. The "wanted" posters featuring photos of health insurance executives that were hung in public places in Manhattan[17] after the murder of Brian Thompson were a form of public denunciation, as were the lists of corporate executives to target that were posted in extremist social media groups.[18]

Denouncement is most harmful when it is done by an extremist influencer with a significant following and who wields significant ideological authority within the extremist movement. The social media account of a high-profile extremist influencer with 100,000 followers will obviously have a much broader reach and impact than one with only a handful of followers. The denouncements of someone widely recognized to have ideological gravitas within the movement obviously bear more weight on impressionable followers than an unknown figure.

Doxing

Doxing is the practice of releasing private information about a target on the internet with malicious intent. This information is obtained through cyber stalking and is released publicly with the intent of encouraging others to harass or attack the target. While doxing by itself does not cause physical harm, it can provide critical personal information to those wanting to do harm to the targets of the doxing—information that can be used to commence the attack cycle.

Doxing is also used as a form of intimidation and can cause intense feelings of fear, as well as psychological stress and pressure on the target. This fear and pressure will often increase dramatically if the target receives threats or harassment at their home, or via their phones—or if they receive threats directed at their family. Often the subject of the doxing is overwhelmed by the personal information contained in the dox which creates a sense of "information shock," the unfounded fear that the person doing the doxing knows everything about the target and has even been conducting extensive physical surveillance on them. We will discuss how to protect oneself from doxing in more detail in Chapter 13.

Harassment

Harassment can take many forms including online trolling, "swatting" calls (whereby a call is made to 911 reporting a serious crime in the hopes that a Swat team will be deployed), and even things such as sending items such as pizzas or pornography to a target's home, or using the target's phone number or email address to sign up for content from pornographic or other objectionable websites. Harassment can also involve vandalism, leaving stickers or flyers near a target's home or office, or even protesting at or near the target's residence, their place of worship or their children's school.

Harassment can be unsettling, and psychologically impactful, especially when harassment activities occur near the target's home and family. Physical harassment is quite often, but not always, preceded by denouncement, doxing, and online harassment.

Physical Attack

A physical attack intended to injure, or kill is obviously the direst threat on this continuum. Attacks can either be targeted against a specific person, e.g., a plot to kill a corporate executive or kidnap a high net worth individual, or against a general target, e.g., a corporate building or asset, or a retail location. The nationwide spree of arson and vandalism attacks against Tesla dealerships due to the denouncement of Elon Musk for his role in the Trump Administration is an example of this.[19]

Contextualization

While we've listed the continuum in terms of severity, threats do not always follow a linear progression along the continuum. For example, an actor can jump right from a grievance to harassment or a physical attack, and conversely, not every grievance leads to doxing, much less harassment or a physical attack.

Unlike the pathway to violence model whereby a single actor progresses through the stages, in the social media threat continuum, different elements of the movement will often execute different stages of the continuum. For example, an extremist influencer can denounce a target, while a "cyber commando" doxes the target and a grassroots extremist begins to plan an act of harassment or an attack. In some cases, the steps may also be taken concurrently, or even out of order, with a doxing occurring after someone has already decided to begin planning an attack or harassment.

Because of these factors, like the other models discussed in this chapter, the continuum is best thought of as an elastic guide to help place threats and actions into context, rather than a rigid framework.

KEY TAKEAWAYS

- Targeted attacks don't just happen. They are the result of identifiable processes.
- These processes identify the elements that enable an attack but also highlight the demands that constrain an attacker.
- There are points during these processes in which those planning an attack are vulnerable to detection. But only if someone is watching for the indications.
- Understanding these models can help those seeking to proactively prevent attacks identify and act upon pre-attack indicators.

NOTES

1 Scott Stewart, "Where the Attack Cycle Intersects the Pathway to Violence," *TorchStone Global*, May 13, 2020, https://www.torchstoneglobal.com/where-the-attack-cycle-intersects-the-pathway-to-violence/.
2 AP News, "What to Know about the Deadly Truck Attack in New Orleans' French Quarter," *AP News*, January 2, 2025, https://apnews.com/article/new-orleans-car-bourbon-street-1685016388d65039ce62e720aab2ba14.

3 National Commission on Terrorist Attacks Upon the United States, "The 9/11 Commission Report," July 22, 2004, https://govinfo. library.unt.edu/911/report/index.htm.

4 Yoko Wakatsuki and Julia Hollingsworth, "Japanese Pop Star Mayu Tomita Sues Government for Inaction over Stalker Who Stabbed Her," CNN, July 12, 2019, https://edition.cnn.com/2019/07/12/asia/ japan-mayu-tomita-sues-stalking-intl-hnk/index.html.

5 ABC News, "Doctor Armed with Assault Rifle Kills 1, Injures 6 at New York City Hospital, Police Sources Say," ABC News, July 2017, https://abcnews.go.com/US/doctor-armed-assault-rifle-kills-injures-york-city/story?id=48378737.

6 Madeline Holcombe, Holly Yan, and Mark Morales, "New Details Emerge in the Virginia Beach Mass Shooting That Left 12 People Dead," CNN, June 2, 2019, https://www.cnn.com/2019/06/02/us/ virginia-beach-shooting-sunday/index.html.

7 Sabrina Tavernise, Amy Harmon, and Maya Salam, "5 People Dead in Shooting at Maryland's Capital Gazette Newsroom," The New York Times, June 28, 2018, sec. U.S., https://www.nytimes. com/2018/06/28/us/capital-gazette-annapolis-shooting.html.

8 Minyvonne Burke, "Buffalo Grocery Mass Shooter Gets Life in Prison during Tense Sentencing Hearing for Racist Attack," NBC News, February 15, 2023, https://www.nbcnews.com/news/us-news/ man-rushes-buffalo-grocery-mass-shooter-emotional-sentencing-hearing-r-rcna70250.

9 Reuters Staff, "Mans Gets Life for Millionaire's Murder in Fraud Scheme," Reuters, January 20, 2012, https://www.reuters.com/ article/world/us/mans-gets-life-for-millionaires-murder-in-fraud-scheme-idUSTRE80J1VN/.

10 Ronald Reagan Presidential Library and Museum, "Assassination Attempt," Ronald Reagan Presidential Library and Museum, accessed April 24, 2025, https://www.reaganlibrary.gov/permanent-exhibits/assassination-attempt.

11 Nicholas Confessore and Karen Yourish, "A Fringe Conspiracy Theory, Fostered Online, Is Refashioned by the G.O.P.," The New York Times, May 16, 2022, sec. U.S., https://www.nytimes.com/2022/05/15/us/replace ment-theory-shooting-tucker-carlson.html.

12 FBI, "Echoes of Columbine," Federal Bureau of Investigation, August 22, 2019, https://www.fbi.gov/video-repository/echoes-of-columbine-2019a.mp4/view.

13 9News, "Student Gunman Who Killed at Least 19 in Crimea School Shooting Dressed like 1999 Columbine Massacre Shooter," 9News, October 18, 2018, https://www.9news.com.au/world/crimea-bomb-ing-college-kerch-multiple-fatalities-injuries/ff7a079c-b64a-4732-baae-3da86534b4d2.

14 Louis Beam, "Leaderless Resistance," *The Seditionist*, February 1992, https://public.websites.umich.edu/~satran/Ford%2006/Wk%202-1%20Terrorism%20Networks%20leaderless-resistance.pdf.

15 Scott Stewart, "Terrorism and the Democratization of Media," *TorchStone Global*, June 11, 2021, https://www.torchstoneglobal.com/terrorism-and-the-democratization-of-media/.

16 Aaron Shaw, "Social Media, Extremism, and Radicalization," *Science Advances* 9, no. 35 (September 1, 2023), https://doi.org/10.1126/sciadv.adk2031.

17 Stephen Pastis, "Here's What We Know about CEO 'Wanted' Posters Appearing in NYC after UnitedHealthcare Murder—as NYPD Investigates," *Forbes*, December 12, 2024, https://www.forbes.com/sites/stephenpastis/2024/12/12/heres-what-we-know-about-ceo-wanted-posters-appearing-in-nyc-after-unitedhealthcare-murder-as-nypd-investigates/.

18 Aaron Katersky, Peter Charalambous, and Josh Margolin, "Executive 'Hit Lists' and Wanted Posters: NYPD Warns about Threats to Executives," *ABC News*, December 11, 2024, https://abcnews.go.com/US/executive-hit-lists-wanted-posters-nypd-warns-threats/story?id=116662519.

19 Jonathan J. Cooper and Gene Johnson, "Violent Attacks on Tesla Dealerships Spike as Musk Takes Prominent Role in Trump White House," *AP News*, March 19, 2025, https://apnews.com/article/tesla-vandalism-musk-trump-domestic-extremism-7576c03393a733eaf34b793e86ad1a6f.

CHAPTER 11

Looking for and Avoiding Trouble

In the case studies featured the first eight chapters of this book we noted several times how practicing an appropriate level of situational awareness could have helped the victim detect the threat actor as they progressed through their attack cycle. So, it is only natural that we begin this chapter on looking for and avoiding trouble with a detailed examination of situational awareness. We will then look at the enemies of situational awareness, situational understanding, and reacting to danger.

To start things off, we define situational awareness as a person simply paying attention to what is happening in the environment around them to identify and avoid potential threats and dangerous situations. Many people think that situational awareness is only something that trained agents like the authors can do, but nothing could be farther from the truth. Situational awareness is more of a mindset than a highly refined skill, and *anyone* can practice good situational awareness if they have a little bit of instruction, and the will and discipline to pay attention to the world around them.

As we noted in Chapter 9, mindset, discipline, and will are critical because complacency, denial, boredom, and distraction often prevent people from practicing an appropriate level of situational awareness for the environment they find themselves in. Then as we noted in Chapter 10 on understanding predators, threats don't just magically appear. There are almost always some sort of warning signs that can be observed and acted upon to avoid danger. Situational awareness is the tool that allows people to proactively notice threats before they can fully develop.

THE LEVELS OF AWARENESS

People typically operate in one of five distinct levels of awareness. There are various ways to describe these levels—"Cooper's Colors" is an example of a system frequently used in law enforcement and military training.[1]

 DOI: 10.4324/9781003647744-12

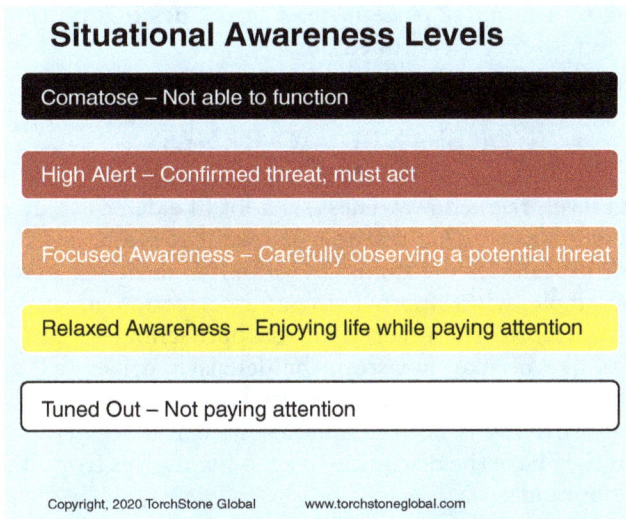

Situational Awareness Levels

Comatose – Not able to function

High Alert – Confirmed threat, must act

Focused Awareness – Carefully observing a potential threat

Relaxed Awareness – Enjoying life while paying attention

Tuned Out – Not paying attention

Copyright, 2020 TorchStone Global   www.torchstoneglobal.com

FIGURE 11.1 Situational awareness levels. Used with permission of TouchStone Global, accessed April 24, 2025, https://www.torchstoneglobal.com/case-study-online-threat/situational-awareness-levels/.

However, during Scott's decades of teaching situational awareness to civilians, he has found that they often have trouble relating to Cooper's colors. Therefore, he's developed a five-tiered system based on the different degrees of attention people practice while driving to describe the levels of awareness, since driving is something that most people do and can readily relate to.

The five levels are: "tuned out," "relaxed awareness," "focused awareness," "high alert," and "comatose" (Figure 11.1).

TUNED OUT

The first level, tuned out, is when someone is not paying attention to what is happening around them. People experience this while driving when they are in a familiar environment, listening to a favorite song on the radio, daydreaming, or flirting with a passenger. Tuned out can become even more dangerous when the driver is distracted by their cell phone or even texting while driving.

A person experiences tuned-out driving when they arrive somewhere without really thinking about their trip—or possible hazards along the route. Most people have caught themselves (or in the authors' cases, our wives have caught us) missing a turn because they were "on autopilot" and driving to a familiar place instead of the destination they actually needed to go to—they were tuned out.

RELAXED AWARENESS

The second level, relaxed awareness, is a lot like defensive driving. This is a mental state in which a driver is relaxed but is also watching to see what the other vehicles are doing and looking ahead for potential hazards. For example, when approaching an intersection, a defensive driver will pay attention to the other vehicles approaching it, and if another driver looks like he may not stop, the defensive driver will tap on the brakes to slow down and avoid a potential accident.

Defensive driving is not tiring, and one can drive defensively for a long time if they have the discipline to keep themselves from slipping into the tuned-out mode.

While practicing defensive driving, a driver can still enjoy the trip, look at the scenery, and listen to the radio, but they cannot allow themselves to get so engrossed in those distractions that they ignore everything else. When someone is in a state of relaxed awareness, they can take time to smell the roses, but they look to ensure there is no bee in the rose before bringing it up to their nose.

FOCUSED AWARENESS

The next level of awareness, focused awareness, is like driving in hazardous road conditions. When a person is driving on icy or slushy roads—or the pothole-infested roads populated by erratic drivers that exist in many developing countries (or northern states in the winter) they must keep both hands on the steering wheel while focusing on the hazards in their path. They can't afford to take their eyes off the road or let their attention wander. There is no time for cell phone calls or other distractions.

The level of concentration required for this type of focused driving makes it extremely tiring and stressful. A drive that would normally seem routine is exhausting under these conditions because it demands prolonged and total concentration.

HIGH ALERT

The fourth level of awareness is high alert. This level generally induces an adrenaline rush, a prayer, and a gasp for air all at the same time. This is what happens when a car runs a stop sign in front of you, a deer runs into the road, or a truck veers into your lane.

High alert can be scary, but people are still able to function at this level—they can hit the brakes and keep their car under control. In fact, the adrenaline rush one gets at this stage can sometimes aid their reflexes. One struggle associated with this level is keeping the amygdala, sometimes referred to as "the lizard brain," from taking over and reducing a person's ability to think rationally and diminishing their fine motor skills.

COMATOSE

The last level of awareness, comatose, is what happens when one literally freezes at the wheel and cannot respond to stimuli, either because they have fallen asleep or, at the opposite end of the spectrum, because they are in shock and unable to respond.

It is this panic-induced paralysis that is most important to consider in terms of situational awareness. In this state, the brain ceases to process information, and one simply cannot react to the unfolding situation. Many times, when this happens, a person can go into denial, believing "this can't be happening to me," or the person can feel as though he or she is observing the event rather than actually participating in it.

Often, the passage of time will seem to go into slow motion or grind to a halt. Crime victims frequently report experiencing this sensation and often note they were frozen and unable to act as a crime unfolded.

FINDING THE RIGHT LEVEL—AND SUSTAINING IT

Now that we've defined the five levels of awareness, we can focus on identifying which levels are ideal for a given situation. The body and mind require rest to function properly, so sitting in your home in the tuned-out mode while watching a movie or reading a book is not only perfectly acceptable—but necessary. Unfortunately, however, some people allow themselves to slip into a tuned-out level of awareness in decidedly inappropriate environments, e.g., while using an ATM, or walking to their car at night in a deserted parking garage.

If you are tuned out while driving and something unexpected happens—say, a child runs into the road or a car ahead stops quickly— you generally either do not see the hazard in time, or you panic and cannot react in time to avoid hitting it. This reaction—or lack of reaction— occurs because it is difficult to quickly change mental states, especially when the adjustment requires moving several steps, e.g., from tuned-out to high alert. Going back to the driving analogy, this jump in mental states is akin to trying to shift a car with a manual transmission directly from first gear into fifth, which causes the vehicle to stall out.

Indeed, many times when people are forced to make the mental jump from tuned out to high alert, they panic and their brains stall, going straight to the comatose level and they are unable to take any action. While training does help people become more adept at moving up and down the alertness continuum, it is difficult even for highly trained individuals to transition from the tuned-out to the high-alert level. This difficulty is why law enforcement and military personnel receive extensive situational awareness training and are frequently reminded to practice appropriate situational awareness.

It is important to note that situational awareness does not mean being paranoid or obsessively concerned about security. Indeed, hyperawareness is as destructive to personal security as complacency and denial. Humans were simply not designed to operate in a state of focused awareness for extended periods, and high alert can be maintained only for very brief periods before exhaustion sets in. As noted above, the body's fight-or-flight response can be very beneficial if it can be controlled. However, when it gets out of control, a constant stream of adrenaline and stress is simply not healthy for the mind or body, and the burnout it causes serves to actually hamper awareness. Operating in a constant state of high alert is not sustainable, and all people, even highly skilled operators, require time to rest and recover.

When away from the safety and security of one's home, the basic level of situational awareness that should be practiced is relaxed awareness. This is a state of mind that can be maintained indefinitely without the stress and fatigue associated with focused awareness or high alert. Relaxed awareness is not tiring, and it allows a person to enjoy life while also helping them protect themselves and their family.

When a person is in a time and place where there is any sort of potential danger (which can be pretty much anywhere), they should go through most of the day in a state of relaxed awareness. If they spot a possible threat, they can "shift up" to a state of focused awareness and take a careful look at the potential threat while also looking for other threats in the area.

If the potential threat proves innocuous, they can shift back down into relaxed awareness and continue on their way. If, on the other hand, the potential threat becomes a probable threat, detecting it in advance allows them to take action to avoid it. In that case, elevating to a higher alert may become unnecessary because they were able to avoid the threat at an earlier stage.

Once a person is in a state of focused awareness, they are far better prepared to handle the jump to high alert if the threat does begin to further develop. Now, if someone must venture into an extremely dangerous area, it is obviously prudent to practice focused awareness while there.

For example, if there is a specific section of highway where many kidnappings occur, or if there is a part of a city that is controlled and patrolled by criminal gangs, it is logical to practice this heightened level of focused awareness. This allows a person to be prepared to ratchet up to a state of high alert in case they notice an indicator of a pending attack. However, once they safely get through that area, they should then consciously shift back down to a state of relaxed awareness to recharge.

ENEMIES OF SITUATIONAL AWARENESS

While anyone can practice situational awareness, there are several pitfalls that hamper a person's ability to do so. Perhaps the first obstacle to situational awareness is ignorance. This can be ignorance of how to practice situational awareness, or even that it is necessary to do so. If you've read this far in the book, you no longer have ignorance as an excuse, so let's examine some of the other impediments.

DENIAL

Perhaps the most pernicious enemy of situational awareness is denial. Sometimes, denial can be a form of thoughtlessness or a simple refusal to face the mere possibility that a threat can exist. However, denial can also take the form of an intellectual equation, in which we allow ourselves to make an incorrect assessment based on faulty assumptions.

Over our long careers, we have talked to many people who were victimized due to denial. Perhaps one of the most memorable cases for Scott was an American energy executive who was kidnapped in Manila in 1992.[2] After a bloody police rescue operation resulted in freeing him from a brutal two-month captivity, Scott had the chance to debrief the executive about his ordeal. During the debriefing, Scott learned that the day before the executive was abducted, the same burgundy Mitsubishi Pajaro his kidnappers used to abduct him had attempted to cut his car off in traffic at the same exact place and time. That first day, his driver had been able to steer around the assailant's vehicle and continue the drive to the office.

Scott asked the executive why he didn't take any additional security measures to protect himself after that first failed attempt. He replied that he didn't do anything because at that time he did not perceive it to be a kidnapping attempt. He didn't consider himself to be an attractive target and he didn't think the time and place were appropriate for a kidnapping attempt. He figured it was just a very reckless driver. The executive's denial cost him dearly. Let's look more closely at some of the different types of denial.

"IT CAN'T HAPPEN TO ME"

Like in the Manila example above, this form of denial entails denying the possibility that you could be targeted for some type of harm. For example, the American construction company owner in Guatemala we mentioned earlier in this book. Many people simply don't consider themselves wealthy enough to be targeted by kidnappers or robbers, but some kidnapping gangs may consider a few thousand dollars a good take. For many street criminals, a purse, smartphone, gold chain, or pair of expensive sunglasses is considered worth the effort for a snatch and grab or mugging. In many parts of the world the smartphone we think little of, is worth a month's wages to a local person. Similarly, the man sitting alone at a bar on a business trip who is approached by an attractive woman may wrongly consider himself to be not important enough to be targeted by a honey trap—or conversely wrongly perceive himself as being more attractive than he actually is. This could result in the man being drugged and robbed, express kidnapped or blackmailed into an act of corporate espionage.

As we've seen from the wide range of targets in recent terrorist and active shooter attacks, social status, ethnicity, or religion may not matter to an assailant. Indeed, they might not even think about any particular person as an individual at all. Instead, all that a person represents is an additional tally in the final body count. The truth is, we are all potential targets for some sort of bad actor; so yes, it *CAN* happen to you.

"IT CAN'T HAPPEN HERE"

Because of our past experiences of being safe in certain locations, we tend to take our security for granted when we are at one of them. Such "comfort zones" can include our homes, offices, schools, or places of worship. Since we consider these places to be safe, we tend to dismiss the signals of potential danger when our senses bring them to our attention.

There have been several incidents in recent years in which this type of location-based denial has occurred. Victims have heard the sound of gunfire but dismissed the sounds as something else because their mental filters told them "those can't be shots." Yet tragically, like in the Pulse Nightclub shooting, those really were shots, and locational denial resulted in people hesitating to respond appropriately, resulting in many of them being killed or wounded.[3]

In the larger picture, there is also the mistaken perception that bad things only happen in other parts of the world and not in "safer" places like the United States, Europe, or New Zealand. This not only applies to terrorism, but also to other crimes and threats. For example, one may harbor a doubt that a potential new romantic partner is genuine but then dismiss that doubt because of the mistaken belief that honey traps can only happen in Beijing or Moscow.

Recent experience is, sadly enough, slowly but surely modifying our blind trust in our security in "safer" places such as the United States and European countries. When our senses alert us to potential danger, we need to ask ourselves, "Why *NOT* here?"

IT CAN'T HAPPEN NOW

"Not now" is a close cousin of "not here." This is the denial that an incident can take place on a certain date or at a particular time of day. While it is true that many criminals prefer to work under cover of darkness, broad daylight does not offer total protection. In fact, as seen in the case studies contained in the first eight chapters of this book, many kidnappings and assassinations happen in daylight during the morning home-to-work commute. As illustrated by the Manila incident I mentioned earlier, in an intentional attack such as a kidnapping, the assailants will know where you'll be and when you'll be there. Because of this, it is important to refuse the urge to believe "this can't happen now." It *CAN* happen now.

IT CAN'T BE HIM

Discriminatory—or non-discriminatory—behavior can also be a form of denial. This happens when a victim dismisses the threat a person or group of people may pose because the victim is concerned with making an inaccurate judgment based on a potential attacker's identity—be it race, culture, economic status, ethnicity, or religion. This concern about not wanting to appear to be prejudiced or fear of offending someone can cause us to disregard warning signals causing us to wrongly conclude: "It Can't be him."

To be clear, we do not condone prejudice or profiling, and we certainly don't advocate for it as a security technique. However, all individuals must be assessed based on their actions and demeanor, not their identity, and we can't allow a person's identity to lead us to a false assessment.

Sometimes reality does indeed reflect a stereotype, and conversely sometimes people with identities we deem non-threatening are. For example, many of serial killer Ted Bundy's victims did not consider him to be a potential threat, due to his charm, manners, and good looks.[4]

It is important not to deny that someone might be an attacker based solely on who they are—judge them by their behavior and the signs and signals they send. Yes, it *CAN* be him.

DISTRACTION: TUNING YOURSELF OUT

Distraction is often closely linked to denial and can be just as deadly. Someone is far more likely to become distracted and allow themselves to slip into a tuned-out state of awareness if they have a "not me, not here, not now" mindset.

Anyone who takes a subway or bus to work daily knows how easy it is to spot people so engrossed in their book, newspaper, or screen that they have no idea what is happening around them. It is also becoming even more common to see people totally engrossed in their screens as they walk down the street. This type of distraction makes it difficult to observe hostile demeanor and other indicators of the attack cycle progressing as a threat emerges. These signs can sometimes be subtle, but even in cases where they are blatant, you simply can't see them if your eyes are intently focused on something else.

A person's sense of hearing can help them identify threats they can't see—threats behind them or concealed by the dark or physical obstructions. But not if they can't hear them due to auditory distractions. This is exemplified in people who run or walk with headphones on and can't hear threats approaching from behind. For instance, in October 2016, Mexican federal judge Vicente Antonio Bermudez Zacarias was assassinated while jogging with his headphones on. The auditory distraction allowed a gunman to run up from behind and shoot him in the back of the head at point-blank range.[5]

We've also noted that in some nightclub shootings, such as at the 2015 attack against the Bataclan Theater in Paris[6] and the 2017 assault on the Reina nightclub in Istanbul,[7] survivors reported that the loud music made it difficult for them to hear gunfire—and even when they recognized the gunfire for what it was, the music then made it difficult to determine where the shots were coming from so victims could determine which way to run.

And these days visual and aural distractions often go hand in hand. We see people everywhere—in the park, on the street, on mass transit—who are both visually and aurally consumed in a game, movie, or TV show on their mobile device. There are times and places where it is appropriate to allow yourself to tune out in this way, but out in public is not one of them.

Practicing appropriate situational awareness doesn't mean people can't read a book on the subway, go to a club, check their email in a park, or listen to music on a run. But there are certain times, places, and situations where those things are inadvisable, and people who do them must be careful not to allow themselves to slip into the tuned-out state of awareness.

So, go ahead and check your email on the subway—but pause occasionally and use your eyes to scan the people in the car, especially after a stop when new passengers enter. Does someone that boarded display demeanor indicating they deserve additional observation? If so, don't return to your device or reading material until you're certain that person isn't a potential threat. If, after more observation, the person does appear to be a threat, you are then prepared to take action to avoid that person rather than getting caught off guard.

Alcohol consumption can also serve to impair a person's senses, judgment, and ability to physically respond to a threat. In fact, many criminals, such as rapists, muggers and express kidnappers intentionally target people who have become impaired by alcohol consumption. Some criminals will also slip drugs into people's drinks to further incapacitate them. We're not saying that people shouldn't have a glass of wine with dinner. However, when one is drinking in a public place, they should do so in a measured and more cautious manner than they would if they were safely locked inside their home.

We encourage people to enjoy life when they are out in public, we just caution people not to allow their minds to become so distracted that they miss signs of a potentially dangerous situation. Instead, practice an appropriate degree of situational awareness.

SPOTTING HOSTILE SURVEILLANCE

Hopefully by this point our readers understand that surveillance is a critical part of the attack cycle, and that threat actors are vulnerable to detection as they conduct surveillance if the target is practicing an appropriate level of situational awareness. With those two facts established, the natural question that arises is "what are people supposed to be looking for?" Let's answer that question now.

As we noted in Chapter 9, most attackers have poor surveillance tradecraft. Yet, despite this, they are able to succeed in launching attacks because the majority of people simply aren't looking for surveillance and therefore miss even inept surveillance efforts. Tradecraft is an espionage term that refers to operational techniques used in the field. Tradecraft elements are as much an art as a skill and they require a degree of finesse to conduct them properly. We see tradecraft skills as being like learning to play a musical instrument. One can listen to music, read books on music theory, and take lessons, but becoming a skilled musician requires a great deal of time and practice.

This is absolutely true for surveillance tradecraft. It takes time and practice on the street for someone to become a skilled surveillance operative who is hard to detect. While there are some terrorist operatives and high-end criminals who have received extensive training and have mastered the surveillance art—like the RAF terrorists who conducted the Herrhausen attack—most hostile actors simply do not devote the time necessary to become adept at surveillance. They display terrible demeanor, use sloppy techniques, and lack finesse during their surveillance. This makes them easy to pick out—but again, only if someone is looking for them.

TEDD

When we received training in spotting hostile surveillance while we were special agents, our instructors used the acronym "TEDD" to illustrate the elements that can be used to identify surveillance. In the decades that have passed since we received that training, we have found TEDD to be a sound guide for anyone seeking to detect hostile surveillance of any kind. TEDD stands for Time, Environment, Distance, and Demeanor.

If a person sees someone repeatedly over time—in different environments and at a distance from where they last saw them—or if they notice someone who displays poor surveillance demeanor, then that person can assume he or she is under surveillance. For example, if you see someone on your morning commute to work and then see the same person while shopping that evening at the mall in a different part of town, there is a good chance that person is following you.

Skilled hostile actors conducting surveillance over an extended period may cloak their actions by changing their clothing, wearing wigs, or other light disguises. They may also use different vehicles or license plates, and thus watching for mistakes in demeanor is critical for detecting hostile surveillance. It is therefore important to focus on things that cannot be changed as easily as clothing or hair, such as a person's facial features, build, mannerisms, and gait. Additionally, while someone can change the license plate on a car, it is not as easy to alter other aspects of the vehicle such as scratches and dents in the body.

As noted in some of our case studies, particular attention should be paid to people who are seen near known locations, such as a person's residence or office, and at choke points and potential attack sites along routes regularly taken, like the Turkey Creek Bridge in the Coors case study.

While the time, environment, and distance correlations are applicable for stalking predators, they may not apply to ambush predators. Because of this, demeanor is the most critical element of TEDD people should focus on.

KEYING IN ON DEMEANOR

Demeanor is the outward behavior a person displays to those watching him or her. The key to good surveillance tradecraft is mastering the ability to display an appropriate demeanor for the environment one is in. However, displaying good demeanor is not intuitive. In fact, we believe many of the things one must do to maintain good demeanor while conducting surveillance are counter to human nature.

At its heart, surveillance is watching someone while attempting not to be caught doing so. As such, it is an unnatural activity, and a person doing it must deal with strong feelings of self-consciousness and of being out of place. Because of this, people conducting surveillance frequently suffer from what is called "burn syndrome," the belief that the people they are watching have spotted them. The feeling of being "burned" will cause untrained surveillance operatives to do unnatural things, such as hiding their faces or suddenly ducking into a doorway or turning around abruptly when they unexpectedly come face to face with the target.

People inexperienced in the art of surveillance find it difficult to control this natural reaction.

Because of this, intelligence, law enforcement, and security professionals receive extensive surveillance training that includes many hours of heavily critiqued practical exercises, often followed by field training with a team of experienced surveillance professionals. This training emphasizes and reinforces maintaining proper demeanor. Even experienced surveillance operatives must deal with the natural feeling of being burned, but training can help one behave normally while experiencing the burn syndrome. A trained surveillance operative possesses the ability to maintain a demeanor that appears calm and normal even though their insides are screaming that the person they are surveilling has seen them.

PROPER COVER

In addition to doing something unnatural or stupid when feeling burned, another common demeanor mistake made by untrained people when they are conducting surveillance is the failure to use proper cover for action and cover for status. Cover for status is a person's purported identity—his costume. A person can pretend to be a student, a businessman, a repairman, etc. Cover for action explains why the person is doing what he or she is doing—e.g., sitting on that bench waiting for a bus.

Proper cover for status and cover for action makes the presence of the person conducting the surveillance appear natural in that specific environment at that particular time. When done right, the surveillance operative fits in with the mental snapshot subconsciously taken by the target as the target goes about his or her business. They do not stand out from the environmental baseline.

An example of bad cover for status was seen in the Coors kidnapping when Corbett was dressed in city clothes standing next to his bright yellow car in the Colorado countryside. Corbett also had no cover for action. He was just lurking at the bridge. By contrast, the Herrhausen attackers showed very good cover for status and cover for action when they dressed in running outfits in the morning near a park with a running trail.

For the most part, however, inexperienced operatives conducting surveillance practice little or no cover for status and cover for action. Like Corbett they just lurk and tend to look totally out of place. There is no apparent reason for them to be where they are or doing what they are doing. In addition to plain old lurking, other demeanor giveaways include a person moving when the target moves, communicating when the target moves, making sudden turns or stops, or even using hand signals to communicate with other members of a surveillance team or criminal gang.

Bad demeanor can be summed up by the acronym JDLR—Just Doesn't Look Right. But in addition to major demeanor mistakes, sometimes bad demeanor manifests itself in more subtle forms. Some people who are experiencing burn syndrome exhibit almost imperceptible behaviors that the target can sense more than observe. It may not be something that can be clearly articulated, but the target just has a gut reaction gets the unsettling feeling that there is something wrong or "creepy" about the way a certain person looks at them or is behaving. Innocent bystanders generally do not exhibit demeanor that triggers such feelings, and we encourage people to trust their gut and act when they encounter such a situation rather than succumb to denial. There is often little to lose by taking such action, other than perhaps a little time and effort, and avoiding a potential problem is always the right thing to do.

Another important demeanor indicator is a person's eyes. How a person looks at you—or doesn't—can provide a good indicator of their intent. Are they looking at you with a hostile, drop-dead look? Do they have a thousand-yard stare? Are they avoiding your gaze? It has been said that the eyes are the window to the soul, and over the years when we have worked on the street we have found this to be very true.

It takes intelligence officers months or years of training and practice to become highly proficient at detecting surveillance conducted by professional surveillance operatives, and there are many tricks of the trade. However, almost anyone can learn to spot surveillance by poorly trained criminals or terrorists—it is not difficult if one has the will and discipline to look.

OODA

We've examined how to look for potential threats, let's now consider how to avoid or mitigate them. This is where the concept of OODA comes in. OODA is an acronym that stands for Observe, Orient, Decide, and Act.

The concept of OODA was first developed during the Vietnam War by U.S. Air Force Col. John Boyd[8] as a method to help his fellow pilots become more effective in dogfights. The system achieved its initial, narrow goal of shortening pilots' decision and action processes, which resulted in a dramatic increase in dogfight success by American pilots during the war.

In subsequent years, people in other fields have recognized the merits of OODA and have applied it in a wide variety of nonmilitary settings, to include topics such as corporate decision-making[9] and medical triage procedures.[10] The system is also a useful tool for enhancing personal security; and while law enforcement and security officers frequently receive OODA training, I believe civilians can also benefit from it.

OODA LOOP

The process of consciously observing, orienting, deciding, and acting—the OODA Loop—creates links between the awareness of one's surroundings in a dangerous situation and the actions necessary to escape it by staying one step ahead of an adversary. Because of this, we consider OODA to be the bridge that connects situational awareness with action.

While teaching OODA, Scott has often had students ask him, "but don't people's brains naturally work this way?" To which the answer, yes, as humans, we often unconsciously follow the pattern of OODA in reacting to stimuli. But by moving through this pattern *consciously*, people can accelerate the process and gain an advantage over opponents who are not engaging in deliberate OODA decision-making. In other words, a person can get inside the OODA loop cycle of their attacker by

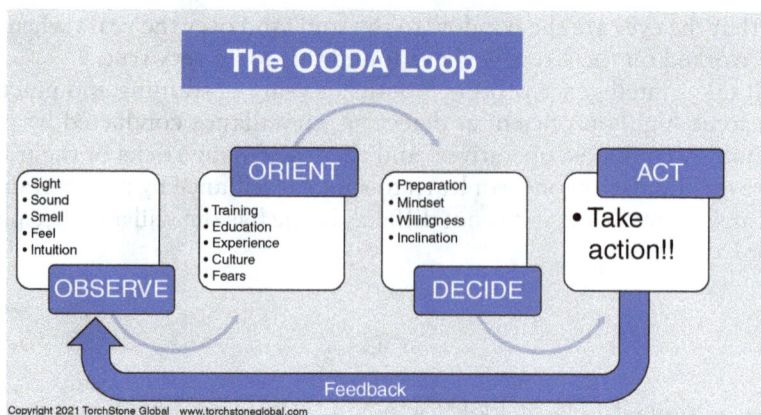

FIGURE 11.2 The OODA loop. Used with permission of TouchStone Global, accessed April 24, 2025, https://www.torchstoneglobal.com/avoiding-the-deadly-oh-oh-loop-with-ooda/.

processing through the cycle more rapidly. Furthermore, by making the process a conscious one, they are less likely to explain away or deny a warning sign that they observe.

Finally, in many cases, people in stressful situations find themselves caught in what we call an "OO loop"—endlessly observing and orienting without making a decision or taking action. This quickly becomes an "Oh-Oh" loop because it causes them to freeze, often resulting in a very bad outcome. Consciously progressing through the OODA loop protects them from entering an Oh-Oh loop by forcing them to make a decision and then act.

Now, can sometimes the decision be not to act? Yes! But in such a situation the person has consciously made the decision not to act instead of being frozen in an Oh-Oh loop where they *can't* act. There is a significant difference between these two states.

It is also critical to recognize that in any dangerous situation OODA is not a one-time action but a continuous loop: As an attacker reacts to the victim's actions, the victim must observe that reaction, and then rapidly orient, decide, and act based on the reaction. The OODA cycle must continue in this manner until the situation is resolved (Figure 11.2).

UNPACKING OODA

The first "O," Observe, is fairly straightforward. Observing is essentially practicing good situational awareness. The more observant a person is of their surroundings, the more likely they are to notice and react to subtle signs of danger, rather than just the obvious ones. This often allows them to proactively spot emerging threats and avoid them, rather than just respond to them.

It is important to note that observation includes all the senses, not just sight. The sound of approaching steps, a gunshot, or screeching tires; the smell of smoke, gunpowder or gasoline; the taste of something strange in a drink; or the feel of a crowd beginning to panic and move; can all indicate danger. We'd also like to include intuition or one's "gut feelings" in observation. As noted in the previous section on recognizing surveillance, sometimes a person's senses can pick up subtle things that their subconscious recognizes as danger, even if their conscious mind is not able to articulate what they are. Over the decades, we have interviewed countless victims who have told us they had a "funny feeling" or a "bad feeling" about a person or situation but chose to ignore those feelings and were victimized. Always trust your gut.

The second "O," Orient, is a bit more complex. Orient doesn't mean determining what direction one is facing like when a person orients themself using a compass. Rather, in the practice of OODA, orienting means the process of a person placing themselves and their observations into the proper context in relation to their circumstances. This meaning of orient is the same one used to define a university orientation program designed to familiarize incoming students with their new environment.

Thus, in OODA, orienting is the process of quickly determining where a person stands in relation to their environment and other actors in an ambiguous or rapidly changing situation. It means the person must conduct a rapid analysis using a number of filters such as education, training, experience, culture, upbringing, fears, and even faith, to put their observations into the appropriate context. In other words, it is quickly turning the things observed while practicing situational awareness into situational understanding. It is this orientation process that equips a person to quickly make a decision, "D."

The "D," Decision, is shaped by factors that include the person's preparation and mindset, as well as their willingness and inclination to do certain things. For example, they may have a deep personal conviction against using violence against another person, or against using lethal force against someone who is conducting a purely economic crime. But ultimately, the decision step is critical because it is what prompts a person to act, "A" and saves them from being caught in an Oh-Oh loop.

In real-life situations, quite often the decision a person makes may not be a "textbook" decision. But by acting and doing something—almost anything—the victim is forcing the attacker to react to that action, and if the attacker is not consciously practicing OODA, the victim might be able to get inside their loop cycle.

PRACTICING OODA

As noted above despite its origins as a tool for fighter pilots, a person doesn't have to be a Top Gun ace to employ OODA. Like situational awareness, anyone can practice OODA if they have the will and discipline to do so. Employing OODA does, however, take some practice, and one way to learn to use it is to consciously employ it during your everyday activities like driving to work, going shopping, taking a run, etc. For example:

Observation: I am about to use an ATM on the street after dark.
Orientation: I know from experience, natural instinct, and security training that this is a time and place of heightened risk. Because of this, I should consider increasing my situational awareness.
Decision: I am going to shift from a relaxed level of situational awareness into focused awareness.
Action: I watch out for danger.

Then, if the person sees something that catches their attention, they can run the OODA loop again.

Observation: Two men began to walk down the street behind me after I left the ATM.
Orientation: I know robbery is common in this city and those men saw me leave the ATM. I don't see any weapons or blatantly bad demeanor, but they could be potential muggers.
Decision: I need to continue to focus on them and do something to see if they are following me, or if they are just casual pedestrians.
Action: I pick up my pace and cross the street at the next intersection.

Then, based on the observation of how the two men react to the change of pace and street crossing, the person will run another OODA loop to decide whether they need to take further action and continue the OODA process, or if they can relax until something else causes them to reengage the OODA process.

On its face, the concept of OODA may seem overly facile, but over the decades we have found that simple guidelines and processes are very helpful during tense situations. Stress, and the fight-or-flight response it provokes, has a discernible effect on human physiology. One consequence is that blood rushes away from the brain to the limbs—often impairing rational thinking in the process—a condition often referred to as "lizard brain." OODA is simple enough that a person can use it even under considerable duress—such as when one is in an aerial dogfight or caught in a confrontation with a street criminal. Plus, the experience of countless soldiers and law enforcement officers has proved that consciously running the OODA process can help defeat lizard brain by keeping the rational parts of the brain functioning, especially when combined with tactical breathing.[11]

A great example of using OODA to get inside an attacker's loop was the May 26, 1997, attack against our friends and former colleagues Denny Williams and John Hucke by a terrorist group called Egypt's Revolution in Cairo. The ambush involved two terrorists in a car armed with a pistol, and a third dismounted terrorist armed with an AK-47. The attackers planned to use the armed man in the car to trap victims at a choke point (an underpass) and then kill them as they sat pinned in by the attacker's car and rush hour traffic.

The ambush began to unfold as the attackers hoped, and they were able to initially trap Denny's Peugeot station wagon in the kill zone and open fire. As the terrorists opened fire on the car, Denny used his training and experience to almost instantly orient himself. He realized that if the car remained where it was, they were going to die in a hail of gunfire. He then quickly decided to "get off the X" and use his car as a weapon. While traffic would not allow him to move forward, and the attacker's car prevented him from driving into the outside lane, Denny thought outside the box and floored the pedal, driving the Peugeot up and over the curb and then he pointed the vehicle directly at the dismounted terrorist to use has car as a weapon. Seeing the Peugeot coming right at him, the dismounted attacker quickly threw down his rifle and ran away. The two attackers in the car also quickly departed the scene. Denny's training, and his ability to use OODA to rapidly orient, decide, and act undoubtedly saved his and John's lives that day.

In addition to being a warrior, Col. John Boyd was a philosopher. He and many others have taken the OODA Loop to very complicated, almost metaphysical levels. There's nothing wrong with that, but for the purposes of personal security, OODA's greatest strength is its simplicity, the way it enables people to observe activity by hostile parties, analyze the information, make appropriate decisions, and quickly implement a course of action. If a person can learn to consciously and rapidly process their observations, make rapid decisions, and then act—they will be way ahead of their opponent in almost any situation.

SITUATIONAL UNDERSTANDING

Situational understanding is closely related to, but different from situational awareness. Situational awareness allows one to see what is happening, while situational understanding allows the observer to understand why it is happening, while also allowing the observer to comprehend the implications and consequences of the event—the "so what?" Situational understanding also makes it possible to identify trends and foresee emerging events.

Situational awareness and situational understanding are both intertwined with the concept and practice of OODA. Situational awareness is what allows one to observe their environment, while situational understanding is what allows one to rapidly understand those observations in order to determine their implications—the "orient" of OODA. This orientation then permits the person to make a decision and act quickly.

But situational understanding is not something inherent. While intuition, upbringing, and culture play a role in developing one's situational understanding, it generally requires additional time and effort for a person to gain detailed knowledge of their environment and the actors operating in it.

In terms of effort, developing situational understanding requires gathering all the information needed to achieve a thorough foundational knowledge of the operating environment and then using that knowledge to craft a solid baseline threat assessment. This applies not only to a person's home environment, but also to the locations they visit. It is important that a person conduct the research necessary to not only develop a solid understanding of the customs and norms of the population at their location but also obtain insight into threat actors operating there, their typical modus operandi, and the types of crimes and attacks they conduct.

In terms of time, experience—and especially experience operating in a person's current environment—is invaluable. Practicing good situational awareness over time allows one to develop a good sense of the "normal now," which assists in spotting anomalies, as well as providing context for observations.

These building blocks of research, assessment, and experience serve to shape a person's perception and interpretation of a particular incident or situation, allowing them to place it into the proper context—this is situational understanding. Placing events into the proper context then provides the insight and foresight required to shape effective decision-making.

Let's now look at an example of how situational understanding can help someone understand events and react appropriately in different environments. Consider, if you will, the case of a man walking down the street who becomes surrounded by three bad actors who converge on the victim. One of the bad actors draws an edged weapon and the group then attempts to force the victim into a car that pulls up to the curb.

Yes, we know it is better to spot such teams before they deploy for an attack, and then quickly act to avoid the situation, but for our purposes here, let's just imagine that for whatever reason, our victim did not spot the team until they deployed, and they were able to get the drop on him at the attack site. In such a situation, the context, and the decisions to act made by the victim, could be very different depending on the victim's situational understanding of their environment.

If, say the person was walking down the street in Sao Paulo, Brazil, a place where express kidnappings by criminal gangs are common, the likeliest outcome of the attack is a relatively quick ordeal resulting in the loss of money. Attempting to resist the kidnappers could help prevent the loss of some money, but it could also result in a serious injury or death. In such a situation, unless the victim is a super-human former SEAL like the fictional character Scot Harvath, he might prudently decide the best course of action is to not resist and to comply with the demands of three armed abductors. Hopefully, the victim has limited what he is carrying on his person and the amount of money in the bank account his ATM card is linked to, so the potential losses from the express kidnapping are not nearly as bad as a stay in the hospital or a trip to the funeral home if he resisted and was seriously wounded or killed.

If, however, the person was walking down the street in Mosul, Iraq, a very different environment—the implications of the situation are also very different. In Iraq and Syria, Islamic State operatives and criminal gangs aligned with them have kidnapped foreigners, held them under brutal conditions—for years in some cases—and beheaded them in others. In this environment, the victim's situational understanding is likely to prompt him to act differently from the victim in Brazil. Instead of complying with his abductors, the victim may decide to resist, viewing the initial abduction to be his best chance of escape before the kidnappers are able to restrain him and take him under total physical control. He may be stabbed and seriously injured during the escape attempt, but he is also likely to be seriously injured or killed during captivity, so deciding to take a calculated risk to "get off the X" and escape from the attack site is quite reasonable in this situation.

In these two different environments, situational understanding helps contextualize the very different implications and consequences of a kidnapping for our notional victim, allowing them to make quick and informed decisions.

When practiced together, situational awareness, situational understanding, and OODA provide a powerful toolset that allows a person to see trouble before it can develop and then quickly take action to avoid a bad situation.

KEY TAKEAWAYS

- Situational awareness is something anyone can, and everyone should, practice. Many people are victimized because they were not practicing an appropriate level of awareness for their situation.
- Paranoia and hypervigilance can be as harmful to security as being tuned out.
- Most people should be in a state of relaxed awareness most of the time they are away from home.
- Denial: "not me," "not here," "not now," "not him," can be deadly, as can distractions such as cell phones, because they prevent people from practicing an appropriate level of situational awareness.
- Most hostile actors are very bad at surveillance and can be detected by people practicing good situational awareness.
- Trust your intuition or "gut feelings"!
- Consciously performing the OODA Loop can allow a victim to outthink an attacker.
- While situational awareness is important, situational understanding is what permits someone to quickly place their observations into context to make a quick decision and act appropriately.

NOTES

1 Cooper's Colors are outlined in Jeff Cooper's book *Principles of Personal Defense*. Jeff Cooper, *Principles of Personal Defense* (Boulder: Paladin Press, 2006).
2 Bob Drogin, "Manila Commandos Free Kidnaped Californian: Philippines: Dramatic Series of Bloody Raids Leaves 14 People De," *Los Angeles Times*, March 19, 1992, https://www.latimes.com/archives/la-xpm-1992-03-19-mn-5915-story.html.
3 Madison Park and Chandrika Narayan, "Orlando Shooting Survivors Describe Scenes of Chaos," *CNN*, June 13, 2016, https://www.cnn.com/2016/06/12/us/orlando-shooting-as-it-happened/index.html.
4 Dan Sewell, "Bundy's Deadly Charm Still Polarizes, 40 Years Later," *Khou.com*, February 9, 2019, https://apnews.com/article/cd9e9b2f3e504338a280d3a39ba0e279.
5 Chuck Goudie, "Judge in El Chapo Case Assassinated While Jogging," *ABC7 San Francisco*, October 20, 2016, https://abc7news.com/el-chapo-joaquin-guzman-extradition-to-us/1565301/.

6 BBC, "Paris Attacks: France Remembers Night of Terror amid Jihadist Threat," *BBC News*, November 13, 2020, sec. Europe, https://www.bbc.com/news/world-europe-54924051.

7 BBC, "Istanbul New Year Reina Nightclub Attack 'Leaves 39 Dead,'" *BBC News*, January 1, 2017, sec. Europe, https://www.bbc.com/news/world-europe-38481521.

8 Robert Coram, "John Boyd - USAF, the Fighter Pilot Who Changed the Art of Air Warfare," www.aviation-history.com, 2002, http://www.aviation-history.com/airmen/boyd.htm.

9 Mark Bonchek and Chris Fussell, "Decision Making, Top Gun Style," *Harvard Business Review*, September 12, 2013, https://hbr.org/2013/09/decision-making-top-gun-style.

10 Stephen Borstelmann, "OODA Loops – a Definition and Thoughts on Application to Healthcare - Volume to Value," *Volume to Value - The Healthcare Blog of Stephen M. Borstelmann MD*, February 21, 2014, https://n2value.com/blog/ooda-loops-a-definition-and-thoughts-on-application-to-healthcare/.

11 John Kifner, "Gunmen Would 2 Americans in Egypt," *The New York Times*, May 27, 1987, https://www.nytimes.com/1987/05/27/world/gunmen-wound-2-americans-in-egypt.html.

CHAPTER 12

A Man's Home
Is His Castle

One thing that has remained constant throughout human history, regardless of location and culture, is the desire to feel safe in one's own home and to protect those who live there. Whether the home was a simple log cabin on the American frontier or a majestic Bavarian castle, keeping one's family safe from harm has always been important. For some families, residential security might simply entail locking the doors for the night and activating the alarm in home mode. For others, in a higher threat environment, residential security measures may be far more complex and involve armed security officers. But as we've illustrated in the case studies contained in this book, having an appropriate plan for residential security, and using the security equipment present in the home is critically important no matter the owner's profile and the location of the home.

Like any effective security program, residential security planning must begin with an assessment of the threats that must be protected against. In the case of residential security, it is important to assess both the threats directed against the owner, and the general environment where the home is located. These assessments provide the residents and security professionals advising them with the information they require to make informed choices, beginning with foundational decisions such as selecting a residence location, and then flowing all the way down to more specific decisions about fences, locks, cameras, and alarms. It is best to purposefully design a home with security measures in mind, but security consultants can conduct assessments of existing homes and make security recommendations. Scott conducts numerous residential security assessments for clients every year.

Obviously, these decisions will also be guided by the amount of funding available for residential security, the owner's risk appetite, as well as aesthetic considerations. But bearing these considerations in mind, the ultimate objective of a residential security program is to keep the residents of the home safe by deterring hostile actors, detecting those who are not deterred, and then denying entry, or at least delaying any bad

 DOI: 10.4324/9781003647744-13

actor who does decide to attack the residence long enough that the police or security can respond.

PERSONAL BASELINE THREAT ASSESSMENT

Before beginning to design and implement any security program, it is important to first conduct a thorough baseline assessment of the threat faced by the person being protected, in this case, the owner of the residence. As the name indicates, baseline threat assessments are foundational assessments conducted to create as complete a picture as possible of the existing threat level facing the owner and will typically examine factors that could bring hostile attention to them, any known threats, and the universe of threat actors who could pose potential threats. By identifying, analyzing, and describing the existing threat level, baseline threat assessments are useful tools for determining what security measures are appropriate to protect against the identified or potential threats.

The first element to assess is the owner's public profile. Naturally, high-profile people, whether celebrities, business executives, or high net worth individuals, are far more likely to attract the attention of threat actors than the ordinary homeowner. If the property owner has large numbers of fans and admirers, they face an increased probability of unstable individuals developing an unhealthy focus of interest in them. It is not unusual for stalkers and fence jumpers to appear at the residences of such people.

Obviously, large numbers of detractors and critics also increase the possibility of negative attention and hostile action being directed toward the owner, especially if the owner is featured in conspiracy theories or is denounced or doxed on social media as part of the social media threat continuum. The owner's business dealings can also draw hostile attention, especially if they work for, or are on the board of a company that is controversial for some reason. Investments in contentious companies, industries, or technologies can also trigger negative attention, as can the acquisition of a company that is a lightning rod for criticism. Social activities such as providing financial support to controversial organizations, serving on the boards of controversial organizations, or even making donations to politicians, can also draw adverse interest to the property owner.

In addition to including known and documented past threats and incidents, the assessment must also account for abnormally aggrieved customers, disgruntled former employees, and unstable individuals who have a fixated focus of interest in the owner. Another factor to consider would be activist or protest campaigns targeting the owner, the owner's company, or directed against other companies in the same sector. Some activists will also target companies doing business with their primary target company or sector as a way to exert additional pressure on their target. For example, environmental extremists have targeted executives of companies in the financial sector for providing financing to energy companies.[1]

ENVIRONMENTAL BASELINE THREAT ASSESSMENT

A measured and informed residential security program also requires a baseline assessment of the security environment where the residence is located, that includes the current and historical trends for factors such as crime, terrorism, civil unrest, and natural disasters. This assessment must examine data for the nation, the city, and the specific neighborhood where the residence is located.

In addition to factors that have a short-term impact, such as crime, consideration should also be given to factors that can cause longer disruptions. This can include events such as civil unrest, violent protests, martial law, or government-imposed curfews that could leave residents isolated and, perhaps, without basic supplies and services for a prolonged period. As we've seen during recent hurricanes, wildfires, and floods, even affluent areas can become isolated and cut off. A good residential security plan will provide self-sufficiency to help mitigate the impact of disruptions to infrastructure and transportation, as well as a plan for evacuation in a worst-case scenario.

The effectiveness of local law enforcement and emergency response personnel, and the location of police stations, fire stations, and trauma centers must also be factored into the environmental baseline assessment. Security plans must account for situations where the police and other first responders are unlikely to respond in a timely manner—or not at all. This is particularly applicable to people like Anne Bass, who live in remote areas where it may take hours for first responders to arrive. The layout of the property the residence is located on, and the geography of the neighborhood around the property also play important roles in the environmental assessment.

As seen in the Aguilar case study in Chapter 3, even within neighborhoods with lower crime rates, like Bel Air, some areas are more attractive to criminals and potential attackers than others because they offer easy access to the neighborhood from the outside and an easy escape from the neighborhood after a crime. The Aguilar residence was located on the edge of Bel Air, close to the freeway. The National Institute of Justice has commissioned several studies in which incarcerated residential burglars were questioned about how they decided which homes to target.[2] These studies identified several factors that dramatically increase the probability of a residential burglary. The homes most likely to be targeted are:

1. Not equipped with a burglar alarm system.
2. Located within ¼ mile of a major thoroughfare.
3. Situated adjacent to a wooded area, railroad tracks, or a park.
4. Located on a corner lot or cul-de-sac.
5. More expensive than other homes in the area.

Neighborhoods with trees and bushes, abandoned houses, vacant lots, construction, and busy roads can also help threat actors to blend in while they conduct pre-operational surveillance. In the 1992 kidnapping and murder of Exxon CEO Sidney Reso, the kidnappers used a construction site adjacent to the Reso residence to conduct their pre-operational surveillance against Mr. Reso.[3] Local ordinances or homeowner association covenants that restrict the construction of fences and walls, or the use of other security measures, such as window grates or exterior lighting, should also be considered in the environmental baseline assessment.

Now that we've covered the personal and environmental baseline assessments, let's examine the distinct layers of residential security and the elements contained in each layer.

CONCENTRIC LAYERS OF SECURITY

Effective residential security planning utilizes a layered approach that begins on the outside and works its way inward. We find it helpful to think of a residence as having five distinct rings or layers of security. The security measures employed in the five layers should be complimentary and mutually supporting.

These layers are:

1. The neighborhood or area around the residence outside of the property line
2. The property line
3. The perimeter of the grounds or yard
4. The exterior of the residence
5. A shelter or safe haven inside the house (Figure 12.1)

These layers should be designed in a manner that will deter a criminal or intruder and cause them to select an easier target. But if the criminal is not deterred, security measures must then detect the intruder, deny them quick entrance into the home, and then delay them until first responders can arrive.

FIGURE 12.1   The layers of residential security. Shutterstock.

These are the four D's of physical security: Deter, Detect, Deny, and Delay. They are often augmented by a fifth D, Defend.

THE FIRST LAYER—THE AREA OUTSIDE THE PROPERTY LINE

Police provide the first layer of protection for most neighborhoods in developed countries. In some places, the police are augmented by the efforts of neighborhood watch programs, which can either be composed of neighbors who volunteer to watch each other's homes, or private security guards who have been retained to patrol the neighborhood.

In more affluent neighborhoods or high-threat locations, residential security teams at the homes of the residents can also help secure the first layer. In such a case, it is recommended that residential security teams communicate with the teams at other residences in the neighborhood to share information about observations and threats.

If possible, the streets in this first layer should be well-lit at night to discourage criminal surveillance and activity.

THE SECOND LAYER—THE PROPERTY LINE

The second layer starts with a clearly delineated property line, which should be marked as private property, and this layer extends to the residence's grounds or yard. When possible, the property line should include physical barriers, such as a wall, fence, or hedge, that serve to discourage casual or accidental intrusion. Obviously, such barriers should be constructed with consideration to aesthetics and the surrounding environment. Scott's residence in Guatemala was surrounded by a ten-foot wall topped with razor wire, but this type of perimeter would not be acceptable or appropriate in many neighborhoods in the United States or Europe. However, there are some very attractive anti-climb fences on the market that can be augmented by alarms to detect if the fence is being cut or if someone is attempting to scale it.

There are also some very good systems that can be used to detect the movement of a person crossing a perimeter line. CCTV systems are also becoming more capable and affordable, and many CCTV systems have infrared or thermal capability, and the software packages that comes with some of these systems can help discriminate between animal and human movement—a plus in areas with lots of deer or other wildlife.

In particularly dangerous environments, or in case of a serious threat, security personnel should patrol the outer perimeter between the property line and the yard. These can include armed or unarmed security guards who are on foot or in patrol vehicles. Guard dogs also make excellent patrol and detection assets, especially when paired with an armed handler.

THE THIRD LAYER—THE PERIMETER OF THE GROUNDS OR YARD

On a large residential property like Anne Bass's 1,000-acre Rock Cobble Farm, there may be quite a bit of distance between the property line and the outer perimeter of the residence's grounds or yard. In these cases, there will often be an additional fence or wall delineating the yard from the rest of the property, and this wall or fence forms the third ring of defense. In cases where there is no fence to mark this layer, additional sensors and cameras can be used to create the security layer. Often times this area will be better lit than the rest of the property or have motion-activated lighting. Proper lighting and CCTV coverage can be very effective deterrents, causing would-be criminals to select an easier target.

In a densely packed urban environment, there may be only a few feet between the property line and the outer walls of the house and rings two and three are condensed into one ring because the property line is the yard perimeter. In other cases, there may be no wall at all. In a large urban area like Manhattan, many residences are apartments or co-ops that require different residential security considerations.

In some cases, an upper-floor apartment in a well-secured building can be a wise choice for housing because the building management assumes the cost and burden of perimeter security, rings 1–3. A well-secured apartment building is essentially a condensed version of a gated community. Such living provides a degree of anonymity, while access is controlled by the use of security cards or doormen.

But even in this scenario, it is not unusual for residents facing a high threat to employ a covert protection team to watch layer 1, the street around the building, to attempt to spot pre-operational surveillance, or an attacker about to deploy against the building, or the principal when they leave the building.

When the residence is in a multi-tenant building, the quality of the building's security system and personnel should be taken into consideration, as should the risk of living in close proximity to someone who is a high-value target, and who has the potential to draw threats to the building and potentially increase the risk to other tenants.

Another issue with apartment living is that building management may not allow residents to add a security system or make other security upgrades to their units such as placing a camera in the hall outside the apartment door, or replacing substandard exterior apartment doors, locks, and jambs. Many times apartment management will also require residents to provide them with keys and alarm codes so they can have access to the residence for maintenance or in case of an emergency. In such cases, it is important to check how the keys and alarm codes are stored, who has access to them and what vetting procedure the building has for its employees.

THE FOURTH LAYER—THE EXTERIOR OF THE RESIDENCE

The exterior of the residential structure, the walls, doors, and windows of the residence, constitute the fourth ring of residential security. This layer should be protected to the highest extent possible and, in many places, can be legally defended by force if necessary. This layer consists of passive measures such as wall construction, window and door design, locks, and security procedures, as well as active defenses, like alarms, detection systems, and security personnel.

Special attention should be paid to the strength, quality, and installation of doors and locks. A high-quality deadbolt can be very effective, and a double-cylinder deadbolt should be used if the lock is located near any window that would allow a person to break the window to access the lock. Vulnerable windows can also be augmented with security film to make them more difficult to break. A simple slide bolt into the floor can serve to fortify a door. Ideally, locks should be selected and installed by specialists.

However, the best lock in the world, even when set in a sturdy metal or solid core wood door, can easily be kicked in if it is set in a cheap wood frame with a thin jamb and short screws. When we were law enforcement officers conducting arrest and search warrants, we observed that the jamb was almost always the weakest part of the door locking ensemble. They were usually the first thing to go when we broke down a door. Jambs must be carefully evaluated, and there are several commercial products available to remedy this common weakness and strengthen door jambs to make them more difficult to kick in. Of course, even the best locks and jambs are useless if doors are left unlocked!

Close attention should also be paid to windows, especially those on the ground floor, or that can be easily accessed by climbing. The locks that come standard on most residential windows are easily broken if the window is pried open with a crowbar, and even decent pry-proof locks on ordinary glass windows can be circumvented by shattering the window itself. In many recent home invasion robberies, criminals have gained access to the residence by shattering a sliding glass door using a brick, a hammer, or the type of spring-loaded glass punches commonly used by first responders to shatter car windows. Shatter-resistant windows or clear shatter-resistant films applied to windows help mitigate this threat. But as illustrated by the home invasion of former House Speaker Nancy Pelosi's San Francisco residence, even laminated high-security windows can be breeched by an assailant with tools if the attacker is given enough time.[4] Such measures can provide a delay to allow the residents to run to a safe haven and call for help, but they will not prevent a determined attacker with tools from entering.

Because of this, in locations with critical threat levels, or a resident facing a critical threat, ground-floor windows can be barred, as can any higher window that can be reached if the intruder climbs up a wall or tree. Accessible sliding glass doors can also be protected by sliding metal grates. However, in situations where windows and doors are secured with metal bars, emergency releases should be installed to facilitate an escape in case of fire.

A robust residential alarm system is another important component of this layer of security. Doors and windows should be alarmed with contact sensors, and these should be augmented with motion detectors and glass-break sensors. The alarm system should be backed up with battery power in case electric power is lost or disconnected. A cell phone backup is also recommended in case the phone or internet lines go down or are cut.

It is critical to remember that even the best alarm system is useless if residents do not use it. We strongly recommend that residential alarms be used in the "home" mode when the occupants are sleeping and may not hear an intrusion such as a window being smashed. In the above-mentioned Pelosi home invasion, Mr. Pelosi was sleeping and did not hear the attacker smash through the security windows of the home's French patio doors. Had the alarm been set in home mode, it would have tripped when the door was opened.

Residential alarm systems must be simple to use and the residents must be trained so they are comfortable using the system in both home and away modes. We recommend that the residential alarm system be set up to feature a silent duress alarm signal that will alert the monitoring company if the resident is forced to turn the alarm off under duress. Often times the duress code is the regular alarm code entered in reverse order on the keypad.

"Panic alarms" should also be discreetly placed in strategic locations around the residence such as the master bedroom, the home office, the safe haven, and other areas deemed appropriate based on the residents' lifestyle patterns. An intrusion into the residence itself must always be treated as an extreme emergency until security responders can clear the residence.

In terms of passive security measures in this layer, wherever possible, landscaping such as hedges should be kept away from walls near windows and doors or kept trimmed short so that they will not conceal a potential intruder as they either wait to ambush a resident, or as they work to defeat physical security measures. Another passive defense is having the perimeter of the residence itself flooded with light. Motion-activated security lighting is a good deterrent, especially when paired with CCTV coverage. In situations where security lighting is not allowed, or the residents do not want it for aesthetic reasons, infrared lights can be utilized for a more low-key approach.

As was highlighted in the case studies contained in the first eight chapters of this book, sometimes threats can emerge from within the residence, whether it is a threat to the family's privacy, or to their safety. As we saw in the Anne Bass and Tushar Atre case studies, insiders have an opportunity to learn the security protocols at a residence, scope out the security system in place (if any), and learn where valuables are kept. Because of this, it is extremely important that household staff, contractors, and vendors be properly vetted before being hired, and then required to sign non-disclosure agreements. Care should be taken to hide door codes and other sensitive information from people without a need to know. Had Tushar done that, his attackers would have had to break in rather than enter his residence using the door code.

When a staff member leaves or is dismissed, a thorough offboarding procedure must be followed that ensures any keys, ID cards or fobs they possessed are returned to prevent them from being used. This was not done in the Anne Bass case. Any issued electronic devices like phones and computers must also be returned Furthermore, all gate codes, alarm codes, and Wi-Fi passwords issued to the employee should be immediately disabled when they leave.

THE FINAL LAYER—THE SHELTER

If an intruder is able to breach the fourth layer and gain entry into the residence (or if they even appear to be attempting to breach the fourth ring), occupants should move immediately to the final ring of protection, an interior shelter, sometimes also called a refuge or safe haven. The location of the shelter may vary depending upon the threat and design of the residence. Some residences may contain more than one.

In some instances, the shelter may simply be a section of the residence that can be locked off by a substantial interior barrier, like the "rape gates" that are a regular feature in South African homes. In other cases, a bedroom, bathroom, bomb shelter, tornado shelter, or even a large closet can be equipped with robust doors and locks to serve as a shelter.

The concept is to have an area that provides an additional barrier that is intended to further delay an intruder from getting to the occupants. High-net-worth families frequently install a dedicated and hardened safe room in their home capable of withstanding a prolonged assault and that can provide a substantial delay. While not every residence requires a purpose-built safe room with a heavy steel door and Kevlar reinforced walls, every residence should have some interior shelter the family can retreat to in the case of an emergency. This shelter should be centrally located on the sleeping floor or the part of the residence where bedrooms are located.

The safe room should be stocked with materials and supplies that the residents might need during an emergency. This includes first aid supplies and medications residents might need immediately. Auxiliary light sources, such as flashlights or battery-powered lanterns, will be needed if all sources of power have been interrupted. A high-intensity tactical flashlight with a strobe capability can also prove quite useful in a home intrusion. Drinking water and an emergency food supply, such as energy bars, are also good to have in an emergency. These emergency items can be stored inside "go bags" that can be readily grabbed if the family needs to vacate the premises for some reason.

Fire is a killer, and the safe room should also be stocked with a smoke hood for each member of the family in case the house catches fire, or an attacker intentionally sets a fire to attempt to smoke the family out of the shelter. Fred and Sam Katz wrote a book about such an incident that occurred at an American Diplomatic facility in Benghazi, Libya in 2012.[5] The attackers were not able to get to the occupants of the villa, who retreated to a safe haven area, but they lit the villa on fire and the U.S. Ambassador to Libya and an Embassy communicator died from smoke inhalation because the safe have was not equipped with smoke hoods as was required by security standards.

The shelter should contain a means of communication such as a spare cell phone or landline phone. An alarm panel and a monitor to allow the residents to view the CCTV system can also be very helpful.

This brings us to the fifth D, Defend. The shelter can also be equipped with a firearm for defense, although the decision to maintain firearms for self-defense in the home is extremely personal. In the hands of a trained person with the will to use deadly force in an emergency, a firearm can be a very effective tool. If firearms are to be kept in the shelter area, they must be properly maintained and secured inside a gun safe that allows them to be quickly deployed while preventing children and unauthorized people from accessing them. Anyone considering keeping a firearm in their home for self-defense must also ensure they are properly trained in the operation of that specific weapon so that they will be able to use it under extreme stress. Not being able to properly use a firearm, or not having the will to use it, could result in unintentionally arming the intruder, which in our opinion is worse than having no firearm at all.

Some people may opt for less lethal defensive equipment such as pepper spray, a Taser, or the good old Louisville Slugger. But like with firearms, Tasers and spray must be properly stored and the residents must be trained to properly employ them.

Like any security measure, a shelter is useless without a well-thought-out plan to use it, and every plan is useless unless it is practiced. Because of this, families should run drills involving intruder scenarios, just as they conduct drills for fires, earthquakes, floods, and other natural disasters.

KEY TAKEAWAYS

- A measured and informed residential security program requires an assessment of the threat level directed against the owner, plus an assessment of the environment the residence is located in.
- Not every residence needs the same level of security as the White House.
- Residential security should be viewed in a layered approach from the outside in, with each layer complimenting the previous one.
- Residential security measures have four objectives that all begin with the letter D: Deter attackers, Detect those who are not deterred, Deny a rapid entry into the residence, Delay a committed attacker until help can arrive.
- A fifth D, Defend, can be added to a residential security program, but if the owner chooses to use a weapon to defend themselves and their family, they must store it properly and be thoroughly trained in using it.

NOTES

1 Sandra Laville, "Climate Activists Smashed Glass Door of JP Morgan in London, Court Hears," *The Guardian*, February 20, 2024, sec. UK news, https://www.theguardian.com/uk-news/2024/feb/20/climate-activists-smashed-glass-door-of-jp-morgan-in-london-court-hears.
2 Paul F. Cromwell, James N. Olson, and D'Aunn W. Avary, "How Residential Burglars Choose Targets: An Ethnographic Analysis," *Security Journal* 2, no. 4 (1991): 195–199, https://www.ojp.gov/library/publications/how-residential-burglars-choose-targets-ethnographic-analysis.
3 Philip Jett, *Taking Mr. Exxon* (Chronos Books, 2021).
4 CBS Evening News, "Pelosi Home Break-in Caught on Security Cameras," *YouTube*, November 2, 2022, https://www.youtube.com/watch?v=Cv6vtLgKFX0.
5 Fred Burton and Samuel M. Katz, *The Attack* (St. Martin's Press, 2007).

CHAPTER 13

Don't Dox Yourself

When we were growing up, if you wanted to find someone's addresses or phone number you used the telephone directory. Even when we worked as federal agents in the 1980s, it was not easy to locate people. We did have some help from the National Crime Information Center (NCIC) which provided a subject's criminal history plus some biographic information. We also had the National Law Enforcement Telecommunication System (NLETS) that could give us a person's driver license and vehicle registration information. We could access the credit bureaus over a dial-up modem to help find address data listed on credit applications. But oftentimes, we were still forced to use good old shoe leather to track somebody down—but that was before the dawn of the digital age.

Today, finding the information needed to locate almost anyone, including high-profile people like celebrities and business executives, is not difficult for any person who has an internet connection and the desire. Internet search engines have made it possible to quickly search for information on a person contained in countless news publications, websites, chatrooms, social media platforms, and other "open" sources connected to the World Wide Web. And as we will discuss in Chapter 15, artificial intelligence search tools are making it even easier.

The open-source information available about a person is augmented by vast amounts of Personally Identifiable Information (PII) data that is collected by data aggregators and data brokers. These are companies who scrape information from the open internet, but then combine it with public records, and non-public commercial data that is obtained by websites, computer and smartphone applications, warranty registrations, surveys, contests, sensors, and other sources.

Sadly, when most of us agree to the terms of service for an app we install on our smartphone, tablet, or other device, we agree to let the company sell our PII to data aggregators. The information collected by data aggregators can be used by companies for legitimate business functions, such as market research, product development, and compliance reporting, but one of the main objectives of collecting this information

DOI: 10.4324/9781003647744-14

is data monetization—companies make money by packaging and selling people's PII—and they will sell it to anyone.

The lesson here is for people to be aware of what they are consenting to when they install apps and click the "I agree to the terms of service" box, or when they provide personal information to register for a website, or fill out a form for a survey or contest, and when they purchase items. If an app or service is free, including the use of big social media sites like Facebook or LinkedIn, and search engines like Google, the individual user is not the customer—**they are the product.**

According to 360Privacy, there are over 400 publicly available websites that sell consumers' PII on the internet for a fee.[1] Some of the more widely known sites are Intelius, True People Search, Spokeo, and BeenVerified. Anyone with an internet connection can go to one of these sites, and for a few dollars, purchase a report about a person they have an interest in. The report usually contains information such as the subject's address, phone numbers, email addresses, job history, education history, criminal history, professional licenses, relatives, neighbors, etc. It is not hard to see how such a report could be used to do harm to the subject by either cyber or physical threat actors. As we saw in Chapter 4, kidnappers and other threat actors absolutely do take advantage of these services.

Because of this, we both routinely advise our clients to use the services of an information removal company to take their information off data aggregator sites. 360Privacy is the best in class when it comes to information removal and digital executive protection services, and we specifically recommend them.

In Chapter 10 we discussed how extremist influencers and others will "dox" or post the PII of people considered enemies of the extremist movement in an effort to encourage their followers to harass or attack them. The Department of Homeland Security defines doxing as "gathering an individual's personally identifiable information (PII) and releasing it publicly for malicious purposes, such as public humiliation, stalking, identity theft, or targeting for harassment."[2]

In the wake of Brian Thompson's murder, we have seen a concerning uptick in business executives being doxed on social media and internet chat rooms. Posts like: "John Smith, the CEO of Acme company needs to be Luigied. He lives at 123 Main Street, Anytown..." are not uncommon. But doxing is not new; activists and others have been doxing and targeting prominent people at their homes for many years now. For example, consider the protests at the homes of hedge fund managers conducted by anti-capitalist groups like the Hedge Clippers,[3] or the pro-Hamas activists who established a protest encampment that lasted for months outside the home of U.S. Secretary of State Antony Blinken.[4] The authorities have not yet released information indicating how Luigi Mangione located Brian

Thompson to begin physical surveillance on him, but we have little doubt he began his attack cycle with internet searches.

In many cases the information that is used to dox a person is collected by simply running an internet search or by purchasing a report from a data aggregator site. This threat can be mitigated somewhat by hiring the services of an information removal company like 360Privacy, mentioned above. However, the services of a company like 360Privacy are ineffective if the person actually "doxes themself" through careless internet security protocols and practices. That is what we were referring to when we titled this chapter "don't dox yourself."

We understand that for many prominent individuals, building their brand is not only essential for their career progression, but is also needed to help foster the success of their company. In the digital age, entertainers need to use social media and other online outlets to engage their fans and promote their music, movies, or books. Business executives need to have a web presence that includes a biography and photos. Interviews in print magazines, podcasts, news programs, and television shows can do a great deal to increase the profile of the person, their company stock, product sales, or their artistic projects. Taking it one step further, influencers have created an entire industry out of monetizing their social media presence and they simply can't make a living without maintaining a robust online presence.

However, it is critical to maintain a balance between promotion and security. We are not saying people should not post things on the internet or social media. Rather, we are urging people to be intentional and careful about what they post, with an eye toward safeguarding both their privacy and physical safety while promoting their brand. This principle also applies to interviews conducted in print, podcasts, or video formats. People must be careful not to reveal personal information in interviews that could help a bad actor target them or their family.

People who dox themselves by providing information that allows bad actors to identify their location and what valuables they have at the location can prove to be their own worst enemies. Perhaps one of the most highly publicized incidents of this type occurred in October 2016, when armed robbers stole some ten million dollars' worth of jewelry from Kim Kardashian while she was staying at a chic boutique hotel in Paris during fashion week. The thieves targeted her after she posted photos of the jewels and of the hotel she was staying at on her Instagram account.[5] The thieves were also reportedly emboldened by boasts Ms. Kardashian had made on social media that she did not wear fake jewelry, assuring the criminals that the jewels she had in her hotel room were real, and worth the risk they would incur in stealing them.[6]

In another notable incident, rapper Bashar Jackson, who was known by the stage name, Pop Smoke, was murdered in February 2020 in a home invasion at a home he had rented in Hollywood. Five members of a South Los Angeles street gang decided to assault the residence after seeing photos posted to social media by the rapper that allowed them to identify the address of the residence. Other social media posts he made featured photos of jewelry and piles of cash that allowed the gang members to run a cost-benefit equation in which they assessed the risk of a daylight home invasion was worth taking due to the potential proceeds they could gain from the crime.[7]

In a more recent incident, in February 2025, a 22-year-old man from Texas traveled to Ft. Lauderdale Florida and was arrested after breaking into a house that had been rented by a group of popular female OnlyFans content creators.[8] One of the women had posted a video on TikTok showing the exterior of the house several days before the incident, noting that it was the new "@Bop House" the location where she and the other girls were now living and producing pornographic content.[9] That video allowed the obsessed fan from Texas to geolocate the house.

These incidents highlight the importance of high-profile people protecting the location of their residence, but revealing their real-time location can also bring danger. As we were writing this chapter, a Japanese live streamer, Airi Sato, was stabbed to death on March 12, 2025, while she was in the middle of a livestreaming video of herself walking down the street in the Shinjuku area of Tokyo. Ms. Sato regularly posted videos of her daily life on the Japanese livestream platform WhoWatch.[10] Her alleged killer was a 42-year-old man who was a fan of the model, and who reportedly developed a grievance after giving her money she refused to pay back. Her alleged attacker tracked her location by identifying buildings in the background of her video.[11]

In cases where the intent of an attacker is to steal a person's possessions rather than harm the target, criminals will not only seek to identify the target's address but will also use social media or internet research to look for times when the target is not at home. In 2008–2009, a group of robbers called the "Bling Ring" burgled the homes of dozens of celebrities in upscale Los Angeles neighborhoods, choosing to strike when they learned the celebrities were away from home by following posts they made to their social media accounts.[12]

In February 2025, an organized gang of seven Chilean nationals were charged in connection with a string of attacks targeting professional NBA and NFL athletes which began in September 2024. Some of the heists have been quite sizable: NBA player Bobby Portis reportedly lost over $1.5 million in cash and jewelry when his home was targeted in November 2024.[13]

In December 2024, ABC News reported they had obtained a copy of an FBI bulletin that was shared with professional sports leagues warning that organized theft groups were targeting the homes of athletes, and that they had identified nine athletes who had been victimized between September and November 2024.[14] According to ABC, the FBI warned that "These homes are targeted for burglary due to the perception they may have high-end goods like designer handbags, jewelry, watches, and cash." The FBI bulletin also noted the groups "conduct physical and technical surveillance in preparation for these burglaries, **using publicly available information and social media to identify a pattern of life for a prospective victim.** They often know in advance where valuables are kept in a home" (Emphasis added). Finally, the report added that "These preparation tactics enable theft groups to conduct burglaries in a short amount of time. Organized theft groups bypass alarm systems, use Wi-Fi jammers to block Wi-Fi connections and disable devices, cover security cameras, and obfuscate their identities."

This bulletin clearly illustrates how criminals use self-doxing by the athletes to assist them in their attack planning cycle. Posts on social media allowed them to identify and select victims, as well as providing the criminals with information about the layout of the residence and the security systems installed to protect them. When combined with the athletes' publicized schedule, it is not difficult for the thieves to pick a date when the athlete is away.

Other organized criminal gangs have also targeted international sports figures in Europe[15] and South America, tracking the stars via their social media accounts. In some instances, armed thieves have conducted brazen home invasion robberies that have left the athletes shaken and injured,[16] other athletes have been kidnapped.[17] In many or most of these cases, the athletes made posts on social media platforms that assisted the criminals in planning the crimes committed against them.

For the clients we have worked with over the years who have the highest profiles, and draw the most attention, obscuring their residential address is a difficult challenge, because everyone—from paparazzi to neighborhood gossips—knows where they live. Fortunately, such people usually have the resources required to put robust security programs in place, to include residential security teams and executive protection details. In this way they are able to mitigate some of the threats posed by having a known address.

But not everyone requires the same level of security as the highest-profile people. Security programs are not "one size fits all," and many of the people with a lower profile can do quite well without a 24/7 security presence. However, as we noted in Chapter 13, before the appropriate level of security for a particular person can be determined, a solid baseline threat assessment should be conducted.[18] A security program can then be tailored that is appropriate to account for the assessed threat.

We would add that personal preference is also very important. Some people have a higher risk tolerance than others, and they may desire less security than the threat assessment indicates due to concerns over privacy or convenience. However, even in such cases it is important that the person consciously makes the decision in light of the threat assessment, and not in ignorance. Other people are more fearful by nature, and such people may prefer more security than the assessment might deem necessary.

In terms of obscuring their residential address, many of the people who do not draw so much attention can often maintain a low profile and fade into the crowd, especially if they live in an area with a lot of affluent people, like New York or Los Angeles. Of course, this is harder for individuals living in small towns where there are fewer expensive homes. But even then, they should be careful to guard their residential address. If a person buys property in their own name, the purchase will often show up in public records such as county tax rolls. Because of this, we advise clients to purchase property using an LLC or trust with an obscure name that cannot be easily connected to the buyer. We have encountered many cases in which residence was purchased with an obvious name, like "Smith Family Trust" that does little to protect privacy.

Where possible it is also better to use a lawyer's office address or a corporate address for use in official documents, such as SEC filings, political contributions, or charitable gifts. Using the name of an LLC or trust to order items online rather than the high-profile person's name can also help hide their residential address from merchants as well as data aggregators. Even having an assistant order the items in their name using a corporate card will help.

In high-threat cases it is also good practice to have mail and packages delivered to a PO box or an off-site office where it can be collected and screened before being transported to the residence. The June 1980 Unabomber attack that wounded American Airlines President Percy Wood at his home in Lake Forest, Illinois, highlights the threat posed when high-profile individuals receive and open packages at their homes.[19]

But again, all these measures to obscure an address can be rendered useless if the prominent person posts photos on their social media that allows their residence to be geolocated, or that even shows the house number in the photo. Other self-inflicted vulnerabilities can include Strava and other exercise apps in which the privacy settings are not locked down, allowing a bad actor to see their address based on their daily exercise routines, or even use the exercise routes routinely taken to plan an attack.[20]

Residential addresses are not the only pieces of critical personal information that should be protected. There are a whole host of little pieces of information—digital breadcrumbs—that can be pieced together to create a mosaic picture of a person's pattern of life. These can include transactions in apps like Venmo that indicate where a person gets their hair cut, visits a massage therapist, has their child in daycare, or buys a cup of coffee every morning. Venmo privacy settings are default in the open mode, meaning that a person's spending history and the people they are connected to are visible to anyone with a Venmo app.

One time Scott was conducting an executive security assessment for a young tech executive and a public profile assessment (PPA) was included as part of the overall assessment. A PPA (some people refer to them as a digital vulnerability assessment) is where an analyst is provided with the name of a subject and then tasked to collect everything available about them on the open internet. When Scott interviewed the executive, he insisted that he was not on social media. However, the analyst Scott assigned the PPA discovered the executive's brother's Venmo account did not have privacy settings enabled. This open account allowed the analyst to identify the client's internet "handle,"[21] the unique nickname he used for a number of social media and email accounts. These digital breadcrumbs provided a trail that ultimately allowed the analyst to identify several social media accounts belonging to the client, as well as reviews and comments left on various websites using his Gmail account that indicated his hobbies and identified some locations where he spent a lot of time, helping to map out his pattern of life.

The case of the tech executive not only demonstrates the utility of PPAs in identifying and closing down vulnerabilities—the brother subsequently locked down his Venmo account—but it also demonstrates that even if a person takes great care to hide their digital tracks, oftentimes friends and family members can inadvertently dox them. We have encountered many examples where family members have posted family photos with names, or photographs of residences, vacation homes, aircraft with tail numbers, children's schools, and sporting events, among other items on social media that provide significant digital breadcrumbs that can be used by anyone attempting to target a prominent person.

In another case, several years ago the authors were hired to do a security vulnerability assessment of a high-profile tech executive, who was extremely security conscious, and who was highly skeptical that we would be able to find any vulnerabilities. While he was very secure, his children were not. Based on posts made by his children on social media, we were able to easily identify the locations of homes, pictures of vehicles, the tail number of the family's private aircraft, vacation homes, and travel patterns.

Family members, friends, and significant others can provide an opening that allows threat actors to penetrate a person's cloak of anonymity. We have found photos on social media of children of executives boasting of eating steak and lobster on private planes (flaunting their wealth), engaged in underaged drinking, street racing and other illegal activities, or posting during family vacations to ski or visit the beach, signaling not only their real time location but that the family home is empty.

Parents have posted photos of their high-profile child's (or grand-child's) wedding, residence, vacation home, or birthday party, provid-ing threat actors with a date of birth, and in some cases, even a year of birth, that could help fraudsters. Such posts can also serve to assist the attack planning of threat actors such as terminated employees, high-end burglars, activist groups, obsessed stalkers, or even murderers like Luigi Mangione.

Because of these dangers, family members, and even extended fam-ily members, should be provided with age-appropriate training on digital hygiene, what information needs to be protected, and the dangers associ-ated with carelessly posting sensitive information. Family members can even be walked through how to tighten the privacy settings on the various social media platforms they do use, how to enable two factor authentica-tion and what platforms to avoid because they have little or no privacy settings, such as the popular social media photo gallery platform VSCO.

We understand that children today are "digital natives" and are under intense social pressure to have a presence on social media. However, they must be taught how to use these tools appropriately in much the same way they are taught to swim, ski, or drive.

Household staff such as drivers, nannies, cooks, cleaning staff, and landscape workers should also be briefed on the importance of digital hygiene, and restrictions on what information they can post about the family should be clear and even codified in their non-disclosure agree-ments and personal services contracts. Household staff can also be recruited by bad actors in a number of ways, including romance scams, outright offers of money, or by becoming entrapped by a criminal because of a drug debt, or even due to a child's drug debt. Because of this, household staff must be carefully vetted and subject to periodic background investigations.

Outsiders can also post information on the internet that creates sig-nificant vulnerabilities. In addition to the personal information shared in the media by paparazzi, vendors, and contractors who work in the resi-dence can also pose a threat by posting photos of their work. Contractors and vendors should not only have background investigations conducted before they are permitted into the residence,[22] but they should also be required to sign non-disclosure agreements prohibiting them from taking and posting photos of the work they do without the express consent of the homeowner.

Another frequent vulnerability we encounter are real estate post-ings on sites such as Zillow, Realtor.com, Trulia, etc. containing numer-ous detailed photos of a residence before it was purchased by the client. Obviously, photos detailing the home's interior layout, grounds, and security features can be of great value to a bad actor. Because of this we advise clients to have such photos taken down by making a request directly to the website, through an information removal company such as 360Privacy, or if necessary, by a letter sent by a lawyer. Speaking of photographs, we also recommend that people request that Google Earth blur photos of their home that appear in Street View.

As people who live and breathe protective intelligence, monitor criminal trends, and watch for indications of threats directed toward our high-profile clients, we encounter digital vulnerabilities nearly every day, many of which are self-inflicted. The world is dangerous enough as it is. People should not aid threat actors by doxing themselves and should consciously work to reduce other online vulnerabilities.

KEY TAKEAWAYS

- People should assess the vulnerabilities created by online information and data aggregators or hire someone to do it for them.
- Everyone should work to avoid posting critical personal information on the internet, on social media platforms, or in interviews.
- Individuals should make an effort to scrub their PII from data aggregators and other websites or hire a reputable firm to do so.
- Family members and staff should receive age-appropriate training on digital hygiene, what information should be protected, and how to use social media and the internet safely.
- Staff, vendors, and contractors should all sign NDAs and be subject to background checks.
- If events are held at a residence, guests and others should be diplomatically encouraged not to post photos on open social media accounts or websites.

NOTES

1 "Products," *360 Privacy*, 2024, https://www.360privacy.io/product.
2 Office of Partnership and Engagement (OPE), "Resources for Individuals on the Threat of Doxing" (Department of Homeland Security, January 16, 2024), https://www.dhs.gov/sites/default/files/2024-01/24_0117_ope_resources-for-individuals-on-the-threat-of-doxing-508.pdf.

3 Dailymail.com Reporter, "The Hedge Clippers Stage Protest at Daniel Loeb's Hamptons Home," *Mail Online*, July 14, 2015, https://www.dailymail.co.uk/news/article-3160245/Hundreds-angry-protesters-stage-demonstration-Hamptons-home-billionaire-hedge-fund-exec-Cuomo-fundraiser.html.

4 ARLnow.com, "BREAKING: Gaza Protest in Front of Blinken's House Removed by State Authorities | ARLnow.com," *ARLnow | Arlington, Va. Local News*, July 26, 2024, https://www.arlnow.com/2024/07/26/breaking-gaza-protest-in-front-of-blinkens-house-removed-by-state-authorities/.

5 Lindsay Weinberg, "Kim Kardashian Makes Rare Comments on Paris Robbery Nearly 7 Years Later," *NBC Boston*, June 22, 2023, https://www.nbcboston.com/entertainment/entertainment-news/kim-kardashian-makes-rare-comments-on-paris-robbery-nearly-7-years-later/3073669/.

6 Peter Allen, "What REALLY Happened in Kim Kardashian's Robbery Hell: Bound, Gagged and Terrified - the Fullest...," *Mail Online*, March 17, 2025, https://www.dailymail.co.uk/news/article-14499497/What-REALLY-happened-Kim-Kardashians-robbery-hell-Bound-gagged-terrified-fullest-account-Parisian-gang-finally-face-justice.html.

7 Andrew Dalton, "Man Charged in 2020 Killing of Rapper Pop Smoke Pleads Guilty to Manslaughter to Avoid Trial," *AP News*, February 6, 2025, https://apnews.com/article/pop-smoke-killing-corey-walker-plea-f0a9fe1135fa53257a81b689923a7a44.

8 Briana Trujillo, "Man Arrested for Allegedly Burglarizing OnlyFans Model's Fort Lauderdale Home," *NBC 6 South Florida*, February 11, 2025, https://www.nbcmiami.com/news/local/man-arrested-for-allegedly-burglarizing-onlyfans-models-fort-lauderdale-home/3541106/.

9 Kyle Phillippi, "The Bop House Is an OnlyFans Paradise That Pulls Millions per Month," *Vice*, February 10, 2025, https://www.vice.com/en/article/the-bop-house-is-an-onlyfans-paradise-that-pulls-millions-per-month/.

10 WhoWatch, https://whowatch.tv/.

11 Martin Fackler, "Online Influencer Is Killed While Livestreaming in Tokyo," *The New York Times*, March 12, 2025, https://www.nytimes.com/2025/03/12/world/asia/japan-influencer-stabbed-livestreaming.html#.

12 Crime Museum, "The Bling Ring," *Crime Museum*, accessed April 24, 2025, https://www.crimemuseum.org/crime-library/crime-in-the-media/the-bling-ring/.

13 Claudia Levens, "Bobby Portis Had His Milwaukee Bucks NBA Championship Ring Stolen during the River Hills Home Burglary," *JournalSentinel*, February 25, 2025, https://www.jsonline.com/story/communities/north/2025/02/25/milwaukee-bucks-championship-ring-in-bobby-portis-burglary/80058348007/.

14 Aaron Katersky and Josh Margolin, "FBI Issues Warning about Burglaries of pro Athletes' Homes," *ABC News*, December 30, 2024, https://abcnews.go.com/US/fbi-issues-warning-burglaries-pro-athletes-homes/story?id=117197676.

15 James Horncastle, "Roberto Baggio's Villa Broken into by Armed Robbers," *The New York Times*, June 21, 2024, https://www.nytimes.com/athletic/5580680/2024/06/21/roberto-baggio-italy-robbery/.

16 Sky Sports, "Joao Cancelo: Man City Full-back Opens Up about 'Horrific' Home Robbery in December," *Sky Sports*, February 14, 2022, https://www.skysports.com/football/news/11679/12542136/joao-cancelo-man-city-full-back-opens-up-about-horrific-home-robbery-in-december.

17 CBS News, "Kidnapped Soccer Star Rescued after Shootout between Police and Captors in Ecuador Jungle," *Cbsnews.com*, December 6, 2024, https://www.cbsnews.com/news/kidnapped-soccer-star-pedro-perlaza-rescued-shootout-ecuador/.

18 Fred Burton and Scott Stewart, "The Role of Baseline Threat Assessments in Protective Intelligence," *Ontic*, June 26, 2020, https://ontic.co/resources/webinar/the-role-of-baseline-threat-assessments-in-protective-intelligence/.

19 FBI, "Unabomber," Federal Bureau of Investigation (FBI, 2016), https://www.fbi.gov/history/famous-cases/unabomber.

20 Scott Stewart, "Creatures of Habit," *TorchStone Global*, July 14, 2023, https://www.torchstoneglobal.com/creatures-of-habit/.

21 "Handle," *Netlingo.com*, 2025, https://www.netlingo.com/word/handle.php.

22 Background checks are important. In one case involving a past client, background checks were conducted on a work crew only after a remodeling project had begun. The checks disclosed that several of the workers had violent criminal histories, to include sexual assault. They should not have been allowed into a home with young children.

CHAPTER 14

Travel Safety

The first step we recommend for anyone to take before embarking on a trip is to research their destination as thoroughly as possible in the time they have, using all the tools at their disposal. Fortunately, today there is an incredible amount of data freely and rapidly available on almost any destination on the globe. A simple internet query in a search engine for a hotel name and location, or a street address will often uncover a great deal of information about that location including background about the location's history and geography, neighborhood guides, news stories, gossip websites, and blogs. An internet search will also usually produce a map of the area in question, but if not, Google Earth or another mapping tool can be used to quickly provide a general overview of the area in both the map and satellite view modes. Street view photos can also convey a great deal of useful data and should be viewed when available.

For most domestic locations and for destinations in many developed countries, an internet search for the city or neighborhood name +crime data, e.g., "Los Angeles +crime data" can also provide a great deal of useful information. Many municipalities publish their crime statistics by neighborhood, police precinct, or zip/postal code. Some municipalities even provide searchable crime maps that can help a traveler understand crime trends and locations. For areas where crime data is not readily available from government sources, real estate tools can sometimes be used to obtain crime statistics or view crime heat maps.

In addition to looking at crime statistics, it is also prudent to check for planned protests and the history of civil disobedience in the destination, as well as the incidence of natural disasters, such as wildfires, earthquakes, hurricanes, etc. The locations of police and fire stations and the closest hospital and Level 1 trauma center are also important data to obtain.

For travelers going abroad, one of the fundamental steps involved in building the situational understanding needed to keep out of harm's way is to know and understand—in advance—some of the idiosyncrasies of the destination country's customs, culture, and government bureaucracy, as well as the identified security risks. Armed with this knowledge and

DOI: 10.4324/9781003647744-15

guidance, a traveler can plan and implement proper security precautions and recognize trouble as it is developing.

Corporate or academic travelers may also have access to powerful paid research tools such as LexisNexis or International SOS that can also help provide a great deal of detailed information on the destination, and travelers should take advantage of those tools if they are available. High-profile travelers may also have access to a protective intelligence team that can conduct all this pre-travel research for them and then use the information to create a tailored travel risk assessment report.

Americans traveling to locations outside the United States should also always check and see what the U.S. government says about their destination country on the U.S. State Department's travel information page.[1] This page provides a wealth of information about entry, exit and visa requirements, crime and safety, health risks, and travel and transportation inside the destination country. The page also has a place where travelers can register for the State Department's Smart Traveler Enrollment Program (STEP). STEP not only alerts the State Department to a traveler's presence in the country so they can account for them during an emergency but also provides the Department with a channel to push out warnings and advisories to the traveler. We strongly advise American travelers to enroll in STEP and that travelers from other countries enroll in their country's traveler advisory system, such as Australia's SMART traveler.[2]

Embassy and consulate websites can sometimes provide more granular crime and safety information than the main State Department site and are worth checking. The annual country security reports available from the Overseas Security Advisory Council (OSAC) are also a very valuable source for detailed crime and safety information. These reports can be found by searching the OSAC website,[3] or by typing "OSAC country security report (insert destination country name)" into an internet browser. Many OSAC products can only be accessed by OSAC constituents and require a site log-on, but the country security reports and security alerts are available to anyone. We also recommend that American corporations, academic institutions and non-governmental organizations that have foreign locations, or that send travelers abroad, join and participate in OSAC.

It is a good idea for travelers to print out a copy of the State Department travel information sheet and take it with them on their trip. At the very least, travelers should write down the phone number of the U.S. embassy, including the after-hours phone number. This number generally rings into the Marine security guard on duty at the embassy's security command center, normally referred to as "Post One," or to the embassy's duty officer. And yes, we did say write it down, so that it is on paper, and not just stored in a phone or other electronic device that can be lost or stolen. The paper with the embassy contact numbers should also be kept separate from the traveler's wallet, so if the wallet gets lost or stolen the contact information will not be lost with it. We also recommend writing down or printing out the address and contact number(s) for the traveler's hotel and any other local contact information for use in case of an emergency. This information should also be written in the local language. Many hotels have business cards written in both English and the local language with the name and address of the hotel on them.

This written or printed contact information is not only useful in case of a robbery or major crisis. If the traveler maintains all their relevant contact information in their phone and relies only on an app like Google Translate, and then the device is lost, dropped in the water, or simply has a dead battery, they could find themselves in a bit of a mini crisis—especially if they are in a country where very little English is spoken and they do not speak the local language. In such a situation, a sheet of paper or business card with contact information in the local language is invaluable.

Even though we are Americans, we also like to read the travel advice provided by other countries, especially the UK,[4] Canada,[5] and Australia.[6] For some destinations, such as francophone countries it is also worth checking the French Foreign Ministry page.[7] The U.S. State Department's Bureau of Consular Affairs coordinates daily with the governments of the British, Canadian, and Australian governments, and the four countries have pretty much the same big picture of the security environment in a specific country. However, we find the real value to be gained by reading the advisories from other countries is that they can sometimes provide specific, anecdotal data not provided by the American advisories.

For example, one time while compiling a travel risk assessment for a client, Scott noted in a U.K. advisory that British citizens in a particular city had been victimized by local criminal gangs who had begun to engage in "express kidnappings"—something not noted in the U.S. crime and safety information. Even though express kidnappings are a tactic used elsewhere in the region, it was helpful to be able to warn the client of an emerging threat in their destination city.

Another great source of information about the local environment is local contacts. For a business traveler, a contact in their local office, or with a client or supplier company, can often provide a wealth of information if asked. In addition to addressing the normal logistical issues, the contact should be asked for information about the local environment to include local culture, laws, customs, and government bureaucracy. They should also be asked about crime and any other security risks in the area where the traveler will be staying or working. These sources can also often provide helpful information on health issues or natural disasters.

Non-business travelers can ask these same questions of friends or family members, or their hotel, resort, tour operator, or outfitter.

Conditions in a destination country and city can and do change. Because of this, if the research is conducted far in advance of the trip, it should be refreshed shortly before departure to ensure that no critical changes have occurred.

Health information is also something that must be researched prior to travel. In addition to the health information provided on the State Department's travel website, travelers should also consult the U.S. Centers for Disease Control and Prevention's travel health information website.[8] The CDC website provides a wealth of information about vaccinations required for specific countries and regions, and provides important tips about avoiding insect-borne diseases such as malaria and dengue as well as food- and water-borne ailments such as amoebic dysentery. The CDC also issues travel health precautions and warnings as well as information on sporadic outbreaks of dangerous diseases.

We also advise that travelers consult with a doctor or travel health clinic well in advance of their trip to ensure their vaccinations are up to date and that they have time to receive all the required vaccinations for their destination before they depart. The doctor can also prescribe anti-malarial medication or other prescriptions if required. Even travelers in good health need to ensure they have the appropriate vaccinations and should take measures to avoid contracting dysentery and other food- and water-borne illnesses—it is hard to enjoy a vacation if you are sick. Many travel health clinics will also issue handy medical travel kits that contain adhesive bandages and an assortment of over-the-counter pharmaceuticals such as pain relievers and anti-diarrhea medicines. Sometimes these kits will even contain prescription antibiotics for use in case of severe dysentery.

We recommend that all travelers take a first aid kit with them, and if one is not provided by the travel clinic, travelers should purchase or assemble their own kits. At a minimum, the first aid kit should contain basic first-aid items such as alcohol preps, antibiotic ointment, hydrocortisone cream, burn and blister cream, gauze, moleskin, a variety of Band-Aids, a triangular bandage, tweezers, safety pins, and a thermometer. As noted above, a prescription antibiotic for severe dysentery is good to have, in addition to medicines such as loperamide, Pepto-Bismol, pain reliever, diphenhydramine, and allergy medicine. If the traveler has severe allergic reactions to things such as bee stings or seafood, they should also carry an EpiPen at all times. We also recommend the kit include stop-the-bleed items such as a tourniquet, a quick clot bleeding control dressing, a chest seal, and a compression bandage.

Another critical health consideration is insurance. Most people do not realize that their normal U.S. health insurance plans (to include Medicare) do not cover them outside of the country. In some cases, a domestic health insurance plan may cover a portion of the medical care provided overseas, but the patient will normally have to pay the provider at the time of service in cash and then be reimbursed. Most medical providers overseas do not accept American health insurance, and will demand cash up front before providing treatment, which may delay treatment.

In some countries, medical providers can also overcharge uninsured patients, who are left with very large bills. We recommend that travelers purchase travel health insurance that will cover them in the countries they will be traveling to. It is also advisable to ensure that this insurance will cover the cost of medical evacuation if needed. Medical evacuation can cost tens of thousands of dollars. The odds of needing to be medically evacuated are slim, if it is necessary, the cost of not having insurance to cover it can be staggering.

PRE-TRAVEL CHECKLIST

- Conduct internet searches for relevant safety and security information on your destination.
- Check the U.S. Department of State travel page for country-specific information, alerts, and advisories. Print out a copy of the page or write down the contact information for the appropriate embassy/consulate.
- Check the U.S. Embassy and, if applicable, the local U.S. Consulate websites for additional security information.
- Check the British, Australian, Canadian, or other government travel sites for relevant information.
- Check the OSAC crime and safety report for the destination country.
- Register with the U.S. State Department STEP, or your country's equivalent service.
- Check with your doctor to receive any required vaccinations. Acquire a travel first aid kit.
- Check the CDC travel website to make sure your doctor doesn't miss any important vaccinations.
- Check your medical insurance policy to determine if it covers overseas treatment and medevac. If not, purchase travel insurance that does.

WHAT *NOT* TO BRING

There are many fine handbooks and travel guides that provide lists of what travelers should pack. However, in our experience, the crucial issue from a security standpoint is not so much what you should bring with you, but rather *what you should not*. Quite frequently, travelers bring unnecessary items with them on trips that attract the attention of potential criminals and that can cause considerable angst if the item is lost or stolen—like the $450,000 Richard Mille watch we mentioned in Chapters 1 and 3.

In Chapter 10, we discussed the cost/benefit equation that criminals consider before selecting a victim. What a traveler brings with them on a trip can have a significant impact on that criminal equation. Simply put, a criminal is willing to take far more risk to get a $30,000 Rolex than a $30 Timex. Because of this, the first thing we recommend to those packing for a trip is that they try not to take anything with them that will draw undue attention from criminals. We also recommend that travelers do not take anything with them that they are not prepared to lose if confronted by an armed criminal.

Some items are precious, and impossible to replace if they are lost or stolen, and these items could cause the traveler to resist surrendering them. As we've previously noted, economic crime should not be resisted, and your stuff is not worth your life—or even an extended stay in the hospital. In most cases, criminals are just interested in getting the goods and getting away. They are not interested in gratuitous violence, but at the same time, they will not hesitate to shoot or stab someone who resists. If travelers leave precious items at home they not only reduce their attractiveness as targets for criminals, but they also remove the urge to resist surrendering the precious item to an armed criminal.

For many years, Capital One Bank ran commercials for their credit cards with the tag line "What's in Your Wallet?" If we were to ask that question to everyone reading this book right now, we doubt that the majority of people could make a detailed list of everything they are currently carrying in their wallets. This lack of awareness can become a significant problem if a person's wallet is lost or stolen, and they need to cancel and replace all the credit and other items in the wallet. Quite frankly, most people carry far more in their wallets than they need to—or should, especially while traveling.

We know people who carry wallets several inches thick, and such wallets are a veritable treasure trove to a criminal. Not only can the criminals immediately benefit from whatever cash and credit cards are in that wallet, but they can also frequently get enough information to do far more substantial damage to the victim's bank account—or even assume their identity. The damage can be compounded if the victim keeps credit card and ATM PIN numbers written in their wallets—especially if they reuse PINs for multiple accounts. We recommend that people go through their wallets before traveling to weed out unnecessary items and ensure they are carrying only the things needed for the trip.

Overseas travelers should leave all club membership cards and other unnecessary wallet clutter at home. They are not of much use abroad and could even get a person into trouble. Consider the case of Charles Hegna, a U.S. Agency for International Development employee and an accountant, who was killed during the 1984 hijacking of Kuwait Airways flight 221.[9] Mr. Hegna carried a card in his wallet that identified him as a Certified International Accountant (an organization whose initials were "CIA"). In combination with Mr. Hegna's official passport the "CIA card" reportedly brought Mr. Hegna to the attention of the hijackers and he was consequently the first American to be executed during the hijacking.[10] We also recommend travelers remove any unneeded military reserve, veteran, or other identification cards. Social Security cards should never be carried in one's wallet.

Once it is decided what credit/debit cards to take on the trip, the traveler should make a list of the cards they will be carrying along with the account numbers and the phone number to contact the companies in case the cards are lost or stolen. For those traveling abroad, it is important to ensure the phone numbers will work from outside the United States. In many instances, the 1–800 toll-free numbers listed on the back of a credit card to report a lost or stolen card will not work from overseas locations. Travelers should take one copy of this credit card information with them on the trip but keep it in a place separate from their wallet. Since the list has credit card numbers on it, it should be stored carefully, and the card verification code number should not be recorded on the list. A second copy of this information should be left with a trusted individual back home who can be called in case the cards and the list are lost. It can also be helpful to leave a photocopy of the information page of the traveler's passport with the trusted contact in case it is lost, and the information is needed to report it stolen or obtain a replacement. The traveler should also keep a photocopy of their passport information page with the credit card list in a secure place.

While on the topic of wallets, men who carry wallets in their back pockets are prime targets for pickpockets. A front pocket wallet and money clip are more difficult for pick pockets to access. Women travelers should also consider foregoing their normally large wallets for their trip and carry a smaller billfold. We also recommend dividing money into different bundles—one bundle with large bills and another bundle with smaller bills to be used for spending cash. The two should be kept in separate front pockets or places on the body. In this way, anyone watching the traveler pull out cash to buy something will not see a wad of money with large bills.

Laptops, tablets, and smartphones have become essential travel accessories because of the vast amount of information they can hold in a relatively small space. For this reason, they—or even just the information they contain—make a prize catch for anyone with hostile intentions. Travelers should take precautions to not only physically safeguard these devices but also the information they contain. These devices often serve as de facto "electronic wallets," and like physical wallets, many people can't identify everything that is in theirs.

While the loss of a phone or laptop is bad, the loss of the information stored in the device can be even worse if identity or financial thieves can access and use the information stored in them. The best way to protect sensitive information contained in a laptop, phone or tablet is, obviously, to leave the device at home. But if devices are taken on a trip, the owner should treat them like a wallet and make an effort to minimize the amount of sensitive information stored on them. One way to minimize the information carried with the traveler is to use a Chromebook with the data stores on the cloud instead of on the device. In addition to minimizing the data stored on devices, it is also prudent to ensure that all important data on the electronic devices is backed up in another location.

Travelers (and everyone else) should also take advantage of any security features the device has, such as requiring a password to access the device. Commercially available encryption programs to encrypt the information stored on the device can also be used to help protect sensitive information from theft. Two-factor authentication should be enabled on all applications that support it. We also recommend that people use encrypted password vaults that can be used to protect usernames, passwords, and pins. Such a program allows a person to protect all their usernames and passwords while only having to remember one very long robust password. When installed on an encrypted hard drive, these programs give you an added layer of security. If law enforcement agencies have difficulty cracking devices with proper security features enabled, it will also be difficult for most criminals.

Features on the devices that allow them to be tracked if lost or stolen, and wiped remotely should also be enabled before the trip because they cannot be enabled after the device is lost. However, it is important to note that these features do not work in all countries. For example, due to privacy laws, the Apple "Find My" app does not work in South Korea.

Criminals like electronic items like laptops and tablets because of their high value on the resale market. These devices are frequently stolen in airports, hotel lobbies and restaurants, on trains and buses, and even on the street. Therefore, a laptop should never be set down in a place where a thief can quickly snatch it and run. In addition, it is a good idea to carry a laptop in a non-typical bag, rather than its case, which can have the manufacturer's logo on it and screams "steal me, I'm expensive."

For business travelers carrying sensitive proprietary information, such information should be either be stored in the cloud or stored on an external storage device and be kept separate from the rest of the computer. In such a case, if the laptop is stolen, the thief will not get the data, which is likely much more valuable than the machine itself.

SECURITY IN THE AIR

Speaking of devices and data being stolen, terrorism and disruptive passengers are not the only threats facing air travelers. Criminals travel too. During our decades of travel, the authors are astounded at the number of people who leave their personal belongings unattended in the airport terminal and aboard the aircraft. It would not be difficult for a criminal to quickly rifle through a purse or briefcase looking for valuables when someone gets up from their seat to use the restroom. It would be a nightmare for a traveler to arrive at their destination and find their phone or passport had been stolen on the plane. Travelers should either leave the bag containing valuables with a trusted companion, or, if traveling alone, take them into the restroom. If on a plane, placing a bag in the overhead bin is also a better option than leaving it unattended in the seat as it makes it more difficult for a criminal to go through the bag without being observed.

Despite the high level of security normally associated with airports, a lot of crime occurs at or around them. In fact, criminals victimize far more travelers every year than terrorists do. The crime problem at airports stems primarily from the fact that airports present a large concentration of potential victims in one place. This is compounded by the fact that most travelers carry things worth stealing, such as money, jewelry, cameras and electronic equipment. Furthermore, many times travelers are exhausted, unfamiliar with the place and culture, and groggy or perhaps even a little tipsy after a long flight with free alcohol. In other words, many travelers in airports do not practice good situational awareness, which makes airports target-rich environments for criminals.

The airport security barrier makes it more difficult for criminals or terrorists wanting to target travelers to get to the secure, or "hard," side of the airport without boarding passes or airport identification—or to get out after they've committed a crime. Because of this, much more theft happens on the unsecure side than on the hard side. However, that does not mean the "secure side" of the airport is safe from criminals or that travelers can let their guard down once they pass through security. Crime occurs on the hard side of the airport every day, and over the years we have seen clients, friends, and colleagues who let their guard down and were victimized while on the hard side of an airport. Purses, briefcases, and laptop bags are especially sought, and travelers should never hang them on the back of a chair or set them down in a place beside or under a table where they can be easily snatched.

In addition to minimizing the time spent outside of the security hardline at the departure airport, travelers should also minimize the time spent on the non-secure side of the destination airport, and practice good situational awareness while in arrival and departure halls outside of security. This means travelers should check in and proceed through security, and then retrieve their bags and leave the airport, as quickly and efficiently as possible.

Arrival halls are prime areas for criminals to lurk and look for potential victims. They normally focus on people who look lost or who are not practicing good situational awareness. There are often ATMs in airport arrival halls, but it is far better to use an ATM or exchange bureau in the secure area of the airport if possible. If a traveler must use the ATM or exchange bureau in the arrival hall, they should pay close attention to people around them, watch their luggage carefully, and only exchange the minimum amount of cash needed to get to their hotel or destination. Withdrawing or exchanging a large amount of cash in an arrival hall will often bring a person to the attention of criminals. Having pre-arranged transportation is one way to help minimize the time spent in the arrival hall. If using pre-arranged transportation, the driver should be asked to use a codeword, or other symbol on their "welcome board" rather than listing the name and company of the traveler.

Traveling by private aviation is generally safer than flying commercial but is no guarantee of security. People have had items stolen in domestic FBO terminals, and in many overseas destinations, general aviation passengers must still pass through immigration and customs in the main passenger terminal and exit via the arrival hall.

HOTEL SECURITY

Like airports, hotels are prime targets for hostile actors like criminals and terrorists. Even people staying at upscale hotels in major cities can become targets, because criminals know that people who have things worth stealing stay at such hotels. It is no mistake that one of the case studies and several examples and stories we shared in the first eight chapters of this book occurred near high-end hotels. Because of this, travelers should practice a heightened state of situational awareness as they arrive at or depart from their hotel.

One important factor for travelers to consider before booking a hotel is the crime and safety environment in the city and neighborhood surrounding the hotel they plan to stay at. Travelers should then check to see if security of the hotel is sufficient for that specific threat environment. Once they are satisfied with the general security of the area, and the security measures in place at the hotel, the next step is to consider the security of the room they will stay in. Some rooms are safer than others, and it is prudent to choose the safest room possible. Generally, rooms above the second floor are safer than those on the ground floor, because a potential attacker cannot enter via the window or patio. However, due to the possibility of fire, a traveler should avoid going more than five or six stories up so that they are not beyond the reach of a fire department rescue ladder.[11]

Other rooms to avoid in high terrorist threat environments are those near the front of the hotel and those adjacent to the street. An attack against a hotel typically occurs near the foyer or lobby in the front of the building. In addition, in many countries, there is a threat of car bombs exploding on the street. Sometimes these are very powerful and can damage nearby buildings, so distance between the hotel room and the street is a good thing, windows not facing the street are better. Travelers should not hesitate to request another room if they believe the one the receptionist has assigned is not safe.

In high-threat environments it is also best to avoid lingering in high-risk areas such as hotel lobbies, the front desk and entrance areas, and ground-floor restaurants. Western diplomats, businesspeople, and journalists who frequently congregate in these areas have been attacked on several occasions.

Should an attack occur, the best course of action is to avoid going to the primary attack zone. Travelers hearing shots or one explosion should avoid the temptation to run to their windows to see what happened, or worse, attempt to videotape the attack. Instead, they should check their doors and take cover in a place away from the windows. Bathrooms with no windows are a good place to do this. Taking this step reduces the likelihood of being injured by a secondary explosion timed to kill survivors and first responders. In most large bombings, flying glass kills many of the victims. If no immediate danger from smoke or fire is present, unharmed guests should remain in their rooms and stay away from windows until rescue and security personnel arrive to secure the scene.

Like at home, travelers should use any security devices the hotel offers. However, they should not count on them being absolute guarantees of security. Hotel door locks, even the electronic ones are not difficult for thieves to defeat. Because of this, if the hotel room door is equipped with a secondary lock, it should be used. We also recommend traveling with a wedge alarm that can be placed under the door to help prevent entry and warn if someone is attempting to enter. Hotel room safes are also easily defeated and they should not be trusted to secure valuables or sensitive information. These items should either be carried at all times or left with a trusted companion.

Window locks and the locks on doors leading to adjoining rooms are also a concern and should be checked to make sure they work properly. If the traveler can't lock all the doors and windows in their room, they should request another room or move to another hotel.

While in their hotel room, guests should avoid opening doors to unannounced visitors or those claiming to be delivering a package or conducting hotel maintenance. It is best in both cases to tell the caller to wait in the lobby and to check with the receptionist or hotel security before admitting anyone into a hotel room. Most reputable hotels will not send a maintenance person to a guest room unannounced.

Travelers should practice good situational awareness, even while they are inside a hotel or resort. Sadly, many robberies and sexual assaults happen in hotels, and some can even involve hotel staff.[12] If a traveler senses they are being followed or if a stranger is wandering the halls when they plan to enter their room, they should make their way to a busy public area (preferably the lobby) instead of going to their room and notify hotel staff of the incident. A stranger should never be allowed to follow a traveler into their room.

When in an elevator with other people, it is preferable to get on last and to be the last person to press the floor button. If someone around or in the elevator makes the traveler uncomfortable, they should get out of the elevator if they are in a public area of the hotel or press a button that will take them to a public area of the hotel, such as the lobby or rooftop restaurant, rather than get off on the floor their room is on.

Fire is a killer, and hotel rooms should also have sprinklers, smoke detectors, and a phone that allows occupants to dial out. Travelers should also check the location and condition of fire extinguishers and hoses as well as check the emergency exits to ensure they are passable. During our travels, both in the United States and abroad, we have encountered emergency stairwells that were obstructed or even rendered impassible by items stored or stacked in them. We have also seen fire exit doors that have been chained shut due to the criminal threat. Blocked fire exits are very dangerous, and if encountered, the traveler should change hotels.

Speaking of fire, we always travel with smoke hoods. Most fatalities in fires are the result of smoke inhalation and not the flames. A smoke hood can help when evacuating down a smoke-filled hallway or emergency stairwell or can keep the traveler safe in their room until the fire department can evacuate them. Smoke tends to rise, so staying low can also help avoid dangerous gases and fumes. At night, we recommend keeping the smoke hood on the nightstand along with a high-intensity flashlight, the traveler's passport if traveling abroad, wallet, and the hotel room key. This ensures those items are readily at hand if an emergency occurs in the middle of the night.

In the last chapter we discussed how pieces of information that allow a threat actor to connect the dots to put a person at a specific time and location are dangerous. As the Brian Thompson case illustrated, this also applies during travel. Travel itineraries and meeting schedules should be closely protected, and this information should only be provided to people with a clear need to know, and even then, they should only be given the parts of the schedule relevant to their duties.

For high-profile people with easily recognizable names, hotel and restaurant reservations should be made in a pseudonym or the name of an assistant. Where possible it is best practice to have an assistant or security agent check the principal in at the hotel in advance to obtain the key and check the room. This way the principal can bypass the desk, avoid a delay in the lobby, and proceed directly to their room.

In situations where a commercial transportation service is used to pick up a VIP traveler at the airport, the driver should not wait in the airport's arrival hall holding a sign advertising the principal's name and company. As noted above, if a sign is needed to identify the driver, a codeword, pseudonym, or symbol should be used with no company name listed.

While flying on private aviation normally provides more anonymity and privacy to travel. There have been many recent examples of people using flight tracking websites and plane spotter networks to identify and track the aircraft belonging to prominent individuals such as the highly publicized case of the college student who began tracking the flights of Elon Musk[13] and Taylor Swift.[14] Even if the aircraft is purchased using an anonymous LLC, and has a tail number that does not identify the owner, plane spotters or paparazzi will eventually connect it to the owner, as can a threat actor who has access to these same online tools. Because of this, we advise those wishing to use general aviation to use a fractional owner-ship service that will allow them to travel on different aircraft belonging to the aviation company with tail numbers that cannot be connected to them.

KEY TAKEAWAYS

- Traveling to an unfamiliar destination can be exciting, but it can also bring with it unfamiliar risks. Proper research in preparation for a trip is needed.
- Travelers should be very intentional about the things they take with them on a trip. Will they draw the interest of criminal or other threat actors? They must also seriously consider what NOT to bring with them.
- Ambush criminals often select airports and hotels as places to spot potential victims. Travelers must maintain situational awareness when arriving or leaving these locations.
- The secure side of the airport is safer, but not absolutely safe. People can be targeted on the "hard" side of the airport and should maintain situational awareness.
- Travelers should minimize the time they spend on the soft side of the airport.
- Some hotels are safer than others, and some hotel rooms are more secure than others. Travelers should ensure they stay in a hotel with appropriate security for the environment and that their room is in a good location within the hotel.
- Crimes can be committed inside hotels and can sometimes involve hotel or resort staff. Care must also be exercised while inside the hotel and the traveler's hotel room.

NOTES

1 "Travel," *Travel.State.Gov*, n.d., http://travel.state.gov/.

2 "Homepage," *www.smartraveller.gov.au*, accessed April 24, 2025, https://www.smartraveller.gov.au/.

3 "Reports," *Osac.gov, 2019*, https://www.osac.gov/Content/Browse/Report.

4 "Foreign & Commonwealth Office," *GOV.UK*, December 22, 2023, http://www.fco.gov.uk.

5 "Travel and Tourism," *Travel.gc.ca*, November 16, 2012, http://www.travel.gc.ca/.

6 "Homepage," *www.smartraveller.gov.au*, accessed April 24, 2025, https://www.smartraveller.gov.au/.

7 "Country Files," *France Diplomacy*, 2024, https://www.diplomatie.gouv.fr/en/country-files/.

8 "Travelers' Health," *Cdc.gov*, 2025, http://www.cdc.gov/travel/.

9 Thomas Ferraro, "The Bodies of American Hijack Victims Charles Hegna And...," *UPI*, December 12, 1984, https://www.upi.com/Archives/1984/12/12/The-bodies-of-American-hijack-victims-Charles-Hegna-and/2143471675600/.

10 While in the DSS counterterrorism division, we were able to secure a copy of the Iranian government's investigation of the hijacking.

11 Most fire department ladder trucks are 100 feet; however, the distance can be problematic with obstructions and parked vehicles on crowded streets. Additionally, fire department response times vary greatly both inside and outside of the United States.

12 Nadine El-Bawab, "Staff Members at Bahamas Resort Arrested for Drugging, Assaulting 2 American Women: Police," *ABC News*, February 9, 2024, https://abcnews.go.com/US/staff-members-bahamas-resort-arrested-drugging-assaulting-2/story?id=107062795.

13 Dani Medina, "UCF Student Says He'll Stop Tracking Elon Musk's Private Jet on X If He Does One Thing," *FOX 35 Orlando*, June 24, 2024, https://www.fox35orlando.com/news/jack-sweeney-tracking-elon-musk-private-jet-ucf-football-stadium.

14 Jeanine Santucci and Christopher Cann, "Taylor Swift Doesn't Want People Tracking Her Private Jet. Here's Why It's Legal," *USA Today*, February 7, 2024, https://www.usatoday.com/story/news/nation/2024/02/07/tracking-data-for-taylor-swifts-jet-location-is-public-heres-why/72507706007/.

CHAPTER 15

Trends Shaping the Future of Protection and Protective Intelligence

As we look out over the horizon at the future of protection and protective intelligence, we are reminded by several high-profile attacks in the recent past that the old methods threat actors used to conduct attacks have not gone away. Consider the July 2024 sniper attacks against President Donald Trump at the Butler County Fairground; the vehicular assault against a New Year's Eve crowd in New Orleans; or the brazen murder of Brian Thompson on the streets of New York City. These are all examples of simple attacks using familiar tactics that in our assessment could have been prevented.

We have learned over the years that there is brilliance in simplicity, and that simple tactics can be used to take advantage of protection failures that occur for a myriad of reasons, to include human error, denial, complacency, fatigue, missed signals, breakdowns in physical security plans and protocols, and failure to think outside the box—what can a couple guys do if we allow them to carry boxcutters onto an aircraft?

As protectors, we need to do better. As we look toward the future, we must never overlook or forget time-tested, simple tactics. But that will not be easy. As we noted in the introduction, threats to prominent people are rising, and every day protectors are being inundated with threats posted on social media platforms, and requests to protect more executives—especially in the wake of Brian Thompson's murder. Today the demands on security teams have never been higher due to our troubled world. In addition to managing the flood of threats, security teams must deal with old-school problems like wildfires, floods, epidemics, workplace violence, protests, geopolitical tension, hot wars in multiple parts of the world, etc.

So, setting aside all the current things posing risks to prominent people, what do we see as the most significant emerging or forthcoming

DOI: 10.4324/9781003647744-16

threats and what do we think they portend for the future of protection and protective intelligence? Here are our thoughts from a forecasting perspective.

AI

There has been a lot of buzz in the security world about artificial intelligence (AI), and in our view, this attention is warranted. We believe AI is the emerging technology that will have the broadest impact on security and protective intelligence. There are two types of AI, machine learning and generative, and both will impact security and protective intelligence in a variety of ways. We think it is also worth emphasizing that AI, like any technology, can be used to both attack and defend.

For many years Scott ran a fencing club, and he taught hundreds of kids to fence. He views AI to be a tool much like a fencer's saber. A saber can be used to attack an opponent, but it can also be used to parry (block an attack) and to riposte (counterattack). The effectiveness of a saber depends heavily on the skill and technique of the person wielding it. The same will prove true for AI, whether machine learning or generative. AI is just another extension of the computer and is likely to become an important tool for both threat actors and security practitioners. But it will remain just that, a **tool**—and all tools can only be as effective as the deftness and skill of the person using them. Because of this, we encourage security and protective intelligence teams to make a conscious effort to embrace and master AI so that they can first of all understand the capabilities and limits of AI, but secondly so that they will be able to use AI effectively to detect and defeat AI-enabled attacks.

At this point in time, machine learning AI is more mature than generative AI and is already having a substantial impact in the security world. On the attack side, machine learning AI tools make it much easier to comb through massive amounts of data. This means that they can help threat actors collect personal identifiable information (PII) and other sensitive data on celebrities, politicians, executives, and other prominent people that can be used to target them. As we noted in Chapter 13, the rise of the internet has already made stalking someone much easier than before, and AI tools are taking that threat to another level. AI search tools are more powerful than ordinary search engines and can enable even those lacking good internet research skills the ability to scour the surface internet and the deep and dark web for PII and other data and then compile the data to create a targeting dossier. AI tools can also help geolocate photos that prominent people post on their social media feeds.

It is worth repeating here that these AI tools can help a malicious actor gather information to begin their attack cycle, but they are still limited and cannot replace the need for physical surveillance. There are still some things someone planning an attack needs to see in person.

On the defensive side, these same AI-enabled search tools can also help security practitioners quickly identify and create profiles on persons of interest. Reverse image search tools, facial recognition tools can also help in this effort.

Some of the AI-enabled tools can also be used to help search for a client's PII on the internet, deep and dark web so it can either be removed or obfuscated by adding a lot of false data to make identifying the real sensitive data more difficult. It is the cyber equivalent of adding hay to the pile to make it more difficult for a malicious actor to find the needle.

In addition, most of the situational awareness software tools and social media monitoring platforms being used by protective intelligence teams today are powered by machine learning AI. These tools can't replace analysts, but they can make them much more efficient by performing mundane, mind-numbing tasks like scrolling through endless social media posts, and freeing up the analysts to focus on more important tasks like reviewing the results of searches performed by AI tools, to separate the wheat from the chaff, and to place the items identified into the proper context. At the present time, machine learning AI tools lack the ability to understand all the nuances of human communication, and an analyst is still required to identify if a particular post is a genuine threat or just an innocuous comment.

AI programs are also being used to assist security personnel monitor CCTV feeds. Rather than having a person sitting at a console watching dozens of screens looking for activity or suspicious behavior, AI-enabled systems can now be set to alert the operator when there is a specific type of behavior in a specific place, thus relieving a great deal of tedium, and making the operator more effective.

AI AND SOCIAL MEDIA

In addition to the way AI tools can be used to search through an ocean of social media posts for relevant information, the intersection of AI and social media has some other significant implications for protective intelligence. The first is the way the algorithms being used to power social media platforms tend to create ideological echo chambers that reinforce fringe or conspiracy beliefs by recommending similar material to users. There have been a lot of studies conducted on this topic,[1] but if someone doubts the validity of these studies, all they have to do is run a search for something like "the moon landing was faked" in YouTube, TikTok, or some other social media platform, watch a video or two that supports the conspiracy theory, and then watch what the algorithms begin to feed them as recommendations to watch.

In the past, people holding extremist views or believing in fringe ideologies had to make some effort to find materials to reinforce those beliefs. This meant traveling to attend a rally or subscribing to a newsletter published by an extremist movement or ordering materials from their book catalog. With the advent of the internet extremist movements were early adopters of the technology and IRC chat rooms and online bulletin boards were around almost from the start of the internet. As the World Wide Web began to emerge in the late 1980s, extremist websites quickly popped up representing an array of ideologies, including white supremacism, jihadism, and anarchism.

These websites created avenues for isolated people holding extremist or fringe beliefs to instantly connect and communicate with others holding their views across the globe. They were no longer geographically limited. Secondly, the anonymity provided by the internet allowed people to express extremist or fringe beliefs with very little "social cost." They didn't have to worry about being judged and shunned like they did when they tried to share their beliefs with normal people in the physical world. Finally, they could find fellow believers no matter how far their beliefs deviated from the mainstream. These online echo chambers serve to reinforce fringe beliefs and can also serve as a vehicle for extremist influencers to radicalize and operationalize people in these communities as we discussed in Chapter 10 with the Social Media Threat Continuum model. These AI algorithms are channeling people into beliefs and actions far more dangerous than the "Tide pod challenge." Beliefs that can serve to transform them into threat actors.

As we were writing this book, Scott's team identified a poster on the X social media app who prompted the X platform's AI tool, "Grok," to create an anti-Semitic conspiracy theory that named a client as part of a global conspiracy. The poster then concluded that the fake conspiracy theory "must be true" since AI created it.

AI DEEPFAKES

Deepfake audio and videos are another type of AI-enabled threat. We have had clients impacted by deepfake pornographic photos and videos, some of which were very realistic—and very disturbing. We are concerned that such deepfakes will serve to fuel subjects who have an unhealthy sexual fixation on a client and compel them to act out.

We have had other clients who have been targeted by deepfake audio, and even video conference calls, by sophisticated scammers attempting to conduct business fraud by using the deepfakes of the CEO to order money transfers. There is also a proliferation of impostor accounts on social media representing themselves to be prominent people. Many of these accounts interact with fans to scam them out of money. We have had several clients approached by angry people who were convinced that they had been communicating with the client who had stolen money from them, and in some cases is very difficult to convince them they were communicating with an imposter. We believe AI deepfakes are going to be used to make these scams even more believable, and thus more dangerous for prominent people.

Another threat posed by deepfake videos is that they will be used to portray prominent people admitting to participating in some illegal activity or conspiracy theory plot. Imagine a video of a person admitting to being part of the secret Illuminati who are controlling the world, that they participated in orgies held on Jeffrey Epstein's Island, or that they are involved in the ritualistic sacrifice of human babies to remain youthful. Such videos could generate a response much worse than the 2016 "Pizzagate" shooting at a Washington, DC restaurant[2] and result in attacks against the person portrayed in the faked video.

Audio and video deepfakes are becoming steadily more natural and convincing, and there will soon come a time when they will become very difficult to distinguish from communications with the real person. Some companies today are instituting codewords to use for communications involving money transfers, much like a duress code. Only in this case, if an email or verbal communication does not contain the codeword, the money is not to be transferred. Fortunately, there are some companies developing AI tools to help spot AI deepfake communications, but not everyone will have access to these tools, and they will cause significant problems that will likely include violent incidents.

AI-ENABLED CYBERATTACKS

We know that on the information security side, they are very focused on how generative AI tools can help even unskilled hackers write sophisticated malicious code. Certainly, this poses a growing and significant challenge to cybersecurity efforts to protect corporate systems, and proprietary information, and it also poses a threat to the PII of business executives. But beyond the information security threat, we believe that soon, cyberattacks are going to pose a physical threat.

We've already seen some examples of cyberattacks impacting the physical world from government actors who have used tools like Stuxnet to destroy centrifuges used in the Iranian nuclear program,[3] or hackers who have taken control of traffic lights and other devices connected to the internet.[4] High end homes are becoming increasingly integrated with internet-enabled devices to control an array of systems from lights and shades to HVAC systems and door locks. It is only a matter of time before some creative hacker uses AI to help create a code that will cause an electrical device to overload and cause a fire, disable the pilot light on a smart fireplace and turn on the gas, or otherwise devise a way to attack the "smart" home of a prominent person they want to target.

Likewise, cars are becoming increasingly computerized. Thieves have taken advantage of this to steal vehicles,[5] stalkers have hacked car apps to track their targets,[6] and hackers have already demonstrated the ability to take physical control of some models.[7] Car manufacturers are obviously concerned about this and are working hard to protect vehicles from such attacks, but we nevertheless remain concerned that AI can be used to find a novel vulnerability that will result in a physical attack against someone using their own vehicle.

DRONES

For over the past decade, drones have been a hot topic in the security world. One only has to walk the floor at the ASIS GSX or ISC West to see the array of products that have emerged in recent years to detect and disable drones. Our personal favorite defensive solution is the use of trained eagles to hunt drones.[8]

But this interest in drones has risen for a reason. Drones have become cheap and plentiful, and they are appearing in increasing numbers over private estates, corporate headquarters, government facilities, airports, and public events. They have become a serious threat to privacy, proprietary information, and a plain old nuisance. In addition to inquisitive hobbyists, paparazzi have been using drones to pry into the private lives of celebrities. California enacted a law in 2015 to prevent aerial snooping,[9] but it clearly has not ended the practice, as drones have become stealthier and harder to detect.[10] Criminal gangs have also been using drones to conduct surveillance of residences for high-end burglaries.[11]

Throughout history, warfare has resulted in rapid technological advances, and the war in Ukraine has spurred huge leaps in drone technology. In fact, at the time we are writing this, short-range first-person view (FPV) drones are causing some 70 percent of the casualties on the battlefield.[12] In the same way that World War I began the era of air combat and tanks, the Ukraine war has begun the age of drone warfare.

The first advancement that has come out of the Ukraine war is the widespread adoption of 3D printed drones. Workshops all over Ukraine and Russia are printing drones, and some units are even printing their own drones near the front lines.[13] This has resulted in making drones cheaper and easier to acquire, and these small drones are being used by the thousands every day in the war for reconnaissance, attacks, and now we are seeing the emergence of counter-drone drones.

The second leap has been the emergence of FPV drones as weapons. These are drones that are driven by a pilot who wears a headset that allows them to see what the drone's camera is seeing to maneuver the drone beyond line of sight. FPV drones were first developed for drone racing and are fast and robust drones that are extremely maneuverable. This is what makes them so effective at attacking moving targets like vehicles and soldiers. At the beginning of the conflict the smaller drones were being used to conduct reconnaissance for small units and to drop grenades and other small ordnance on targets.

But as the war progressed and drones became cheaper and more plentiful, FPV drones became expendable, and are being used in one-way attack missions, outfitted with a variety of ordnance for attacks against different targets. Some are outfitted with RPG warheads to attack armored vehicles, others are outfitted with fragmentation bombs to target troops, thermobaric munitions are used to attack troops hiding in bunkers or buildings, and the "dragon drones" are rigged to drop molten thermite on enemy soldiers and equipment.

The third major advancement in drone technology during the war has been to make the drones quieter, harder to detect, and more difficult to disable via electronic warfare. New propeller designs allow them to fly more quietly so that the targets have less time to react and take cover. In response to the increase in drone usage, both sides began to extensively employ electronic warfare equipment to jam drone frequencies and protect fighting positions from drone attack. They even began to mount jammers on tanks and other equipment. In response, drone operators began to employ frequency hopping technology to allow their drones to overcome the jamming systems. Electronic warfare systems were improved to help protect against frequency hopping, which led to a further leap of technology, in which drone operators began to use fiber optic strands to control their drones, rendering their drones impervious to radio frequency jamming, while also making it more difficult to identify the drone operator's position since there is no radio transmission to intercept and triangulate. AI is also being used to program drones so that they can launch, conduct a mission, and either attack or return to the launch point. This technology also makes them impervious to jamming equipment and protects the operator from detection.

What do these battlefield advances in drone technology have to do with protection? Everything. It is only a matter of time before these technological innovations are adopted by threat actors to include criminals, terrorists, assassins, and paparazzi. Quiet fiber optic controlled drones will be difficult for security teams to hear, and can stream 4K ultra high definition video, a feature that will be of obvious interest to paparazzi.

Since they do not rely on radio frequency to operate, anti-drone systems will struggle to detect them or locate their operators and like on the battlefield, they will be impervious to anti-drone systems that rely on RF signal jamming.

One of the main factors that has limited the use of drones for attacks outside of battlefield locations remains ordnance. A large percentage of the drones used in the Ukraine war use existing ordnance like RPG warheads, mortar rounds, and 40mm grenades. While drone operators are using a variety of 3D printed munitions for their drones, they are still filling the 3D printed bodies with TNT and other military-grade high explosive filler that is often salvaged from unexploded ordnance recovered from the battlefield, or in some cases, using explosives from military demolition charges.

Military grade explosives and even commercial explosives have become much harder for threat actors to obtain in recent years. This is why we've seen most bombing attacks in the United States and Europe involve low-explosive devices like the pressure cooker bombs used in the Boston Marathon bombing,[14] or homemade explosive mixtures like those used in the July 2005 London bombings.[15] By extension, we can conclude that the ordnance used in drone attacks will most likely also use 3D printed munitions filled with low explosive mixtures or homemade explosive fillers, which will be less reliable and less effective than those filled with military grade explosives. This will help mitigate the threat somewhat, but security teams must still begin to plan for ways to counter the emerging drone threat.

OTHER ELECTRONIC DEVICES

While a great deal of attention is being paid to drones, it is important to recognize that there are other electronic items that are also becoming cheaper and more accessible for threat actors. One of these is hidden cameras. LAPD and other departments in Southern California report that burglary gangs are increasingly using cameras hidden in bushes and trees to monitor the patterns of life in homes they want to target. These cameras are being found both before and after homes have been robbed.[16] These same cameras can be placed to enable surveillance of a target on a frequently used route. This permits them to conduct surveillance of a target's movements and record them to identify patterns, without having to physically expose themselves to detection every time the target vehicle passes.

To date, most of the hidden cameras that have been discovered have been those that use an SD card for memory, or that are attached to another type of memory device to store the images or video. This requires the criminals to return to either recover the devices or swap out the SD card before they can view the images or videos. Cameras are also available that use cellular services or Wi-Fi networks to transmit data, and these cameras can allow criminals to have real-time coverage of a targeted residence or route in the same way Wi-Fi-enabled security cameras allow homeowners to view their homes in real time. Purchasing a cellular plan for such cameras using a false identification would not be difficult for most criminals, nor would obtaining a burner phone to view the camera feeds. Wi-Fi-enabled devices could use a home's own Wi-Fi network if it is unsecured, or secured with a weak password, or even a neighbor's unsecured Wi-Fi network to transmit data.

Speaking of Wi-Fi-enabled surveillance devices, miniature high-quality audio and video surveillance device "bugs" are readily available at spy stores and on the internet. The ease of obtaining these devices, their low cost, and their user-friendliness, have combined to lower the bar of entry for those wishing to use them. This is why there are almost daily arrests of criminal voyeurs for placing hidden surveillance devices in bathrooms, locker rooms, and other places.[17]

The mass-produced and accessible nature of miniature bugs means that they are used by a wide variety of threat actors. This can make it difficult to trace a device back to a specific perpetrator when discovered, especially in a corporate setting. This means that it is often difficult to identify, much less bring legal charges against a suspect for planting the device. Because of these factors, there are many more bugs being discovered today than there are people being charged for placing them, and corporate victims tend to quietly cover up cases where there is no chance of obtaining a conviction.[18]

Bugs can be hidden in many common household or office items— including electrical outlets, power strips, phone chargers, USB cords, and thumb drives. They can also be placed in more traditional items such as lamps, clocks, and smoke detectors. For an added cost, spy shops and bug manufacturers can even build an audio or video device into a custom item, such as a specific piece of art or furniture. These devices can be hardwired, use internal storage devices such as micro-SD cards to store audio and video files, or they can transmit data via Bluetooth, cellular signals, or Wi-Fi.

Speaking of Wi-Fi-enabled cameras, with homeowners turning increasingly to security cameras that transmit on Wi-Fi and home security alarm systems that use Wi-Fi for contact sensors and motion detectors, some criminals have begun to use Wi-Fi jammers to defeat these systems.[19] While these jamming systems are illegal, if a criminal can determine what system the home is using (those yard signs can help) they can obtain a system that is capable of overwhelming the alarm system's Wi-Fi signal. Alarm companies are working to counter this threat by using algorithms that are harder to counter, and many systems are now able to alert when they sense RF interference that may be jamming them, but the best way to avoid this threat is to use wired alarm sensors and security cameras.

But despite these high-tech tools. In the majority of robberies we are seeing, the robbers are old school and will simply smash through a window on the back of the house using a glass punch or a rock, and either hope the alarm was not activated—sadly many people do not use their alarms—or if the alarm does activate, quickly rush into the house grab the items of value they are targeting and get out before the police can respond.

OTHER FACTORS

Aside from these technological developments, we will also see traditional threats continue to evolve or increase in frequency or intensity.

As the July 2024 attack against then-presidential candidate Donald Trump in Butler, Pennsylvania, reminded the world, the sniper threat remains a current and persistent concern for protection teams of U.S. Government officials, and we would also argue, other prominent individuals. We think it is important to point out, however, that the gunman in this case was less than 140 yards from where President Trump was standing,[20] and was using an AR-15 with only a 16-inch barrel and chambered in 5.56mm. Despite the news reports all clamoring about the "sniper attack," the shooter was not a trained sniper, and the weapon he used was not a legitimate sniper rifle. The same is true for the so-called "Beltway Sniper Attacks" in 2002.[21] We believe the threat posed by a real sniper using a heavier caliber sniper rifle is far greater, especially if using a heavy .50 caliber rifle, which trained snipers can use to kill at distances over a mile. These rifles can also punch through most lightly armored vehicles.

We have not yet seen legitimate sniper attacks against prominent people, but we believe it is only a matter of time. As protectors know, the resources to counter this threat, like counter sniper teams and heavy armored vehicle, are simply not there in the private sector and likely never will be. Therefore, innovative solutions need to be considered, to include moving advertised, public events indoors.

As the horrific fires in Malibu and Los Angeles, California have shown, many of which destroyed the homes of prominent people, the threat from fire is growing, and protectors must prepare to mitigate the threat posed by fires. We have seen reports of private estates building their own firefighting capabilities and have long recommended placing smoke hoods in residences and that they also be carried during travel. Fire escape cloaks are also recommended for residences in fire prone areas. Other natural disasters to include hurricanes, floods, earthquakes, and landslides are also having a greater impact and are occurring more frequently. Contingency plans must be created to help mitigate the impact of such events on the principals.

Finally, untangling the complexity of local, state, and foreign regulations is a daunting task for security teams, which range from the licensing and liability of carrying weapons, to specific operating licensing requirements, to learning if a satellite phone or tracking device can even be carried in a particular location. When combined with ever-changing geopolitical events, shifting duty of care requirements and other compliance issues, more than ever security teams need protective intelligence analysts to help them make sense of the world and keep track of changes and emerging threats.

KEY TAKEAWAYS

- Never let thinking about future threats distract from considering tried and tested simple attack methods.
- AI will impact security and protective intelligence in many different ways. Security teams must embrace AI so they can develop the skills needed to effectively use AI to mitigate the threats it poses.
- Advances in drone technology will make their way from the battlefield in Ukraine to other parts of the globe and will present novel threats for security teams.
- With all the focus on cyberattacks and drones, don't lose sight of the threat posed by plain old hidden cameras and bugs.
- Trained snipers pose a very real, persistent threat that most private security teams do not have the resources to counter. Novel approaches must be taken to mitigate the threat.

NOTES

1 Matteo Cinelli, Gianmarco De Francisci Morales, Alessandro Galeazzi, Walter Quattrociocchi, and Michele Starnini, "The Echo Chamber Effect on Social Media," *Proceedings of the National Academy of Sciences* 118, no. 9 (February 23, 2021): 1–8, https://doi.org/10.1073/pnas.2023301118.
2 Merrit Kennedy, "'Pizzagate' Gunman Sentenced to 4 Years in Prison," *NPR*, June 22, 2017, https://www.npr.org/sections/thetwo-way/2017/06/22/533941689/pizzagate-gunman-sentenced-to-4-years-in-prison.

3 Council on Foreign Relations, "Connect the Dots on State-Sponsored Cyber Incidents - Stuxnet," *Council on Foreign Relations*, July 2010, https://www.cfr.org/cyber-operations/stuxnet.

4 Andy Greenberg, "Dutch Hackers Found a Simple Way to Mess with Traffic Lights," *Wired*, August 5, 2020, https://www.wired.com/story/hacking-traffic-lights-netherlands/.

5 CBS New York, "CBS News Investigates: Car Hacking," *YouTube*, September 26, 2023, https://www.youtube.com/watch?v=-BY_wtLQcNY.

6 Hana Carter, "Woman's Creepy Stalker Ex Hacked into Her Car App to Track and Control Her Driving Warning 'You're Lucky Ju...,'" *The Sun*, November 14, 2019, https://www.thesun.co.uk/tech/10349716/stalker-hacked-car-app-control/.

7 Andy Greenberg, "Hackers Remotely Kill a Jeep on the Highway— with Me in It," *Wired*, July 21, 2015, https://www.wired.com/2015/07/hackers-remotely-kill-jeep-highway/.

8 Anna Holligan, "Eagles Trained to Take down Drones," *BBC News*, March 8, 2016, https://www.bbc.com/news/av/world-europe-35750816.

9 Melanie Mason, "California Assembly Approves Limits on Drones, Paparazzi," *SUAS News*, January 30, 2014, https://www.suasnews.com/2014/01/california-assembly-approves-limits-on-drones-paparazzi/.

10 James Hibberd, "Using Drones for Spying, Robberies on Rise: 'It's Gotten Worse,'" *The Hollywood Reporter*, March 21, 2025, https://www.hollywoodreporter.com/lifestyle/lifestyle-news/drones-spying-robberies-solutions-hollywood-1236166714/.

11 Mike Potter, "'Suspicious Drone Activity' | Carmel Police Warn Drones Are Being Used by Criminals to Scope out Homes," *WTHR*, January 29, 2025, https://www.wthr.com/article/news/crime/carmel-police-warn-drones-are-being-used-in-burglaries-department-cops-thieves-casing-homes-privacy-faa-uas-uav/531-6534ab1f-a769-41ac-9c76-de7d6258e28f

12 Marc Santora, Lara Jakes, Andrew E. Kramer, Marco Hernandez, and Liubov Sholudko, "Drones Now Rule the Battlefield in the Ukraine-Russia War," *The New York Times*, March 3, 2025, https://www.nytimes.com/interactive/2025/03/03/world/europe/ukraine-russia-war-drones-deaths.html.

13 Charles Goulding, "Ukraine's Homegrown 1 Million Unit Drone Industry Takes Flight with 3D Printing," *Fabbaloo*, May 4, 2024, https://www.fabbaloo.com/news/ukraines-homegrown-1-million-unit-drone-industry-takes-flight-with-3d-printing.

14 United States of America v. Dzhokhar A. Tsarnaev, Case 1:13-cr-10200-GAO (Mass.2013).

15 British Transport Police, "London Bombings of 2005," *British Transport Police*, 2024, https://www.btp.police.uk/police-forces/british-transport-police/areas/about-us/about-us/our-history/london-bombings-of-2005/.

16 Austin Turner, "Neighbor Finds Hidden Camera in Bushes after Los Angeles Home Burglarized," *Yahoo News*, March 21, 2025, https://www.yahoo.com/news/neighbor-finds-hidden-camera-bushes-130550145.html.

17 Raphael R. Roker and Jordan Gartner, "Man Arrested after Female Coworker Finds Hidden Camera in Restroom, Police Say," *KBTX*, February 6, 2025, https://www.kbtx.com/2025/02/06/man-arrested-after-female-coworker-finds-hidden-camera-restroom-police-say/.

18 Katie Banahan, "A Private Investigator's View into Managing a Targeted Threat," *Ontic* (The Connected Intelligence Podcast, November 3, 2021), https://ontic.co/resources/podcast/a-private-investigators-view-into-managing-a-targeted-threat/.

19 LAPD Wilshire (@LAPDWilshire), "Wilshire area has been subjected to various residential burglaries, involving 3–4 suspects using Wi-Fi jammers as they enter victims' residences. The Los Angeles Police Department is seeking your help to deter such burglaries. #lapd #lapdwilshire @LAPDRodriguez," Twitter, March 4, 2024, 10:31pm, https://x.com/LAPDWilshire/status/1764780841996030209.

20 Emily Mae Czachor, "Maps Show Location of Trump, Gunman, Law Enforcement Snipers at Pennsylvania Rally Shooting," *CBS News*, July 14, 2024, https://www.cbsnews.com/news/trump-rally-shooting-pennsylvania-gunman-snipers-location-maps/.

21 FBI, "Beltway Snipers," *Federal Bureau of Investigation*, 2002, https://www.fbi.gov/history/famous-cases/beltway-snipers.

CHAPTER 16

The Gold Standard of Personal and Family Protection

The protective intelligence (PI)-led executive protection model is now the gold standard of personal and family protection. Much like GPS, the internet, and space flight, the model was first developed and refined in the public sector and then later exported to the private sector where it has become widely adopted. But, to help understand the model, it is instructive to consider how it was created, so let's revisit the history of why the PI-led model was created and how it was refined.

First, we must acknowledge that historically, government protective operations have always been shaped by tragic failures. These failures prompt outrage and calls for reform that spark formal investigations. Really big failures, like the Kennedy Assassination, can even result in investigations by multiple branches of government. After the congressional investigations,[1] Presidential Commissions,[2] and Accountability Review Boards[3] have completed and filed their reports, reforms are made, and money and resources are allocated to address the problems identified in the reports. Then, over time, attention wanes, funds dry up, personnel are cut—and another disaster happens that prompts new changes.

This pattern impacts all government security budgets (and many in the private sector), but it is nowhere more plainly seen than in the history of the Diplomatic Security Service (DSS). We had a front row seat to the roller coaster ride of security boom and bust cycles during our U.S. Government careers. We were both hired as special agents with the DSS as the result of a dramatic increase in funding for Diplomatic Security resulting from the 1985 Inman Commission report that was issued in the wake the security disasters in Beirut and Moscow.[4] But by the Clinton Administration, less than a decade later, attention to Diplomatic Security had waned. The reforms, personnel, and programs added by the Inman

 DOI: 10.4324/9781003647744-17

Commission had helped to prevent or mitigate attacks, and with no smoking holes in the ground where embassies once stood, security was no longer seen as a budget priority. As a result, the Bureau of Diplomatic Security suffered sustained, significant budget cuts which crippled programs and led to a shortage of personnel. During this time of budget cuts, we even had an Assistant Secretary of State for Diplomatic Security who testified to Congress that "terrorism was dead" to justify the Administration's security budget cuts. He made that statement shortly before the 1993 World Trade Center bombing, and long before the chaos and loss of life on 9/11. Of course, the agents knew differently, but we had no voice. That cycle of cuts was ended by the 1998 East Africa Embassy Bombings, and the Accountability Review Board report into those attacks noted that the budget cuts were a significant factor contributing to them.[5] After those horrific bombings, Diplomatic Security budgets grew again.

They also waned again, or at least did not keep pace with dramatically increasing demands in the post 9/11 world, a dynamic that led to the tragedy in Benghazi.[6] This led to another round of budget increases, but sadly, the boom-and-bust pattern in Diplomatic Security funding continues and is in a down cycle as we write this. It is only a matter of time until there is another tragedy.

There are two agencies inside the U.S. Government that were key in the development of modern-day PI–namely, the U.S. Secret Service (USSS) and State Department, DSS. In fairness, many other U.S. Government agencies do conduct protective details, e.g., the FBI, DoD, U.S. Marshals, U.S. Capitol Police, and the U.S. Supreme Court Police; and some have created very good PI operations. Additionally, there are many state-level protective details around the nation that do wonderful work on the protection front, e.g., the Texas Department of Public Safety, Georgia Bureau of Investigation, etc. However, the USSS and the DSS led the way in pioneering the art and science of PI.[7]

Let's first examine the USSS. The assassination of President John F. Kennedy in 1963 was a disaster that resulted in dramatic changes in the processes and protocols of modern-day protection.[8] The Warren Commission report identified several key areas for improvement and specifically noted the concept of "Preventative Protection" as a key failure and area that needed to be improved:

> In attempting to identify those individuals who might prove a danger to the President, the Secret Service has largely been the **passive recipient** of threatening communications to the President and reports from other agencies which independently evaluate their information for potential sources of danger. This was the consequence of the Service's lack of an adequate investigative staff, its inability to process large amounts of data, and its failure to provide specific descriptions of the kind of information it sought.

The Commission then went on to identify a key change that was needed:

> *Protective Research participation in advance arrangements.* --Since the assassination, Secret Service procedures have been changed to require that a member of PRS accompany each advance survey team to establish liaison with local intelligence gathering agencies and to provide for the immediate evaluation of information received from them.[9]

And this key point:

> *Information known about Lee Harvey Oswald prior to the assassination.* -- No information concerning Lee Harvey Oswald appeared in PRS files before the President's trip to Dallas. Oswald was known to other Federal agencies with which the Secret Service maintained intelligence liaison. The FBI had been interested in him, to some degree at least, since the time of his defection in October 1959. It had interviewed him twice shortly after his return to the United States, again a year later at his request and was investigating him at the time of the assassination.[10]

The Commission also discussed the challenges of a central storage location for threats against the President, the importance of having persons of interest data based by geography, and the need to do a better job of sharing intelligence. These protocols have all become fundamental practices of modern PI.

Now, let's take a look at the DSS. After the assassination of two American foreign service officers in 1973 in Khartoum, Sudan—the Black September Organization (BSO) assaulted and seized a group of diplomats attending a party at the Saudi Arabian Embassy,[11] the Office of Security (SY) at the State Department,[12] created a 24-hour command center at Foggy Bottom and beefed-up security of diplomats as best they could, but were greatly hindered by a lack of resources. In those days, agents assigned to embassies, called "regional security officers," were truly regional and were responsible for the security of embassies and consulates located in many countries.

In June of 1976, the U.S. Ambassador to Lebanon, Francis Meloy, and the Embassy's economic counselor Robert Waring, were kidnapped and murdered in Beirut, Lebanon, along with a foreign service national driver.[13] The tragedies continued in February 1979, when U.S. Ambassador to Afghanistan Adolph "Spike" Dubs was kidnapped from his vehicle by armed militants and shot in a hotel room in Kabul, during a botched rescue attempt by Afghan security forces under the control of a Soviet intelligence officer. The exact circumstances of Dubs' murder remain murky given the fact that the abductors took Dubs to a hotel in Kabul and that the one kidnapper who was captured alive was executed before he could be interrogated by the Americans.[14]

These collective murders caused the Office of Security at the State Department to create a Threat & Analysis Group known as "TAG,"[15] along with the evaluation of armored limousine enhancements and communications protocols.[16]

As noted above, the catastrophic bombings of the U.S. embassies in Beirut and Kuwait in the 1980s and the Russian Embassy debacles,[17] resulted in the creation of the modern day DSS, after a series of recommendations were made by the "Inman Commission," to enhance physical security measures of diplomatic locations, which included the establishment and enforcement of security standards and physical security upgrades to facilities, along with the agents required to administer the programs.

The 1980s also saw the creation of the first dedicated Counterterrorism Investigations Branch (known as DS/CR/CT) which we both served in for many years. Fred was one of the first batch of agents assigned to the branch. Our office had a wide remit and was responsible for investigating threats against the Secretary of State and attacks against U.S. diplomats and facilities around the globe, but also included hostage debriefings and the study of how threat actors identify and choose their targets. The branch was expanded into a division in the late 1980s, and Scott joined the unit as part of that expansion. The office was renamed the PI Division in 1992. Our office investigated many international hijacking and kidnapping cases, along with participating in the investigation of hundreds of terrorist attacks such as the first World Trade Center bombing in 1993.

One key PI success our branch had involved a threat actor by the name of Edward Louis Gallo, a decorated Vietnam War veteran.[18] The Wooster, Massachusetts native, who lived with his mother, had a Master's Degree in chemistry, but began to suffer psychotic incidents, and developed a fixation on the President, but became particularly focused on Secretary of State George Shultz, who he believed was controlling his brain using a satellite. In November 1987, after seeing Secretary Shultz interviewed on the "Face The Nation" television program, Gallo loaded up his vehicle with an AR-15 rifle, a sawed-off shotgun, and a full-length shotgun, told his mother he was going to kill Shultz, and drove away.

Fortunately, Gallo's mother reported him to the police and to the DSS Boston Field Office.[19] This likely saved the life of her son, but also probably saved the lives of some of the agents on the Secretary's protective detail and perhaps the Secretary himself. The world witnessed how much damage the untrained John Hinckley was able to do with a cheap.22 revolver when he attacked President Ronald Reagan and his protective detail in 1981.[20] A trained combat veteran armed with an AR-15 and a sawed-off shotgun had the potential to cause far more carnage.

Following an extensive multi-state search for Gallo, his vehicle was located at a sketchy motel in Northeast D.C. in the early hours of the morning. The Metropolitan Police Department SWAT team breached his room and took Gallo into custody. (He was arrested without incident, although an accidental round was discharged by the SWAT team during the entry.)

After debriefing Gallo for many days at the criminal wing of St. Elizabeth's Hospital in Washington D.C., where he was being detained, we learned that he had previously been to the city and had been able to watch and study the motorcade movements of the Secretary of State's protective detail, but he was never seen by any of our agents. Gallo also reported that he had driven by the Secretary's residence in Bethesda, Maryland, at various times of the day, again, without being detected.

Clearly, our traditional form of protection wasn't working.

We obviously needed to re-think how protection was done to find the likes of a committed attacker like Gallo who had not self-identified by making a threatening communication. In other words, we were doing a pretty good job of identifying, assessing and databasing the "howlers"—those who made threats—but we needed to find a way to find the "hunters" like Gallo who did not issue threats before initiating their attack cycle.[21] We studied how other security services worked[22] and how espionage targets were surveilled discreetly and came up with the concept of PI countersurveillance (PICS) or "shadow"[23] teams to look for threat actors stalking our principals at their residences, at work, or while at scheduled events.

Based on our many investigations of past attacks and thwarted attacks, we were absolutely convinced that the attack cycle was a valid model for understanding attack planning, and we knew that by focusing on attack cycle activities and vulnerabilities—especially pre-operational surveillance—we would be able to proactively spot a hunter before they could launch an attack. In sum, the shadow teams gave us a tool to proactively get "left of the boom."

So, we began to deploy shadow teams of special agents trained in countersurveillance and dressed in street clothes to blend into the environment and to watch for people watching our protectees, and protective details. At times, shadow team agents could dress like students, tourists, or even like street people or messengers on bicycles. It's amazing what you can see if you simply stop and look.[24]

Meanwhile, back in the office, other agents would work with our Intelligence and Threat Assessment Division, investigate threatening communications, work to identify suspicious individuals spotted by the shadow teams, work with psychologists to conduct formal threat assessments, and compile files and photographs of known threat actors for BOLO (be on the lookout) face sheets that we would provide to both the detail agents and the shadow teams. The BOLO sheets were essentially the same old school model that agents from the LANCER (JFK) Detail used in the 1960s, it worked, but it wasn't very efficient. Technology solutions in the 1980s were typewriters, index cards, and photocopies. Cell phones were just becoming available and over time, digital solutions have made collecting and passing intelligence far quicker and easier.

The concept became an instant game-changer in the way the DSS protected the Secretary of State and we also began to use PICS to cover high-profile visitors like foreign ministers, the Pope, Nelson Mandela during his first visit to the United States after his release from prison, Princess Diana and Prince Charles on several trips, or Salman Rushdie. It also changed the way we protected events like the Middle-East Peace negotiations, United Nations General Assemblies, and major international summits. The shadow teams were eventually expanded to provide countersurveillance coverage for many high-threat U.S. embassies overseas using local agents who could blend into the environment.

In early 1998, we took the PI-led model to the private sector, after being hired to protect a high-profile business executive and his family. Once word got out about what our team was doing for our principal, we were visited by members of the executive protection teams of many other high-net-worth individuals and families, and the model quickly spread. Today this model has become the gold standard of executive and family protection in the private sector.

Here is what the model looks like today.

INTELLIGENCE-LED

Protective intelligence analysis and tools form the backbone of this model. This obviously means that PI capability is needed. This capability can be achieved by the creation of an internal PI team, or with the support of an outside partner who can provide PI support. Scott's PI team at TorchStone Global provides the PI capability for many of their clients and augments the capabilities of others with limited PI resources.

As noted in previous chapters, one of the first PI tools that is needed to create an appropriate executive protection program is a baseline threat assessment.[25] It is folly to put any security program in place without first obtaining a solid understanding of the threats the program is attempting to counter. Threat levels can vary considerably, even among people holding the same position in the same sector, and it is important to establish the types and level of threats facing the person or organization the program is intended to protect. Not every person requires security at the level of the President of the United States, or even a cabinet officer. Some people don't require executive protection at all, and others only need extra security at certain places and times as dictated by the situation. A baseline threat assessment allows the executive protection program to be "right-sized" to meet the existing threat to the principal. It is also important to recognize that since we live in a constantly changing world, threat levels change and baseline assessments must be regarded as "living" documents that are updated regularly to account for these changes. They are not a "one and done" product.

The baseline assessment must first consider the principal's public prominence. Recognizable, high-profile principals are more likely to attract the attention of threat actors than those with a lower profile. Of course, a principal with many fans—or critics—has a higher probability of attracting unstable individuals who have an unhealthy focus of interest. Some high-net-worth people can fly under the radar, others cannot, meaning they are more likely to be targeted by financially motivated criminals, so the principal's degree of public recognition and prominence is important.

The principal's position can also draw the attention of threat actors if they lead a company that is being targeted by activists, extremists, competitors, or foreign governments. Investments in a company being targeted, doing business with a company being targeted, or serving on the board of such a company can also bring negative attention. Other factors to be considered are if the principal has been mentioned in connection with conspiracy theories or has been denounced as an "enemy" by an extremist influencer. Making charitable donations to a controversial organization or cause, or even publicly speaking out on a contentious social issue can also result in threats and must be factored into the baseline threat assessment.

The baseline assessment must consider the threats posed by the entire array of threat actors to include financially motivated criminals, aggrieved or unstable individuals (to include insiders), activists, terrorists, and even hostile governments.

As we discussed in Chapter 13, public profile assessments identifying what information is available about the principal in the public domain should also be factored into the baseline assessment. An executive whose residential address is readily identifiable is at greater risk than one whose address is not. These assessments not only help inform what information is available on the principal, but can often identify where it came from, identifying vulnerabilities that can be addressed to stop the flow of sensitive information. Even if the source of the information can't be fixed, like in a historical SEC filing, property tax record, or political donation record, knowing where the information came from can at least help protect the principal from information shock if they are doxed, and knowing the information is publicly available to any threat actor is a risk factor that must be considered.

CORPORATE SITUATIONAL AWARENESS

Protective intelligence teams also provide a valuable function by providing situational awareness to security teams by using social media monitoring and alerting tools. These tools can be used to scan the internet and social media feeds for threats against the principal. These online threats can include statements by extremist influencers denouncing the principal, posts doxing the principal, or posts explicitly calling for the principal to be targeted for harassment or attack, like the posts calling for a CEO to be "Luigied." The social media threat continuum model outlined in Chapter 10 helps PI teams place such posts into context.

PI teams also scan the internet for other events that could impact the principal or cause disruption, like vehicle accidents, protests, and natural disasters. The January 2025 wildfires in Los Angeles, and the March 2025 transformer failure that took London's Heathrow Airport offline are examples of disruptive events PI teams helped security teams navigate.

These same tools can also be used to monitor the public media activity of identified persons of interest (POIs). In terms of POIs, it is not only important to look for clearly stated threats to the principal, but also an increase in volume of their mentions of the principal, or changes in the tenor of their mentions of the principal that could indicate a growing obsession, a festering grievance, or that express an intent to travel to meet the principal. Analysts also look for indications of violent ideation or other signs a POI is progressing along the pathway to violence. Databasing the communications and social media posts of POIs rather than discarding them is critical because it allows analysts to assess new communications against older ones to identify changes in frequency and tone suggesting that they are progressing along the pathway to violence. Databased communications can also prove useful evidence if a legal case is initiated against a POI.

Protective intelligence analysts also have an array of tools they can use to identify social media posters to help assess the threat, if any, they pose. They can also help identify and assess anomalous or suspicious people or vehicles spotted by executive protection, surveillance detection, or residential security teams. Databasing suspicious or anomalous people, vehicles, or incidents is a powerful tool, especially if these databases can be integrated with tools like license plate readers to pick up other sightings of the vehicle. Scott's PI team has found Ontic[26] to be an ideal PI tool to database incidents and POIs, monitor social media activity, write reports, and manage investigations.

As an example of the utility of databasing seemingly innocuous incidents, Scott likes to recount a chain of events his team experienced with one of their protectees. During a publicized appearance at an event in Europe, a woman from South America attempted to approach the principal in his hotel room. She was intercepted by the executive protection team, interviewed briefly, and the executive protection team filed an incident report. The PI team received the report, identified the woman, and databased the incident in Ontic for future reference. Several weeks later, the residential security team at the principal's home in the United States encountered a woman attempting to enter the residence. An Ontic database check on her name quickly identified her as the same South American woman who had attempted to approach the principal in Europe. This allowed the residential security team to inform local law enforcement that she had stalked the principal across two continents. These dots could not have been connected without the incident report being filed and databased.

This incident also illustrates the importance of the PI team maintaining close contact with the executive protection team, the residential security team, and the principal's administrative assistants and household managers to collect, assess, and database information.

Other products the PI team can provide to help security management make important security decisions are travel risk assessments and event risk assessments. Even a principal who does not normally need executive protection at home might need it for a trip to a high crime or terrorism threat destination. And while a principal might not have executive protection coverage for a low-profile event held by their company, they might require it if they are attending a publicized event like Brian Thompson, or an event being hosted by a company that is being targeted by an extremist or activist movement.

WATCHING FOR WATCHERS

Due to the many demands for their attention, it can often be difficult for close protection agents to carefully study their environment beyond a very limited bubble around the principal. They may be able to scan the first couple rows of people as they leave a building to walk the principal to the car, but it is very difficult for them to pick up on the person standing at the back of the crowd, or across the street, unless that person displays an overtly hostile demeanor. But as close protection, their job is to watch for those close-in immediate threats. We've worked protective details, so we get this, and as we noted above when discussing the Gallo case, detecting hostile surveillance is a problem for even the best-trained close protection teams.

This inward focus was a major source of the security failure that led to the July 2022 assassination of former Japanese Prime Minister Shinzo Abe. Videos of the attack[27] showed that the team was inwardly focused and did not catch the early stages of the assassin's attack cycle, or even his deployment as he approached Abe from behind with his homemade firearm. Abe's detail agents did not even begin to react until after the first shot was fired, and that proved to be too late: action is always faster than reaction.

By watching from the outside in, instead of the inside out, and focusing on pre-attack behaviors, and specifically the pre-operational surveillance that occurs early in the attack cycle, countersurveillance "shadow" teams can be a very effective tool for proactively exploiting vulnerabilities in the attack cycle to thwart attacks. *It is important to watch for watchers.*

For high-threat protective details, a countersurveillance capability is a must. In addition to observing the people around the detail for signs that they are conducting surveillance, the shadow team can also observe the environment around the residence and office for signs of hostile surveillance, or signs of an attack team deploying.

In cases in which the principal faces less of a threat, diagnostic countersurveillance by a shadow team can be used as an occasional tool to ensure the principal is not under surveillance. In other situations, a shadow team can provide covert protection for the principal, forming an invisible, protective bubble around them as they go about their normal daily routine. That is the type of protection Scott and his partner were doing outside that hotel in Manhattan in the story we shared in Chapter 3 about the criminal who wanted to mug their client for her diamond bracelet. They were a shadow team performing covert protection and had formed an invisible bubble of protection around their client. While she walked down the street, they identified an emerging threat and stepped in to proactively prevent it—and she was unaware the incident even occurred.

There is also a case to be made for covert protection involving shadow teams in high-threat cases, especially when a trip is unannounced, and the principal is not making any public appearances. Sometimes a low-key detail is more secure than a highly visible one because it does not draw attention to the principal. That is how we provided security for Salman Rushdie during his first trip to the United States after the Iranian fatwa against him was announced.[28] We had one special agent from the DSS Protective Liaison office drive Mr. Rushdie in a non-descript sedan, while our shadow team formed an invisible bubble around the vehicle and the locations he visited.

One other advantage to the use of shadow teams is that they are amorphous by nature and are far more difficult for a potential assailant to detect and quantify than traditional overt security measures. Ideally, the shadow team agents should be practicing good cover for status and cover for action while displaying a neutral demeanor, allowing them to be largely invisible on the street—true shadow teams. Because of this, they should avoid directly interacting with the close protection agents.

However, even if one of the shadow team agents does slip up and get identified by a hostile actor conducting surveillance, their presence tends to introduce a great deal of uncertainty into the attack cycle planning.

Are there six shadow team agents, or only two? We have conducted red team exercises against protection teams where we took the role of an attack planner conducting pre-operational surveillance, and in cases where we have spotted one undercover shadow agent working counter-surveillance, we then had to begin to look for others who may or may not have been there. This generated a lot of pressure and uncertainty, and in some cases caused us to identify people as shadow team agents who were not. Quite frankly, in that case, if we were criminals, we likely would have diverted to an easier target, rather than deal with such an ambigu-ous situation. Denying hostile actors the ability to conduct surveillance at will is a powerful tool.

Countersurveillance operations are far less valuable if they're con-ducted without databasing or analysis of what's been observed over time, distance, and in different environments. For example, a shadow team without an analytical element would find it difficult for the agents to rec-ognize when the same person or vehicle has been encountered by differ-ent teams or at different sites. Passdown briefings are often incomplete, and people have perishable memories. Robust reporting and databasing ensure that critical information is retained and readily retrievable so that the dots can be connected.

While countersurveillance efforts are valuable, they can't operate in a vacuum. As noted above, they need to be part of a larger PI program that includes an analytical component, but investigation is also an important and necessary function. Investigations and analyses are closely related yet distinct components that yield a high degree of synergy.

Analysis can help focus countersurveillance operations on the most likely or most vulnerable targets. Social media monitoring and assess-ments serve to supplement the observations of the shadow team and can help identify people or groups the team needs to be watching for.

Once a suspicious person or incident is observed, reported, assessed, and databased, the next PI tool comes into play: investiga-tion. The goal is not just to detect surveillance, but to counter it. That requires verifying that surveillance was indeed being conducted but also identifying the person doing it. This can be accomplished covertly, by having the shadow team follow the person, or more overtly by hav-ing the person interviewed. Nothing rattles a person conducting sur-veillance more than being put on notice that they've been spotted, and in many cases, this may be enough to cause them to divert to another target.

In some cases, an interview is deemed necessary and can determine that yes there was surveillance going on, but it was not related to attack planning. We have experienced instances in which the suspected hostile surveillant was a private investigator following a company employee as part of a divorce or workman's comp case, a process server waiting to catch an employee as they leave the building to walk to their car, and a narcotics detective watching an employee who was suspected of selling drugs. But without an investigative team to interview these people who were identified by the shadow team, it would have been difficult, if not impossible, to determine that they did not pose a threat to the principal.

Another important PI tool is a formal threat assessment by a trained mental health professional. These assessments can be conducted in person to assess the potential threat posed by an insider, or by reviewing the correspondence of an outside threat actor, though obviously an in-person interview will normally yield better conclusions and recommendations. In addition to helping to assess the potential threat posed by a subject, they can also provide important guidance on how best to interact, or not interact, with them, if there are certain phrases or subjects that should be avoided, and potential ways to help them get off the pathway to violence.

Once the PI tools are in place, providing an overarching PI umbrella, the more traditional security components such as a security driver, protection agent(s), and a residential security team can be employed at the appropriate level to mitigate the assessed threat. These measures can be adjusted as the threat level and situation dictate, with a larger security presence when deemed necessary and maybe little to none at other times. Of course, the principal's risk tolerance and preferences must also be considered in making these decisions. A PI-driven executive protection program can be tailored so that it is adaptable to both the threat environment and the principal's lifestyle.

KEY TAKEAWAYS

- Executive protection programs are not "one size fits all" and must be tailored to fit both the threat and the principal's comfort.
- Protective intelligence assessments should drive decisions over the size and style of executive protection programs.
- Protective intelligence programs can use the frameworks of the attack cycle, the pathway to violence, and social media threat continuum to help them proactively identify potential threats and take steps to mitigate them.
- Analysis, investigations, countersurveillance, and psychological assessments are all important tools that work together in a PI program to direct and equip close protection and residential security teams.

NOTES

1 Select Committee to Study Governmental Operations, "The Investi gation of the Assassination of President John F. Kennedy: Performance of the Intelligence Agencies (Book V)" (United States Senate, April 23, 1976), https://www.intelligence.senate.gov/sites/default/ files/94755_V.pdf.

2 "Warren Commission Report: Table of Contents," U.S. National Archives, August 15, 2016, https://www.archives.gov/research/jfk/ warren-commission-report/toc.

3 "Accountability Review Board Documents," *State.gov*, 2017, https://2009-2017.state.gov/arbreport/

4 "Secretary of State's Advisory Panel Report on Overseas Security, June 1998," *1997–2001.state.gov*, June 1985, 1997-2001.state. gov/www/publications/1985inman_report/inman1.html

5 US Department of State, "Report of the Accountability Review Boards on the Embassy Bombings in Nairobi and Dar Es Salaam on August 7, 1998 | Office of Justice Programs," *Ojp.gov*, 2025, https:// www.ojp.gov/ncjrs/virtual-library/abstracts/report-accountability- review-boards-embassy-bombings-nairobi-and.

6 For more on Benghazi read: Fred Burton and Samuel M. Katz, *Under Fire: The Untold Story of the Attack in Benghazi* (St. Martin's Press, 2013).

7 The USSS and DSS also teach protection courses to local and state police agencies around the country.

8 Other major attacks and assassinations on key officials have been previously covered with lots of research and books, e.g., the Lincoln assassination.

9 "Chapter 8," U.S. National Archives, August 15, 2016, https://www. archives.gov/research/jfk/warren-commission-report/chapter-8. html#intelligence.

10 "Warren Commission Report: Table of Contents," U.S. National Archives, August 15, 2016, https://www.archives.gov/research/jfk/ warren-commission-report/toc.

11 "Foreign Relations of the United States, 1969–1976, Volume E–6, Documents on Africa, 1973–1976 – Office of the Historian," *History.state.gov*, June 1973, history.state.gov/historicaldocuments/ frus1969-76ve06

12 Now, the Diplomatic Security Service (DSS).

13 James M. Markham, "U.S. Ambassador and aide kidnapped and murdered in Beirut Combat Sector," *The New York Times*, June 17, 1976, https://www.nytimes.com/1976/06/17/archives/us-ambassador- and-aide-kidnapped-and-murdered-in-beirut-combat.html.

14 AFSA, "The Assassination of Ambassador Spike Dubs — Kabul, 1979 – Association for Diplomatic Studies & Training," *adst.org*, accessed April 24, 2025, https://adst.org/2013/01/the-assassination-of-ambassador-spike-dubs-kabul-1979/.

15 This office is now called Intelligence and Threat Analysis (ITA). 2009-2017.state.gov/m/ds/terrorism/c8584.htm

16 The State Department's security organization was created in 1916 but would not become the Bureau of DSS until 1986.

17 KGB listening devices placed inside the embassy.

18 AP, "Man Held in Threat on Cabinet Member," *The New York Times*, November 4, 1987, https://www.nytimes.com/1987/11/04/us/man-held-in-threat-on-cabinet-member.html.

19 Associated Press, "Mom Tips Police, Man Accused of Threatening Shultz Arrested," *Los Angeles Times*, November 3, 1987, https://www.latimes.com/archives/la-xpm-1987-11-03-mn-18505-story.html.

20 United States Secret Service, "In Remembrance: Forty Years since the Assassination Attempt on President Reagan," *www.secretservice.gov*, 2024, https://www.secretservice.gov/reagan40thanniversary.

21 For more on "Hunters and Howlers," we recommend Fredrick Calhoun's 1998 publication by that name. https://cdn.fedweb.org/fed-96/2/Hunters_and_Howlers.pdf.

22 For example, the British Security Service and Israeli Mossad.

23 We initially called these teams "PICS teams," but after protective detail agents started calling them "pixies" we quickly re-named them "shadow teams."

24 For more on the shadow teams, please read *Ghost: Confessions of a Counterterrorism Agent*, by Fred Burton, 2008, published by Random House.

25 Fred Burton and Scott Stewart, "The Role of Baseline Threat Assessments in Protective Intelligence +," (Ontic and TorchStone), accessed April 24, 2025, https://www.torchstoneglobal.com/wp-content/uploads/2020/06/Ontic-Whitepaper-Baseline-threat-assessments.pdf.

26 "Ontic," *Ontic*, April 23, 2025, https://ontic.co/.

27 Miyazawa (@Miyazawa809588), "High quality footage of the former Prime Minister of Japan, Shinzo Abe, being shot at from behind with an improvised double barreled shotgun," July 7, 2022, 11:57 p.m., https://x.com/Miyazawa809588/status/1545255792902905856.

28 Jay Conley, "Author Recounts Life in Seclusion under Iranian Fatwa," *GW Today*, 2022, https://gwtoday.gwu.edu/author-recounts-life-seclusion-under-iranian-fatwa.

Index

Note: *Italic* page numbers refer to figures.

For Product Safety Concerns and Information please contact our EU
representative GPSR@taylorandfrancis.com
Taylor & Francis Verlag GmbH, Kaufingerstraße 24, 80331 München, Germany

www.ingramcontent.com/pod-product-compliance
Lightning Source LLC
Chambersburg PA
CBHW050226270326
41914CB00003BA/595